TH

COSTA BRAVA

Forthcoming titles include

Baltic States • Chicago • Corfu
First-Time Round the World • Grand Canyon
Philippines • Skiing & Snowboarding in North America
South America • The Gambia • Walks Around London

Forthcoming reference titles include

Chronicle series: China, England,
France, India • Night Sky

Read Rough Guides online

www.roughguides.com

Rough Guide Credits

Text editor: Matthew Teller
Series editor: Mark Ellingham
Production: Andy Turner and Zoë Nobes
Cartography: Maxine Repath and Melissa Baker
Picture research: Mark Thomas
Proofreading: Susannah Wight

Publishing Information

This first edition published June 2002
by Rough Guides Ltd,
62–70 Shorts Gardens, London WC2H 9AH

Distributed by the Penguin Group:

Penguin Books Ltd, 80 Strand, London WC2R ORL.
Penguin Putnam, Inc. 375 Hudson Street, New York 10014, USA
Penguin Books Australia Ltd, 487 Maroondah Highway,
PO Box 257, Ringwood, Victoria 3134, Australia
Penguin Books Canada Ltd, 10 Alcorn Avenue,
Toronto, Ontario, Canada M4V 1E4
Penguin Books (NZ) Ltd,
182–190 Wairau Road, Auckland 10, New Zealand

Typeset in Bembo and Helvetica to an original design by Henry Iles.
Printed in Spain by Graphy Cems.

© Rough Guides 2002
400pp, includes index
A catalogue record for this book is available from the British Library.

ISBN 1-85828-802-9

THE ROUGH GUIDE TO

COSTA BRAVA

by Chris Lloyd

ROUGH
GUIDES

We set out to do something different when the first Rough Guide was published in 1982. Mark Ellingham, just out of university, was travelling in Greece. He brought along the popular guides of the day, but found they were all lacking in some way. They were either strong on ruins and museums but went on for pages without mentioning a beach or taverna. Or they were so conscious of the need to save money that they lost sight of Greece's cultural and historical significance. Also, none of the books told him anything about Greece's contemporary life – its politics, its culture, its people, and how they lived.

So with no job in prospect, Mark decided to write his own guidebook, one which aimed to provide practical information that was second to none, detailing the best beaches and the hottest clubs and restaurants, while also giving hard-hitting accounts of every sight, both famous and obscure, and providing up-to-the-minute information on contemporary culture. It was a guide that encouraged independent travellers to find the best of Greece, and was a great success, getting shortlisted for the Thomas Cook travel guide award, and encouraging Mark, along with three friends, to expand the series.

The Rough Guide list grew rapidly and the letters flooded in, indicating a much broader readership than had been anticipated, but one which uniformly appreciated the Rough Guide mix of practical detail and humour, irreverence and enthusiasm. Things haven't changed. The same four friends who began the series are still the caretakers of the Rough Guide mission today: to provide the most reliable, up-to-date and entertaining information to independent-minded travellers of all ages, on all budgets.

We now publish more than 150 titles and have offices in London and New York. The travel guides are written and researched by a dedicated team of more than 100 authors, based in Britain, Europe, the USA and Australia. We have also created a unique series of phrasebooks to accompany the travel series, along with an acclaimed series of music guides, and a best-selling pocket guide to the internet and world wide web. We also publish comprehensive travel information on our website: www.roughguides.com

Help us update

We've gone to a lot of trouble to ensure that this Rough Guide is as up to date and accurate as possible. However, things do change. All suggestions, comments and corrections are much appreciated, and we'll send a copy of the next edition (or any other Rough Guide if you prefer) for the best letters.

Please mark letters "Rough Guide Costa Brava Update" and send to:

Rough Guides, 62–70 Shorts Gardens, London WC2H 9AH, or Rough Guides, 4th Floor, 345 Hudson St, New York 10014.

Or send email to: mail@roughguides.co.uk Online updates about this book can be found on Rough Guides' website (see opposite)

Acknowledgements

The author thanks everyone who helped with information and advice, especially Anny Linnell, Montse Pericot, Lisa Brown and Laura Alsina from EICA, Jordi Camps and Consol Carós for a renewed acquaintance with Girona's nightlife, Debi Moss, Mrs Betty Rawling and Francina Esteve, Josep Martinez, Pere Compte, Xavi Oliver, and Jacqui, Myriam and Sarah in Cadaqués. Thanks for moral and practical support to Averil and Mervyn Lloyd and Rita and David Armitage. Everyone in the excellent tourist offices throughout the region, especially Isabel Godoy, Anna Suades and Concepció Bascompte. Most of all, I'd like to thank Liz for everything.

The editor would like to thank Polly Thomas for starting the ball rolling, Mark Thomas for picture research, Susannah Wight for proofing, Andy Turner for sharp typesetting and Melissa Baker for outstanding cartography. Also Geoff Howard for guidance and support.

Readers' letters

Many thanks to those readers who took the time to write in with comments, suggestions and updates on the Costa Brava, based on the most recent edition of the *Rough Guide to Spain*: Sheila Adam, Mark English and Marian Hobbs, C.J. Ferns, Sheilah Openshaw, G.A. Parkinson, Sam Robson, Deirdre Timoney, Sandy Wilson, Andy Wood and Liz Shaw.

CONTENTS

Contents

MAP LIST

Map Symbols

-----	International boundary	♜	Castle
--- --	District boundary	⛪	Monastery
▬▬	Motorway	⚘	Gardens
═══	Main road	ⓘ	Information office
───	Minor road	⊠	Post office
▬▪▬	Railway	✈	Airport
▬▬	Pedestrianized street	🅿	Parking
‖‖‖‖‖	Steps	★	Bus stop
───	River		Building
▲	Peak		Church
⚜	Viewpoint		Park
⋙	Rocks		Forest
⌒	Cave		Beach
∴	Ruins		

Introduction

The most unfairly maligned and misrepresented stretch of coast in Europe, the **Costa Brava** has long been derided as a package-holiday, chips-and-sangria destination – an image that is based solely on two or three of the more notorious towns at its southernmost tip. The truth is that this diverse region matches extraordinary natural beauty with a rich cultural heritage, an accumulated legacy of centuries of invading armies that shows itself in a tapestry of walled towns, fortified farmhouses and ancient hilltop villages. The coastline is enchantingly serpentine – Costa Brava means **"Rugged Coast"** – with spurs of the Pyrenees forming wild sea-cliffs. Secluded coves hide between the jagged rocks, where tenacious pines cover the slopes down to the water's edge and extensive sandy beaches provide a breathing space, punctuating the deeply scored shoreline.

In the 1900s, Picasso and Marc Chagall were drawn to the area's beauty, and when **Salvador Dalí** returned to his childhood home here, artists, writers and would-be bohemians trailed in his wake; before the Civil War struck, the Costa Brava had begun to compete with France's Côte d'Azur as a playground for the rich and famous. When Franco's Ministry of Tourism began pushing the area as a holiday destination in the 1950s, with scant regard for

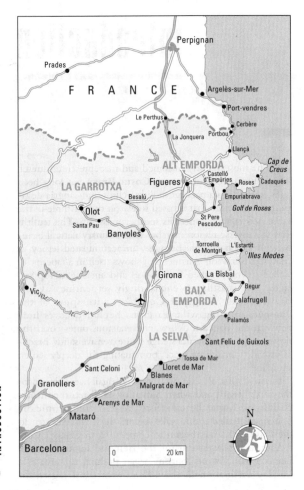

regional sensibilities or the environment, the jetset initially returned, but as sedate fishing towns were devoured and distorted by high-rise hotels, they turned their noses up at the tide of package tourists and moved on.

However, the region's charm had always survived alongside the depredations of the tourist boom, and the locals had long known where to come to see the best of their stunning coastline. When **democracy** returned in the 1970s, so did a Catalan sense of self: these days, the towns of the Costa Brava are increasingly unwilling to sell their soul for tourism. The idealized, emasculated caricature of a pan-Spanish culture that was dreamt up by the impoverished Franco regime, complete with sanitized and wholly alien images of flamenco and bull-fighting, has all but disappeared. In its place, the region is restating and strengthening native values for a more discerning breed of visitor, and the Costa Brava has begun to overturn its largely undeserved foreign reputation as the repository of all that's worst in mass tourism.

Where to go

Diversity characterizes the region's beauty. Capital of the province is **Girona**, a walled medieval enclave that has been fought over every century since it was founded. Coupled with its rich history is a thriving cultural scene and a municipal pride that is palpable in the lanes of its charming old quarter. Inland from Girona, an abrupt change in the terrain marks the volcanic region of **La Garrotxa**, a rolling, flowing landscape in the foothills of the Pyrenees, perfect for rambles through ancient beech woods into the craters of dormant volcanoes.

The southernmost part of the coast, **La Selva**, was most affected by the tourist boom, and remains a place of tour buses and all-day English breakfasts. Despite that, the natural beauty of the area, marked by small coves interspersed with long sandy beaches, is still largely intact in parts and the towns themselves – especially historic **Tossa de Mar** – retain some charm beneath the tourist veneer.

North from here, the coast is at its best. With one or two exceptions, the chic **Baix Empordà** never succumbed to the tourist boom. Here, electric-green pines cluster at the edge of crystalline turquoise coves that are perfect for swimming or snorkelling. Many well-heeled Catalans own second homes here, and the towns, including **Palamós**, **Palafrugell** and **Begur**, are a haven of sophisticated elegance, housing some of the finest restaurants and terrace bars anywhere in Spain. With enormous contrasts between the laid-back charm of **Calella de Palafrugell** and **Tamariu**, the lively chic of **Platja d'Aro** and the unspoilt splendour of **Sa Tuna** and **Aiguablava**, the one constant is an air of refined hedonism.

Further north, the **Alt Empordà** has two markedly different areas. The southern part is dominated by the sweeping sands of the Golf de Roses, flanked at one extreme by the Classical ruins of **Empúries** and at the other by the full-on beach culture of **Roses** itself. A short distance inland lies the county town of **Figueres**, Dalí's home town and dominated by a museum dedicated to him. North of Roses, at the **Cap de Creus** headland, the scenery suddenly changes to become bleak and barren, where the few pines clinging on for dear life above grey-sand coves are bent almost double in the wind. The beautiful seafront village of **Cadaqués** is the main draw, very near Dalí's one-time waterfront residence, beyond which a string of attractive, little-developed coves reaches north along the corrugated coast to **Portbou** on the French border. Inland, the protected **Serra de l'Albera** offers a cool, green and peaceful mountain retreat from the coast.

When to go

Peak season is July and August. Weather at this time is rarely uncomfortably hot, although the influence of the Pyrenees means that conditions can change suddenly. The main towns are full of people but, if you choose your spot carefully, you can still find yourself alone in a tiny cove or enjoying the views from a tranquil mountain-top.

The coast is at its best between Easter and the end of June and then again during September, when temperatures aren't quite so high, the swimming is idyllic and the crowds either haven't arrived or have just left. Girona is perfect to visit any time of the year. Note that from October until Easter many hotels and services – especially in the more tourist-oriented coastal areas – close altogether.

CLIMATE

The table shows average daily maximum temperatures in and the average number of days with rain for each town

	Begur	Girona	Lloret de Mar	Roses
Jan	16°C 2	18°C 8	19°C 5	19°C 2
Feb	16°C 3	19°C 2	21°C 1	21°C 1
March	20°C 6	23°C 8	24°C 4	23°C 6
April	19°C 6	22°C 11	23°C 10	23°C 6
May	22°C 7	28°C 5	26°C 5	27°C 5
June	26°C 5	31°C 7	31°C 3	32°C 5
July	26°C 4	31°C 4	30°C 5	31°C 3
Aug	29°C 3	34°C 2	33°C 3	34°C 1
Sept	25°C 6	30°C 7	29°C 6	30°C 1
Oct	20°C 3	26°C 8	24°C 3	28°C 8
Nov	17°C 3	21°C 3	21°C 4	21°C 4
Dec	17°C 5	20°C 2	19°C 3	20°C 4

BASICS

BASICS

Getting there

The easiest and cheapest way to reach the Costa Brava is to **fly**, with a broad choice of flights and many package options. The only airline operating scheduled flights to **Girona** is the British low-cost carrier Buzz, although there are plenty of flights to **Barcelona**, 100km south, and a handful to **Perpignan**, 70km north in France. From Britain, **rail** travel is relatively quick, although not cheap, and in recent years **driving** has steadily increased in popularity.

Airfares depend on the **season**, with the highest being around July and August; fares usually drop during the "shoulder" seasons – June and September – and you'll get the best prices between October and May (excluding Easter, Christmas and New Year when prices are hiked up). Flying on weekends can sometimes add a premium.

Booking flights online

Many airlines and discount travel websites let you book **online**, cutting out the costs of agents and middlemen. Good deals can often be found through discount sites, as well as through the airlines' own websites.

Ⓦ **www.cheapflights.com**
Flight deals, travel agents, plus links to other travel sites.

Ⓦ **www.deckchair.com** Bob Geldof's online venture, drawing on a wide range of airlines.

- ⓦ **www.etn.nl/discount.htm** A hub of consolidator and discount agent web links, maintained by the non-profit European Travel Network.
- ⓦ **www.expedia.com** Discount airfares, all-airline search engine and daily deals.
- ⓦ **www.flyaow.com** Online air travel info and reservations site.
- ⓦ **www.lastminute.com** Offers good last-minute holiday package and flight-only deals.
- ⓦ **www.skydeals.co.uk** Charter flights to Girona.
- ⓦ **www.travelocity.com** Destination guides, hot web fares and best deals for car rental and accommodation.
- ⓦ **travel.yahoo.com** Incorporates a lot of Rough Guide material in its coverage, with information about places to eat and sleep.

FROM BRITAIN AND IRELAND

For **scheduled flights**, Buzz flies daily to Girona from Stansted (April–Oct) from around £50 return. Booking ahead on any of the other budget carriers can get you similarly inexpensive fares: EasyJet flies to Barcelona from Luton, Gatwick and Liverpool (with connections from Belfast and Scottish airports); Go serves Barcelona from Stansted and Bristol; and Ryanair flies to Perpignan from Stansted (with connections from Prestwick and Dublin). The larger carriers – British Airways, BMI British Midland and Iberia – fly to Barcelona from Heathrow, Gatwick, Birmingham and Manchester for between £110 and £200; Iberia also flies from Belfast; and both Iberia and Aer Lingus fly from Dublin for around €140.

Numerous **charter flights** operate in summer to Girona (often referred to simply as "Costa Brava airport"). It's also possible to find flights in the winter, especially around Christmas and New Year. Although many are block-booked by travel agents, there are normally seats free; last-minute deals can be around £100, although expect to have to travel at any time of the day or night.

Don't rule out **package holidays** – seven-day deals can cost as little as £150 – but bear in mind that you'll often have little choice over accommodation or even location; that said, there's nothing to stop you ditching the package once you've arrived. Some **tour operators** also offer interesting cultural, sports and culinary packages.

Airlines in Britain and Ireland

Aer Lingus UK ⊤ 0845/973 7747, Republic of Ireland ⊤ 01/886 8888, ⓦ www.aerlingus.ie.

BMI British Midland UK ⊤ 0870/607 0555, Republic of Ireland ⊤ 01/283 8833, ⓦ www.flybmi.com.

British Airways UK ⊤ 0845/773 3377, Republic of Ireland ⊤ 1800/626747, ⓦ www.britishairways.com.

Buzz UK ⊤ 0870/240 7070, ⓦ www.buzzaway.com.

EasyJet UK ⊤ 0870/600 0000, ⓦ www.easyjet.com.

Go UK ⊤ 0845/607 6543, ⓦ www.go-fly.com.

Iberia UK ⊤ 0845/601 2854, Republic of Ireland ⊤ 01/407 3017, ⓦ www.iberia.com.

Ryanair UK ⊤ 0870/156 9569, Republic of Ireland ⊤ 01/609 7800, ⓦ www.ryanair.com.

Flight agents in Britain and Ireland

Cheapflights
ⓦ www.cheapflights.co.uk. Searches for the best bargains to Girona and offers some online booking.

Dial-a-flight UK ⊤ 0870/333 4488, Republic of Ireland ⊤ 01/617 7556, ⓦ www.dial-a-flight.com. Scheduled and charter flight bargains (including flights to Girona and accommodation).

First Choice UK ⊤ 0870/750 0499, ⓦ www.holidays.co.uk. Flight-only booking service, with summer offers to Girona.

Flightbookers UK ⊤ 020/7757 2444, ⓦ www.ebookers.com. Low fares on an extensive selection of scheduled flights.

North-South Travel UK ⊤ 01245/608291, ⓦ www.northsouthtravel.co.uk. Excellent discount fares, with profits used to support projects in the developing world, especially the promotion of sustainable tourism.

Trailfinders UK ⓣ 020/7628 7628, Republic of Ireland ⓣ 01/677 7888, ⓦ www .trailfinders.com. Efficient and well-informed agent.

Travel Cuts UK ⓣ 020/7255 2082, ⓦ www.travelcuts .co.uk. Budget, student and youth travel.

Tour operators in Britain and Ireland

A Taste of Spain Spain ⓣ 0034/932 103 504, ⓦ www.atasteofspain.com. Cooking holidays in Catalan farmhouses.

Bridgewater Travel UK ⓣ 01299/271717, ⓦ www .bridgewatertravel.co.uk. A good selection of villas, apartments and farmhouses throughout the Costa Brava.

Exodus UK ⓣ 020/8675 5550, ⓦ www.thisamazingplanet.co. uk. Walking and cultural tours of La Garrotxa and Dalí country.

Explore Worldwide UK ⓣ 01252/760000, ⓦ www .explore.co.uk. Walking holidays staying in small hotels.

Fahy Travel Republic of Ireland ⓣ 091/594747, ⓦ www .fahytravel.ie. Good selection of last-minute bargains.

Golf in the Sun UK ⓣ 01327/350394, ⓦ www .golfinthesun.co.uk. Golfing holidays at three- and four-star hotels in the Baix Empordà.

Hidden Trails UK ⓣ 0870 /134 4283, ⓦ www.hiddentrails .com. Horse-riding holidays in La Garrotxa and the Alt Empordà.

Inn Travel UK ⓣ 01653/629000, ⓦ www.inntravel.co.uk. Excellent Costa Brava and Pyrenees walking holidays. Walk from inn to inn while your luggage is carried ahead.

Longmere Golf UK ⓣ 020/8655 1101, ⓦ www.atlgolf.demon .co.uk. A range of golfing holidays and accommodation in the Baix Empordà.

Magic of Spain UK ⓣ 0870 /027 0480, ⓦ www .magictravelgroup.co.uk. Upmarket hotel and villa holidays, often in out-of-the-way places.

Martin Randall Travel UK
ⓣ 020/8742 3355,
ⓦ www.martinrandall.com.
Small-group cultural tours and gastronomic holidays in Girona, Figueres and the Costa Brava.

The Real Spain (Citalia) UK
ⓣ 020/8686 0677,
ⓦ www.citalia.co.uk. High-quality hotels, villas and apartments in less populated areas.

Spanish Harbour Holidays UK
ⓣ 0870/027 0507,
ⓦ www.spanish-harbour.co.uk.
A very good site offering villas, apartments and hotels in the unspoilt Baix Empordà.

Travel Club of Upminster UK
ⓣ 01708/225000,
ⓦ www.travelclub.org.uk.
Villas and apartments in the Baix Empordà.

Vintage Spain UK ⓣ 01954/261431, ⓦ www.vintagetravel.co.uk. Specialists in renting country houses, most with pools, in the Baix Empordà and inland.

BY CAR

Going by **car**, the main decision is whether to take two days to schlep all the way across France or pay more for the 24-hour **ferry** crossing (Feb–Oct only) to the Spanish coast. Ferry prices vary depending on the day and period of travel, but a return to Bilbao or Santander for a car and two adults, including a cabin, is likely to be around £520. Add at least €50 for motorway tolls: both arrival ports are a full day's drive from the Costa Brava (roughly 600km). By contrast, crossing to and from France costs around £200 by ferry or £140 by **Eurotunnel**, to which you should add €360–600 for *autoroute* tolls, meals and accommodation on the long drive there and back.

FROM BRITAIN AND IRELAND

7

Ferry operators and Eurotunnel

Brittany Ferries UK ⓣ0870
/536 0360, Republic of Ireland
ⓣ021/427 7801, ⓦwww
.brittanyferries.co.uk. Cork to
Roscoff (March–Oct); Poole to
Cherbourg; Portsmouth to
Caen or St Malo; Plymouth to
Roscoff (year-round);
Plymouth to Santander
(March–Oct).

Eurotunnel UK ⓣ0870/535
3535, ⓦwww.eurotunnel
.com. Shuttle train for vehicles
and their passengers between
Folkestone and Coquelles,
near Calais (every 15–45min;
35min). Book ahead or buy
your ticket at the toll booths
(junction 11a off the M20). It's
cheaper to travel Mon–Fri
10pm–6am.

Hoverspeed UK ⓣ0870/524
0241, ⓦwww.hoverspeed
.co.uk. Dover to Calais;
Newhaven to Dieppe.

Irish Ferries Republic of Ireland
ⓣ01/661 0511, ⓦwww
.irishferries.com. Rosslare to
Cherbourg or Roscoff
(March–Sept).

P&O Portsmouth UK
ⓣ0870/242 4999,
ⓦwww.poportsmouth.com.
Portsmouth to Cherbourg, Le
Havre or Bilbao.

P&O Stena Line UK ⓣ0870
/600 0600, ⓦwww.posl.com.
Dover to Calais.

Sea France UK ⓣ0870/571
1711, ⓦwww.seafrance.com.
Dover to Calais.

BY TRAIN

Trains from London arrive in Paris at the Gare du Nord, from where you'll have to cross the city: night trains to Girona depart from the Gare d'Austerlitz, day trains from the Gare de Lyon. You may also have to change midway (at Narbonne or Montpellier). Journey time from London is at least 12 hours, and point-to-point return fares start around £210; a **rail pass** might work out cheaper. Note, though, that exploring the Costa Brava by train is not a viable option (see p.24).

Eurostar ⓣ 0870/160 6600,
  ⓦ www.eurostar.com.
  Passenger trains direct from
  London Waterloo to Paris
  Gare du Nord, via Ashford in
  Kent and the Channel Tunnel
(3hr). The cheapest return
costs £79 (restrictions apply).
Rail Europe ⓣ 0870/584 8848,
  ⓦ www.raileurope.co.uk.
  Tickets and passes for
  European train travel.

FROM NORTH AMERICA

From North America, **scheduled flights** nonstop to
Barcelona are run by Delta from New York. American
Airlines, Continental and Iberia all fly from New York and
Los Angeles via Madrid, while Air Canada, British Airways
and Iberia fly from Toronto via London. Expect to pay
US$900–980 from New York, US$1200–1375 from LA, or
C$1220–1360 from Toronto. **Tour operators** offer reason-
ably imaginative holidays, mainly taking in Girona and Dalí
country.

Airlines in North America

American Airlines ⓣ 1-800
  /433-7300, ⓦ www.aa.com.
Air Canada ⓣ 1-888/247-2262,
  ⓦ www.aircanada.ca.
British Airways ⓣ 1-800/247-
  9297, ⓦ www.britishairways
  .com.
Continental ⓣ 1-800/231-0856,
  ⓦ www.continental.com.
Delta ⓣ 1-800/241-4141,
  ⓦ www.delta.com.
Iberia ⓣ 1-800/772-4642,
  ⓦ www.iberia.com.

Flight agents and tour operators in North America

Air Courier Association
  ⓣ 1-800/282-1202,
  ⓦ www.aircourier.org. Courier
  fares to Madrid.
Auto Europe ⓣ 1-800/223-
  5555, ⓦ www.autoeurope
  .com. Air-hotel deals and car
  rental.

FROM NORTH AMERICA

Butterfield and Robinson
ⓣ 1-800/678-1147,
ⓦ www.butterfield.com.
Biking and walking holidays,
staying in luxury hotels,
starting and finishing in
Barcelona.

EC Tours ⓣ 1-800/388-0877,
ⓦ www.ectours.com. A
variety of package tours,
including Girona and Figueres.

**International Association of
Air Travel Couriers** ⓣ 561/
582-8320, ⓦ www.courier.org.
Courier flight broker.

Petrabax Tours ⓣ 1-800/634-
1188, ⓦ www.petrabax.com.
Escorted tours, hotels,
historic inns and property
rentals in Girona.

Travel Cuts ⓣ 1-800/667-2887
or 416/979-2406, ⓦ www
.travelcuts.com. Youth
specialists.

FROM AUSTRALIA AND NEW ZEALAND

There are no direct **flights** from down under to Spain, the
only option being to make one or two stopovers on the
way. Fares from Australia are around A\$1050, from New
Zealand about NZ\$1700. **Tours** are also limited: some
operators will put together a package, but these can be
expensive – it's often more economical to book accommodation separately from your flight.

Airlines in Australia and New Zealand

Alitalia Australia ⓣ 02/9244
2400; New Zealand ⓣ 09/302
1452, ⓦ www.alitalia.it.
British Airways Australia
ⓣ 02/8904 8800; New
Zealand ⓣ 09/356 8690,

ⓦ www.britishairways.com.
Japan Airlines (JAL) Australia
ⓣ 02/9272 1111; New
Zealand ⓣ 09/379 9906,
ⓦ www.japanair.com.

Agents and operators in Australia and New Zealand

Flight Centre Australia ⓣ 13 1600, ⓦ www.flightcentre .com.au. New Zealand ⓣ 0800/243544, ⓦ www.flightcentre.co.nz. Discount agent.

IB Tours Australia ⓣ 02/9560 6932. Customized tours of Spain, as well as car rentals and city stays.

Ibertours Australia ⓣ 03/9670 8388 or ⓣ 1800/500016, ⓦ www.ibertours.com.au.

Escorted and solo tours to rural and city areas of Spain, plus help in organizing study trips.

STA Travel Australia ⓣ 1300/ 360960, New Zealand ⓣ 0800/874773, ⓦ www .statravel.com.au. Discount agent.

Thomas Cook Australia ⓣ 13 1771, New Zealand ⓣ 09/379 3920.

Red tape and visas

EU citizens need only a valid national identity card to enter Spain for up to ninety days; UK citizens, lacking an ID card, need a passport. US, Canadian, Australian and New Zealand citizens don't need a visa for a stay of up to ninety days, but do require a valid passport. **Visa** requirements can change, and it's always advisable to check the current situation before you travel.

Spanish embassies abroad

Australia 15 Arkana St, Yarralumla, Canberra, ACT 2600 ☎02/6273 3555.

Canada 74 Stanley Ave, Ottawa, ON, K1M 1P4 ☎613/747-2252, ⓦwww.docuweb.ca /SpainInCanada.

Ireland 17a Merlyn Park, Ballsbridge, Dublin 4 ☎01/269 1640.

UK 39 Chesham Place, London SW1X 8SB ☎020/7235 5555.

USA 2375 Pennsylvania Ave NW, Washington, DC 20037 ☎202/728-2330, ⓦwww.spainemb.org.

Embassies and consulates in Spain

Australian Pl Descubridor Diego de Ordas 3, 28003 Madrid ☎914 419 300, ⓦwww.embaustralia.es.

Canadian c/Nuñez de Balboa 35, 28001 Madrid ☎914 233

250, ⓦ www.canada-es.org.
Consulate in Barcelona ⓣ 933
170 541.

Irish Paseo de la Castellana 46-
4, 28046 Madrid ⓣ 915 763
500.

New Zealand Pl de la Lealtad
2-3, 28014 Madrid ⓣ 915 310
997.

UK c/Fernando el Santo 16,
28010 Madrid ⓣ 917 008 200,
ⓦ www.ukinspain.com.
Consulate in Barcelona ⓣ 933
666 200.

US c/Serrano 75, 28006 Madrid
ⓣ 915 872 200,
ⓦ www.embusa.es. Consulate
in Barcelona ⓣ 932 802 227.

Information, websites and maps

The **Spanish National Tourist Office (SNTO)** has information on general matters such as accommodation and climate, but virtually nothing of practical help on Girona and the Costa Brava. Far better information is available from the **Patronat de Turisme Costa Brava Girona**, either directly or via their website.

Local **tourist offices** (Oficines de Turisme), sponsored by the Patronat de Turisme, are very efficient; we've pinpointed them where relevant. They stock free, top-quality information and maps and generally have helpful staff who can advise on accommodation, trips and activities.

SNTO offices

Australia and New Zealand
178 Collins St, Melbourne
ⓣ 03/9650 7377, ⓔ sales
@spanishtourism.com.au.
Canada 2 Bloor St West #3402,
Toronto, ON, M4W 3E2
ⓣ 416/960-3131, ⓦ www
.docuweb.ca/SpaininCanada.

UK 22–23 Manchester Sq,
London W1M 5AP
ⓣ 020/7486 8077, brochure
requests ⓣ 0906/364 0630,
ⓦ www.tourspain.co.uk.
USA 666 Fifth Ave, New York,
NY 10103 ⓣ 212/265-8822;
also in Chicago and LA;
ⓦ www.tourspain.es.

Patronat de Turisme Costa Brava Girona

**Patronat de Turisme Costa
Brava Girona** c/Emili Grahit

13–15, 17002 Girona ⓣ 972
208 401, ⓦ www.cbrava.es.

THE COSTA BRAVA ON THE INTERNET

Most towns have official **websites** as well as unofficial ones. Besides the Patronat de Turisme, there's a handful of general sites in English – plus plenty in Catalan – with information on the region.

ⓦ **www.cbrava.es** The most complete site for the whole area, with good links to museums and accommodation.

ⓦ **www.costabravainfo.com** Rather uneven site sticking to the coast, but has decent town descriptions plus some listings.

Ⓦ **www.costabravanord.com**
Activities, accommodation
and eating from Platja d'Aro
to Portbou.

Ⓦ **www.dlleure.com** Primarily
an accommodation site, this
also has very good information
on each town and what to
expect there, plus listings of
restaurants and bars.

Ⓦ **www.publintur.es** A tourist
guide to Catalonia with a
good section on the Costa
Brava; especially good on the
natural parks.

Ⓦ **www.tourspain.es** The
Spanish tourist board site,
with a small overview of the
region.

MAPS

Our **maps** and the free maps handed out by the tourist
offices should be enough for most needs, although a **road
map** will help you explore more fully. The best are
Catalunya Comarques, covering the whole of Catalonia, or
the more detailed *Costa Brava Comarques de Girona*, both
published by Distrimapas Telstar and available at most local
newsagents for around €3.60.

Detailed 1:30,000 maps of the **natural parks** can be had
free from each park's information office. The most reliable
1:50,000 **walking** maps are the series of sheets covering
each *comarca*, or area (Baix Empordà, Alt Empordà, La
Garrotxa, and so on), published by the Institut Cartogràfic
de Catalunya (around €7.20) and available at better
newsagents or the outlets listed below.

Map outlets

In Catalonia

Altaïr Gran Via 616, 08007
Barcelona Ⓣ 934 271 171,
Ⓦ www.altair.es.

Ulysus c/Ballesteries 29, 17004
Girona Ⓣ 972 211 773.

In the UK

Blackwell's 53 Broad St, Oxford OX1 3BQ ⓣ01865/792792, ⓦwww.bookshop.blackwell.co.uk.

Stanfords 12–14 Long Acre, London WC2E 9LP ⓣ020/7836 1321, ⓦwww.stanfords.co.uk.

In North America

Map Link 30 S La Patera Lane #5, Santa Barbara, CA 93117 ⓣ805/692-6777, ⓦwww.maplink.com.

World of Maps 118 Holland Ave, Ottawa, ON, K1Y 0X6 ⓣ613/724-6776, ⓦwww.itmb.com.

In Australia and New Zealand

Mapland 372 Little Bourke St, Melbourne ⓣ03/9670 4383, ⓦwww.mapland.com.au.

Specialty Maps 46 Albert St, Auckland ⓣ09/307 2217, ⓦwww.ubd-online.co.nz/maps.

Insurance
and health

Y ou'd do well to take out an **insurance** policy to
cover against theft, loss and illness or injury. Before
paying for a new policy, however, it's worth checking whether you're already covered: some home insurance
policies may cover your possessions when overseas, and
many private medical schemes include travel cover. Student
health coverage often extends during the vacations and
beyond.

A typical policy provides cover for the loss of baggage,
tickets and cash or cheques, as well as cancellation or cur-
tailment of your trip. Most exclude "dangerous" sports –
scuba diving, windsurfing or trekking – unless you pay
more. If you take medical coverage, ascertain at what point
benefits will be paid, and whether there's a 24-hour emergency number you can call. When securing baggage cover,
make sure that the per-article limit will cover your most
valuable possession. If you need to make a claim, keep all
receipts. If anything is stolen, you must obtain an official
statement from the police, called a *parte*.

ROUGH GUIDES TRAVEL INSURANCE

Rough Guides offers its own travel insurance, customized for our readers by a leading UK broker and backed by a Lloyd's underwriter. It's available for anyone, of any nationality and any age, travelling anywhere in the world.

There are two main Rough Guide insurance plans: Essential, for basic, no-frills cover; and Premier, with more generous and extensive benefits. Alternatively, you can take out annual multi-trip insurance, which covers you for any number of trips throughout the year (with a maximum of sixty days for any one trip). Unlike many policies, the Rough Guides schemes are calculated by the day, so if you're travelling for 27 days rather than a month, that's all you pay for. If you intend to be away for the whole year, the Adventurer policy will cover you for 365 days. Each plan can be supplemented with a "Hazardous Activities Premium" if you're going to indulge in sports considered dangerous, such as scuba diving. You can buy or get an online quote at ⓦ www.roughguides.com/insurance, or by phone at UK freefone ☎0800/015 0906; US toll-free ☎1-866/220-5588; or, at usual international rates, ☎+441243/621046.

HEALTH

Hygiene standards on the Costa Brava are high and the water is perfectly safe to drink. The only likely blights may be an upset stomach or a touch of the sun.

For minor complaints, go to a **pharmacy** (*farmàcia*); there are plenty in the major towns, identifed by a green or red cross outside. Most keep usual shop hours (Mon–Sat 9am–1pm & 4–8pm), and they all display the rota indicating which one locally is open 24 hours. For more serious cases, head to the **CAP** (*Centre d'Atenció Primària*, or

Primary Healthcare Centre) in larger towns, where you'll often find English-speaking staff; we've listed these where applicable, along with each **hospital** (*hospital* or *urgències* in Catalan) with an out-patients' department.

In emergencies, call ⓣ112.

If you're relying on free treatment under Spain's reciprocal health arrangements with other EU countries, tell ambulance staff and hospital medics to avoid being treated (and billed) as a private patient. Always carry a photocopy of your **E111** form, available free from main UK post offices, or from the local health board in Ireland.

Dentists are all private: you'll pay around €55 for a filling. The local Yellow Pages (*Pàgines Grogues*) will have a list, or ask at your hotel or tourist office.

Costs and money

C atalonia is the wealthiest region in Spain, and the Costa Brava is in the richest province in Catalonia: **costs** of accommodation (apart from package hotels), shopping and eating out are among the steepest in Spain, though still fairly economical compared to northern Europe.

If you **stay** in a *pensió* or *hostal* and buy picnic food, you can get by on around £30/US$48 a day. Staying in a three-star hotel, eating out and not skimping on nightlife can double this. For £85/US$136 a day, you can live in considerable comfort. At even the top end of the scale, **eating out** offers excellent value: a meal in a top restaurant will set you back about £20/US$28. **Drinks** are cheap and measures are generous by northern European standards, but prices can mount up, especially at a club or if you're being served on a terrace.

For details of tipping, see p.55.

One other cost to bear in mind is IVA **sales tax**, which ranges from seven percent on meals and accommodation to sixteen percent on luxury goods – sometimes it's quoted in prices, at other times it's added to the final bill.

Full-time students are eligible for the International Student ID Card (ISIC), which entitles you to special travel fares and **discounts** at many attractions. Anybody aged 26 or less qualifies for the International Youth Travel Card, and teachers can get the International Teacher Card, both of which carry ISIC benefits. Check Ⓦ www.isic.org for outlets selling the cards, all of which cost in the order of £6 or US$22.

MONEY

The currency of Spain, and of eleven other EU countries, is the **euro**, made up of 100 cents (*cèntims* in Catalan). There are notes of €5, €10, €20, €50, €100, €200 and €500, and coins of 1c, 2c, 5c, 10c, 20c, 50c, €1 and €2.

Spanish **banks** are slow, bureaucratic and expensive, but they're still the best places to change money, with lower commissions than elsewhere. **Bureaux de change** stay open outside bank hours, but either charge higher commissions or are commission-free at a much less favourable exchange rate. Hotels and campsites will often exchange money, but at uncompetitive rates.

**Normal banking hours are Mon–Fri 9am–2pm;
in winter, banks are also open Sat 9am–1pm.**

CARDS AND TRAVELLERS' CHEQUES

Credit and **debit cards** are the most convenient way to obtain holiday currency. They can be used to withdraw cash from ATMs (cash dispensers) or over the counter (subject, possibly, to a transaction fee): Mastercard and Visa are accepted just about everywhere but American Express may not be taken in some places. ATMs are widespread and your bank will able to advise on whether you can use your **debit card** in them.

Travellers' cheques, by contrast, can be expensive, but are secure. Most brands are accepted, and the usual fee for buying them is one or two percent. Keep the purchase agreement and a record of cheque serial numbers safe and separate from the cheques; report lost or stolen cheques immediately (there'll be a phone number provided with your cheques); most companies claim to provide replacements within 24 hours.

Visa TravelMoney (ⓦwww.visa.com/pd) combines the security of travellers' cheques with the convenience of plastic. It's a disposable debit card, charged up before you leave home with whatever amount you like, and usable in any ATM that accepts Visa. Citicorp, and Thomas Cook/Interpayment outlets, sell the card worldwide (see the website). When your money runs out, you throw the card away. You can buy up to nine cards to access the same funds – useful for couples or families travelling together. Visa's 24-hour customer service centre can be reached from Spain on ⓣ900 951 125.

Getting around

The Costa Brava has a very good **public transport** system, with **buses** linking all the minor and major towns, mainline **trains** running through the region and **boats** plying almost the full length of the coast. If you want to explore the region in depth, though, you'll really need a **car** or **motorbike**.

BY BUS

The region's extensive **bus** network is reliable and inexpensive. All inter-town services are run by the **Sarfa** company (℡ 902 302 025, Ⓦ www.sarfa.com). Between the main towns comfortable buses run roughly hourly 7am–9pm, with between two and ten buses a day to smaller towns. In summer, additional local services run to some of the beach towns.

Timetables are available from Sarfa ticket offices (*taquilla*), bus stations and tourist offices. It's possible to buy **tickets** for inter-town services on the bus, but to be sure of a seat it's best to buy them in advance at the bus station (some tourist offices also sell tickets). **Fares** average out around 10c per kilometre: a one-way fare (*anar*) from Girona to Cadaqués is €6.25, Barcelona–Begur is €11.09, and L'Escala–Palamós is €3.31. Return tickets (*anar i tornar*) cost exactly double.

Larger **bus stations**, such as those in Girona and Figueres, have marked bays, while smaller ones usually have only one or two stops; they all display route maps showing the start and finish points of each line, and all buses display their destination on the front. Where a town doesn't have a station, buses leave from outside the Sarfa office (see list below).

Larger towns also have good **local buses**, going around town and to outlying beaches. Tickets – bought from the driver – are very cheap, generally around €0.60 flat rate.

Sarfa bus company offices

Begur Pl Forgas 6 ☎972 622 446; **La Bisbal** c/Voltes 10 ☎972 640 964; **Cadaquès** c/St Vicens ☎972 258 713; **Castelló d'Empúries** Hotel Emporium ☎972 250 593; **L'Escala** Avgda Ave Maria 26 ☎972 770 218; **Girona** Estació Autobusos ☎972 201 796; **Lloret de Mar** Estació Autobusos ☎972 364 295; **Pals** Turisme, Pl Major 1 ☎972 637 380; **Palafrugell** c/Torres Jonama 73–79 ☎972 300 623; **Palamós** c/López Puigcerver 7 ☎972 600 250; **Platja d'Aro** Estació Autobusos ☎972 826 787; **Roses** Gran Via Pau Casals ☎972 150 585; **St Antoni de Calonge** Turisme, Avgda Catalunya ☎972 661 714; **St Feliu de Guíxols** c/Llibertat 1 ☎972 321 187; **Tossa de Mar** Estació Autobusos ☎972 340 903.

BY TRAIN

The **train** isn't a viable way to explore, as the only line runs from Barcelona past the coastal town of Blanes north inland to Girona, on to Figueres, and from there to the border via Llançà and Portbou. It's a good way of getting from one end of the Costa Brava to the other, but not for accessing coastal or inland towns.

BY CAR OR MOTORBIKE

Driving your own vehicle, you're able to reach the most secluded – and attractive – towns and beaches. However, driving can sometimes seem a free-for-all, with round-abouts used as overtaking spots, hard shoulders as an extra lane, and most drivers barrelling over pedestrian crossings. The quality and quantity of road signs can vary, giving very little warning of hazards ahead. That aside, **driving rules** mean that you must wear a seatbelt, mustn't cross an unbroken white line in the middle of the road – even if everyone else does – and must stop at a "Stop" sign. At junctions, unless a sign says otherwise, **give way to the right**. All drivers must carry two hazard triangles, a recognized first-aid kit and a set of spare bulbs.

The fastest **road** is an *autopista*, for which you pay at a staffed or automatic toll (*peatge*). The **A7** is the main route, running inland from Barcelona to the French border (and on to Perpignan as the French A9), while the **A19** hugs the coast from Barcelona to Blanes. All other roads are free. Those labelled "N" followed by a Roman numeral are national routes: the **N-II** shadows the A7 all the way along (you might sometimes see "CN-II" used in addresses, instead of the standard "N-II" used on road signs). Local main roads are denoted with a "C", and smaller roads with a "GI".

It's worth paying the A7 tolls (roughly €6 from Barcelona or Perpignan to Girona): in summer especially, the N-II gets packed and offers no advantages of scenery over the *autopista*.

Main roads are very good, but some of the side roads can be a little hairy and are sometimes little more than dirt tracks. **Speed limits** are 60kph on urban roads, 90kph on minor roads, 100kph on main roads and 120kph on *autopistas*; hefty spot fines are handed out for breaking them. Random drink-drive **breath tests** are common.

Fuel is the cheapest in Europe. There are two types of unleaded (*sense plom*), usually labelled "98" and "95" and always with green pumps; leaded Super-Plus (97 octane); and diesel (sometimes *gas-oil*), usually with black pumps.

Motoring organizations

Australia: AAA Ⓦ www.aaa
.asn.au.

Canada: CAA Ⓦ www.caa.com.

Irish AA Travel Ⓦ www
.aaireland.ie.

UK: AA Ⓦ www.theaa.co.uk;
 RAC Ⓦ www.rac.co.uk.

US: AAA Ⓦ www.aaa.com.

CAR AND MOTORBIKE RENTAL

Dozens of companies offer **car rental**, which is cheaper than in most European countries. To rent, you need to be over 21, have been driving for at least a year and have a valid licence. **Prices** vary greatly; for a small saloon, budget on €32–40 a day with unlimited mileage, although you can sometimes get better rates with agencies that deal with local firms, such as Autos Abroad. You'll have to leave a credit card imprint or pay a hefty cash deposit. **Fly-drive** deals can be good value: in the UK, for example, Iberia offers cars from £120/180 a week (low/high season).

A **motorbike** lets you explore areas that might otherwise be inaccessible, and is especially good for some of the rougher tracks in the north of the Costa Brava and inland areas. You can rent from local agencies in most large towns on a sliding scale: €24 for 4hr, or €50 for a 12hr day.

International car rental companies

Autos Abroad Ⓦ www
   .autosabroad.com.
Avis Ⓦ www.avis.com.
Budget Ⓦ www.budget.com.
Europcar Ⓦ www.europcar.com.

Hertz Ⓦ www.hertz.com.
Holiday Autos Ⓦ www
   .holidayautos.com.
Thrifty Ⓦ www.thrifty.com.

BY BOAT

Numerous **boats**, ranging from large open-topped water-buses to simple craft with room for a dozen people, chug up and down the coast between Easter and the end of October. They usually operate on short stretches and count less as an efficient means of getting around than an unhurried way of trying out new beaches while getting a passing view of the coastline. **Tickets** are available from booths on the beach, where you'll also find timetables. Fares vary depending on the type of boat but, as a guide, a trip from Blanes to Sant Feliu de Guíxols – nine stops and three main towns away – costs €12.50 return.

Accommodation

Although many visitors to the Costa Brava opt to have their **accommodation** included as part of a package deal, the region boasts everything from campsites of all prices and sizes, through self-catering apartments to luxurious, spectacularly sited hotels. A recent development is a network of *turisme rural* houses, an imaginative alternative to more traditional forms of self-catering. Accommodation is cheap in comparison with other European countries and normally of a high standard.

A lot of hotel rooms in more popular towns are block-booked by agencies, but this still leaves plenty for indepen-

ACCOMMODATION PRICE CODES

Accommodation in this guide has been graded on a scale of ❶–❾, indicating the cost of the least expensive double room in high season. Prices take IVA tax into account.

Apartments (which are usually rented by the week) and turisme rural houses (which may be rented on a weekly or nightly basis) are graded according to the nightly rate for two adults.

❶ under €30	❹ €60–75	❼ €120–150
❷ €30–45	❺ €75–90	❽ €150–180
❸ €45–60	❻ €90–120	❾ over €180

dent travellers – along with the range of self-catering accommodation. Although it's possible to turn up and find a place to stay even in high season (July, Aug & Easter), it's highly advisable to **reserve**. Cheaper hotels in coastal resorts tend to close in winter.

Online bookings

Four local associations monitor quality across types of accommodation. The **Provincial Hotel Federation** (Ⓔ fphg@gna.es) is the only one that doesn't offer online booking; while the **Tourist Apartment Association** (Ⓦ www.apartamentos-ata.com), **Girona Rural Tourism** (Ⓦ www.costabrava.org/rural), and the **Girona Camping Association** (Ⓦ www.campingsgirona.com) all do.

You can also make online reservations for local hotels, apartments and *turisme rural* houses through **Eoland** (Ⓦ www.eoland.com) and **Dlleure** (Ⓦ www.dlleure.com).

FONDAS, PENSIONS, HOSTALS AND HOTELS

The Spanish system of categorizing accommodation is fiendishly complicated. The Catalan government recognizes two types – hotels and *pensions* – although all lists and the establishments themselves still use the range of old names. Nonetheless, you'll find that categorization has no bearing at all on **character**. A nominally downmarket *pensió* or *hostal* could as easily be in a historic building as a modern block, while you'll come across three-star hotels occupying anonymous beachfront hulks and graceful old mansions alike. We've made an effort to highlight the region's more characterful establishments.

Least expensive of all is a **fonda** or a **pensió**; the two are more or less interchangeable – *fonda* is an old term which is dying out – with the *pensions* divided into one- and two-star establishments, all usually comfortable and well maintained. You can find en-suite rooms at both one- and two-star places; they're to be expected if you're paying more than about €50. Traditionally, *pensions* served meals (and some still require you to take half board), but they're increasingly offering only B&B.

Next up the price scale is a **hostal**, traditionally categorized from one to three stars; almost all have en-suite bathrooms and many compare favourably with hotels. You might also see the term *hostal-residència*, which used to denote that the place was a *hostal* that offered only B&B, although these are now being reclassified as *pensions*. There's a great deal of overlap, as a two-star *pensió* can be equivalent to a one- or even two-star *hostal*, while some upmarket three-star *hostals* are being reclassified as hotels. Many places use both names.

More expensive still is a **hotel**, graded between one and five stars. All have en suites, normally to a very high standard, although some have simpler facilities: there's little difference between a one-star hotel and a *pensió*. Three-star hotels, however, are noticeably more sophisticated, and four- and five-star hotels are safely ensconced in the luxury bracket.

As for **cost**, a simple double with shared bathroom is around €30 in the winter, or as much as €50 in the summer. A double room in a three-star hotel will set you back between €78 and €90, while more luxurious places can charge upwards of €180.

APARTMENTS AND TURISME RURAL

In recent years the Catalan government has demanded higher standards of **self-catering** accommodation and, as a result, the quality of apartments and villas has risen sharply, as have prices. The latest arrival is a network of **turisme rural** houses wherein you can rent a room by the night, and share some facilities with the owner, or take the whole house (you'll normally be expected to do so by the week). Most are in charming old buildings, some with gardens and pools, and they usually represent an economical alternative to hotels.

CAMPING

Camping is popular with Catalans, and there are countless sites all over the Costa Brava. Facilities tend to be very good, with clean toilets and showers, shops, bars, restaurants and swimming pools, and many offer mobile homes or cabins to rent. As a general rule, a one-star site charges €15–18 for a pitch, vehicle and two adults, a two-star site €18–27. Most close November to Easter. An international camping carnet gives some discounts and insurance cover, buyable from motoring organizations or clubs such as the UK Camping and Caravanning Club (ⓦ www.campingandcaravanningclub .co.uk) or the US Family Campers and RVers (ⓦ www.fcrv .org).

It's illegal to camp, or even sleep, on the beach. Inland, you can sometimes pitch a tent in the mountains – but not within the natural parks – although you should make sure you're not on private hunting land (denoted by a white sign with a black border and gun); consult local tourist offices in advance.

ALBERGS DE JOVENTUT

The region's five **Albergs de Joventut** (youth hostels) – in Girona, Figueres, Banyoles and Olot, and on the beach between Empúries and L'Escala – are affiliated to Hostelling International (HI) and of a very high quality. The one in Girona offers doubles and triples as well as eight-bed dorms, while the others have dorms sleeping four to twenty.

All reservations are through the Catalan arm of HI (see below); if you aren't an HI member in your home country, you can join at any Catalan hostel for €18. Prices range from €10 to €24, the most expensive being for doubles at the Girona hostel.

Hostelling organizations

Australia ⓦ www.yha.com.au.

Canada ⓦ www.hostellingintl.ca.

Catalonia ⓦ www.gencat.es /catalunyajove.

England & Wales ⓦ www.yha .org.uk.

Ireland ⓦ www.anoige.ie.

New Zealand ⓦ www.yha.co.nz.

Northern Ireland ⓦ www.hini .org.uk.

Scotland ⓦ www.syha.org.uk.

USA ⓦ www.hiayh.org.

ALBERGS DE JOVENTUT

Food and drink

T ainted by popular images of chicken-and-chips and sangria, **food** on the Costa Brava nonetheless has depth: traditional cooking closely wedded to regional products has created a very distinctive cuisine. The variety of vegetable, meat, fish and seafood dishes is matched only by a supremely sinful sweet-tooth.

EATING

Catalans are demanding diners, and it's not hard to find good local cooking amid the tourist fare. The Costa Brava has a superb cuisine based on fresh **fish** and **seafood**, usually cooked very simply, either grilled or baked in salt or cooked as a stew with potatoes and tomatoes in the tasty dish *suquet*. **Meat** is served grilled, and a range of cured meats and **cheeses** accompany *pà amb tomàquet* (bread liberally smeared with tomato, olive oil and salt). **Veggie** dishes are often based on aubergines, peppers or wild mushrooms.

There's a menu reader, in Catalan and English, on pp.363–367.

One of the idiosyncrasies of Costa Brava cooking is **mar i muntanya** cuisine. Meaning literally "sea and mountain", this is an appetizing way of combining seafood with land produce, such as squid stuffed with meatballs, or rabbit and crayfish. In the mountainous La Garrotxa region, the hearty **cuina volcànica** ("volcanic cuisine") is based around a combination of any of eleven core ingredients, from such ordinary items as potatoes and beans to more exotic boar and truffles. Anyone with a sweet tooth will meet their match in the subtle **desserts**, while the fabulous local **pastries** are perfect in the afternoon with a cup of coffee.

Unless you're in a hotel which dishes up a good buffet, **breakfast** (*esmorzar*) is better taken in a café or bar, and will include coffee, toast or croissant, orange juice and even a slice of *tortilla* or a sandwich. In winter, **lunch** (*dinar*) might be a huge affair lasting hours, but in the summer most people tend to have a salad and grilled fish or order the **menú del dia**, a set meal. Also on offer are *plats combinats*, roughly akin to mixed grills. The **evening meal** (*sopar*) is normally eaten late: restaurants start buzzing around 9pm and many locals won't eat until 10pm.

Snacks, usually in the form of huge sandwiches, can be eaten at most times of day at a café or bar. **Tapas** are not a Catalan tradition, but a lot of bars serve small portions of different dishes, which you can cobble together to make an appetizing meal. Latest trend is for Basque tapas bars, where each *tapa* is held onto bread by a toothpick; you're charged by the number of toothpicks on your plate.

To give an idea of costs, each place we've reviewed is placed in one of four **price categories**, relating to the cost of a full meal (starter, main course, dessert, half a bottle of wine and coffee): budget (under €15 per person), inexpensive (€15–20), moderate (€20–30) or expensive (over €30).

For details of tipping, see p.55.

Opening hours vary, but daytime cafés and bars operate from 8 or 9am to 10pm or later. Restaurants are open

EATING

between roughly 1 and 4pm and then again from, say, 8pm to around midnight. Some, especially those on the beach, stay open all day, while in summer it's common to find a lot of the upmarket restaurants opening in the evening only.

Bars open at around 8pm, but don't really get under way for another couple of hours, and stay serving drinks until 3am. These times shift for clubs and discos (the terms are interchangeable, although they're generally referred to locally as *discoteques*), which usually open from 10pm to around 6am.

Through the summer, most places on the coast stay open all week; in winter, they tend to either close one day a week or open at weekends only. Inland towns generally stick to one day off a week all year round. Most places display a sign in Catalan saying which day they close (*Tancat* followed by the day).

Reservations aren't normally necessary; we've given phone numbers for those places where it's a good idea.

DRINKING

Spanish **wines** are reasonably inexpensive. The thing to look for is a Designation of Origin (DO) label on the back of the bottle, denoting that the wine has satisfied the quality assessment carried out by the relevant regional wine control board. Prices for a bottle are around €6–9. Rioja is the most famous **red wine**, and for overall taste and finesse is unbeatable. The Costers del Segre DO offers the subtle Raimat wines, while wines from another Catalan region, Priorat, are gathering clout. The local Costa Brava wine is the DO Empordà, which is a bit raw but drinkable with a meal.

Catalonia produces the best **whites** and **rosés** in the country, notably Peralada, from the north of the Costa

Brava, and the smooth Penedès wines from south of Barcelona. The most famous Catalan wine is sparkling white **cava**; the best-quality ones – such as Juvé i Camps and Recaredo – are often only sold locally.

Long drinks are popular, especially the universal "Gin-Tònic" and the even more common Cuba Libre; you might like to try one with Spanish Caribbean rums (*ron*) such as Cacique from Venezuela or Havana Club. The region also has some interesting mariners' drinks brought back from the Americas, including **Lumumba**, brandy with chocolate milk (served hot in winter). A must-try for the late evening is **Cremat**, a concoction of rum, brandy, cinnamon and lemon peel brought to you blazing in an earthenware dish: you keep it burning by stirring with the ladle provided, adding a cup of coffee immediately before serving. The longer you let it burn, the subtler the flavour. Other local drinks are the rather sickly **ratafia**, made in the mountain areas and served with cakes, and sweet **moscatel** wine, drunk on special occasions such as the *castanyada* (see p.47).

Ever popular, **sangria** (chilled red wine with lemonade, sliced fruit and ice) is a good low-alcohol alternative at lunchtime, but quality can vary greatly between towns, especially in the more touristic southern part of the coast; the awful pre-bottled stuff is to be avoided. A refreshing variation is *sangria de cava*, made with local sparkling white wine.

Beer (*cervesa*) is invariably lager and served either as draught or in quarter- or third-litre bottles, the most common brands being the equally good Estrella and San Miguel. Some of the beach towns serve beer – including British brands – in pint glasses, but it's much more usual to drink the smaller Spanish draught *canya* (normally served in quarter- or third-litre measures).

DRINKING

The usual drinks from other regions in Spain are easily available, including **sherry** (*Xeres/Jerez*), ranging from the dry *fino*, through medium-dry *amontillado* to sweet *oloroso*, (terms you should use when ordering). Catalan **brandy** (*conyac*), especially Torres, is very good. For an after-dinner drink, the Basque *patxaran*, made from anis with sloes, is excellent, as are the slightly sweeter **fruit liqueurs**, in particular apple, peach and pear (*licor de poma/pressec/pera*).

As far as **soft drinks** go, all the usual suspects are readily available. A couple of local favourites are very refreshing in the summer heat, especially *orxata* (*horchata* in Castilian), a chilled milky drink made from tiger nuts. Equally cooling is *granissat*, an iced drink usually made with lemon or coffee (*granissat de llimona/café*), but occasionally with more exotic mixes.

In the mountains and the northern part of the coast, tap water is very good and clear, but it gets increasingly chlorinated as you go south, where you might prefer the bottled variety.

Coffee (*café* or *café sol*) will always be served black unless you specify otherwise. For a larger, weaker cup of black coffee, ask for a *café doble* or *café americano*. Breakfast is usually a large white coffee (*café amb llet*), while after meals, the smaller *tallat*, coffee with a dash of milk, is a good digestive. For black coffee with brandy or rum, ask for a *carajillo* and specify *amb conyac* or *amb ron*; brandy or rum added to a small white coffee is a *trifàsic*. Decaffeinated coffee (*descafeinat*) usually comes in a sachet, although some places serve espresso decaff – ask for *descafeinat de màquina*. **Tea** is normally poor, made by steam-heating water and a bag together; you might do better with a **herbal tea** or infusion, especially camomile (*camamilla*), mint (*menta*) or lime (*tilla*).

DRINKING

37

GASTRONOMIC FESTIVALS

The Costa Brava's gastronomic festivals see the main restaurants in all the towns creating traditional dishes with local ingredients. Celebrations normally run over a period of around four weeks, unless otherwise stated, and are the perfect opportunity to sample the best in regional cooking.

Jan–Easter

Calella de Palafrugell – Garoinada (Sea Urchin Festival); Jan, Feb or March.
Roses – La Cuina de Roses; two weeks of Feb during Carnival.
Pals – La Cuina de l'Arròs (Rice Cuisine); mid-March to mid-April.

Easter–June

Castell-Platja d'Aro, **Sant Feliu de Guíxols** and **Santa Cristina d'Aro** – La Cuina del Bacallà (Cod Cuisine); late April & May.
Girona and surrounding area – Setmana Gastronòmica Gironina (Gastronomy Week); second week of April.
Begur – Peix de Roca de Begur (Rock Fish); mid-April to early June.
Calonge-Sant Antoni and **Palamós** – La Gamba (Festival of the Prawn); mid-April to late June.
Peratallada – Mostra Gastronòmica de Productes de l'Horta (Garden Produce Show); mid-April & May.

Castell-Platja d'Aro, **Sant Feliu de Guíxols** and **Santa Cristina d'Aro** – La Cuina de Faves, Pèsols i Suquet d'Escrita (Broad Bean, Pea and Suquet of Ray Festival); May.

L'Estartit and **Torroella de Montgrí** – Tastets de Mar (Seafood Tasting Festival); mid-May to mid-June.

Castell-Platja d'Aro, **Sant Feliu de Guíxols** and **Santa Cristina d'Aro** – La Cuina del Peix Blau Ganxó (Blue Fish Dishes Festival); June.

Roses – Suquet de Peix (Fish Suquet Festival); late June.

Sept–Dec

Castell-Platja d'Aro, **Sant Feliu de Guíxols** and **Santa Cristina d'Aro** – La Cuina del Bolet (Mushroom Cuisine); late Sept to early Nov.

Peratallada – Mostra Gastronòmica de l'Aviram (Poultry Cuisine); late Sept & Oct.

Girona and surrounding area – Setmana del Bolet (Mushroom Week); first week of Oct.

Calonge-Sant Antoni – Menú de la Badia (Bay Menu Festival); Oct–Dec.

Palamós – Ranxo de Pescadors (Fishermen's Fare); mid-Oct to mid-Dec.

Olot – Mostra de Cuina Volcànica de la Garrotxa (Garrotxa Volcanic Cuisine); second week in Nov.

Palafrugell – El Niu (a complex dish with dried cod, cod tripe, wild fowl and, sometimes, squid); first week of Dec.

Communications

Phone connections from the Costa Brava are efficient but expensive. The **postal** service is reasonably reliable, and burgeoning internet cafés make keeping in touch by **email** a feasible option from most towns.

POST

Postal services work fairly well through the year, but get clogged in the summer, when you should allow a week for items to reach places in Europe, two weeks or more for elsewhere. All large towns have a **post office** (*Correus*; generally Mon–Sat 9am–1.30pm); these spawn long queues but are the only places from which you can send parcels. For stamps and sending letters or postcards, you're better off going to a **tobacconist** (*estanc*; Mon–Fri 9am–1pm & 4–8pm, Sat 9am–1pm).

PHONES

You'll find **public phones** in towns and villages all over the Costa Brava, all with instructions in English; most take coins, but some accept only phonecards, which can be bought from any tobacconist for €5 or €10. The España

USEFUL NUMBERS

To call the Costa Brava from abroad
Dial your international access code (00 from the UK, Ireland and New Zealand; 011 from the US and Canada; 0011 from Australia) followed by 34 for Spain, followed by the nine-digit number.

To call abroad from the Costa Brava
For the UK, dial ☏ 0044; for Ireland, ☏ 00353; for the US or Canada, ☏ 001; for Australia, ☏ 0061; for New Zealand, ☏ 0064 – then the area code (minus the zero if there is one), then the number.
Operator services ☏ 1009.
Domestic directory enquiries ☏ 1003.
International directory enquiries ☏ 025.

Mundo card, also available from tobacconists for €30 (details on ☏ 900 902 902), lets you call Europe or North America at discounted rates. One convenient way to phone home is via a **phone charge card**, most of which are free to obtain from phone providers but relatively expensive to use. They let you make calls from most hotel, public and private phones using an access code and a PIN number, with the cost charged to your home account.

There are no **area codes** in Spain: you dial all nine numbers for landlines (which start with a 9) and mobile phones (which start with a 6). Off-peak rates apply Mon–Sat 8pm–9am, and all day Sunday.

Mobile phones

If you want to use your own **mobile phone**, check with your provider in advance whether it will work abroad; you may have to inform them before leaving in order to get international access switched on. This may incur a charge.

PHONES

You're also likely to be charged for incoming calls, and there may be different price brackets for outgoing calls; also check whether you can text and retrieve messages while you're away. ⓦ www.gsmworld.com has details of compatibility between networks.

EMAIL

On the coast and in the large inland towns you'll generally find a choice of **internet cafés**. Most are fairly hi-tech joints, but you'll sometimes find a computer or a coin-op screen in a corner of an ordinary bar. **Prices** are usually €3–3.60 per hour.

The two big names for a free **email** address – among thousands – are YahooMail (ⓦ www.yahoo.com) and Hotmail (ⓦ www.hotmail.com).

Opening hours, holidays and festivals

There's a great deal of variability in **working hours**. Normal opening times for **shops** are Mon–Sat 9am–2pm & 4–8pm, although in smaller towns many shops will close on Saturday afternoon. On the coast in the summer, shops usually operate daily 10am–2pm and 5–10pm. **Banks** are open Mon–Fri 9am–2pm; in winter, they're also open Sat 9am–1pm.

A normal week for a **museum** is Tues–Sat 9am–2pm and 4–8pm, while **churches** are usually open similar hours during the week and then only for masses at the weekend. Some village churches are kept locked, in which case the key will generally be held by the neighbours.

PUBLIC HOLIDAYS

Spain has ten national **public holidays** a year, which are supplemented by five regional ones; in addition to this, each town and village has its own *Festa Major*, or patron saint's day (see below). On a public holiday (*festiu*) all shops and businesses close, public transport runs one-third of its normal service, and museums and public buildings follow Sunday hours. In coastal resorts, though, most businesses trade as usual.

National and regional holidays

Jan 1 New Year's Day (Any Nou)

Jan 6 Epiphany (Reis)

Good Friday (Divendres Sant)

Easter Monday (Dilluns de Pascua)

May 1 Labour Day (Festa de Treball)

June Corpus Christi

June 24 St John's Day (Sant Joan)

Aug 25 Assumption (Assumpció)

Sept 11 Catalan National Day (Diada)

Oct 12 Spanish National Day (Pilar/Hispanitat)

Nov 1 All Saints (Tots Sants)

Dec 6 Constitution Day (Constitució)

Dec 8 Immaculate Conception (Immaculada Concepció)

Dec 25 Christmas Day (Nadal)

Dec 26 Boxing Day (Sant Esteve)

FESTIVALS

Combining religious ceremony with surprisingly large doses of pagan ritual, each Catalan town's **Festa Major** involves noise, merrymaking and plenty of dancing. Many include traditions such as the **gegants** ("giants"), originally mascots for craftsmen's guilds – pairs of effigies up to 12m tall (a king and queen, or shepherd and shepherdess) swirling through the streets, attended by the *capgrossos* ("bigheads"), smaller effigies with oversized caricature heads, to the tune of ancient wind instruments and drums.

Fire plays a significant role, especially around Sant Joan's Eve on June 23, when bonfires are lit and spectacular fireworks displays are held; the best is the week-long **fireworks festival** in Blanes. More eye-catching still are the *correfocs* ("fire runs"), when bands of devils prance through the streets under a rain of sparks while drummers beat out a hypnotic rhythm.

Two annual festivals stand out. **Setmana Santa** (Easter) is marked by elaborate and colourful processions in most towns, while **Carnestoltes** (Carnival), in February, is a frenzy of pure hedonism.

Many towns stage **music festivals** throughout the summer, ranging from classical and world music to jazz and traditional. The more established ones in Torroella de Montgrí and Peralada attract some big names, especially from the classical world, while the newer ones tend to have a parallel street music element, imbuing the town with a spontaneous party atmosphere.

Sardana and havaneres

All through the year, you're likely to stumble across the **sardana**, the traditional dance, being performed in the open. The dancers form a circle which anyone can join until it gets too unwieldy, when some members break off to form new circles. The steps are complicated, with dancers only keeping time by strict counting. Accompanying them is the *cobla*, a band made up of five woodwind musicians, five brass players and a double-bassist, who create the distinctive keening shrill of *sardana* tunes.

More stirring still are the **havaneres**, sea shanties brought back from Cuba by sailors, which tell of lost loves and faraway ancestors. Concerts are staged throughout the summer, top event being the stunning *cantada d'havaneres* festival held every June in Calella de Palafrugell.

FESTIVALS

FESTIVAL CALENDAR

January

20–21 Tossa de Mar celebrates its *Vot del Pelegrí* (the Pilgrim's Vow), a colourful maritime procession commemorating the end of the plague in the fifteenth century.

February

Lent *Carnestoltes* (Carnival). Banned under Franco, the re-instated celebrations are especially fun at Platja d'Aro's glittering procession, one of the most spectacular in Spain.

March/April

Setmana Santa (Easter). The most interesting celebrations are the colourful *Manaies* procession in Girona, dating from 1566, when superbly attired Roman soldiers march through the Barri Vell on Wednesday of Easter week and Good Friday, preceding the procession of the Virgin. A macabre celebration is the *Ball dels Morts* (Dance of the Dead) in Verges, when five skeletons dance through the streets, while Besalú's Good Friday procession features Jesus and the Apostles chanting a hymn.

May

First fortnight Flower Festival in Girona's Barri Vell.
Last weekend Palafrugell's Spring Festival, started as a way of getting past Franco's ban on Carnival, features music and a procession.

June

24 The *Festa de Sant Joan* sees bonfires lit all over Catalonia; especially lively in Palamós, where music, dancing and fireworks run from the previous Friday to the Sunday following June 24.

July

July & Aug Peralada Music Festival, with an eclectic programme including leading classical musicians and cabaret stalwarts.

All month Maritime processions in Palamós, Llança and Lloret de Mar.

First Sat Calella de Palafrugell's *Havaneres* festival, where the sea shanties attract 40,000 spectators.

Second Sun Olot's *Aplec de la Sardana* is one of the largest *sardana* festivals in the region.

Last two weeks International Fireworks Competition in Blanes.

24–26 Lloret de Mar's *Ball dels Almorratxes*, as part of the town's *Festa Major*, features an ancient ritual dance between couples, culminating in the girl dashing a jar to the ground to fend off the boy's advances.

August

All month International Music Festival in Torroella de Montgrí.

First three weeks Cadaqués classical music festival.

September

All month Sant Feliu de Guíxols' Porta Ferrada Music Festival.

7–8 Olot's *Ball dels Gegants* (Dance of the Giants) is the high point of the lively local *Festa de la Tura* festivities, famed for its high jinks and procession.

11 Catalonia's national day *La Diada*.

Second weekend Cadaqués' spectacular *Regates de Llaguts i de Vela Llatina* fills the bay with billowing sails.

October

29 The holidays of the patron saint of Girona, Sant Narcís, run from the Friday before Oct 29 to the Sunday after. A cultural programme is complemented by music together with craft stalls, funfair and *sardanes*.

31 The eve of All Saints is celebrated everywhere with the *castanyada*, a feast of roast chestnuts and moscatel wine.

FESTIVALS

47

Sports and outdoor pursuits

Y ou'll find countless opportunities for **outdoor pursuits**. Activities range from the sedate pleasures of walking and golf to arduous mountain treks or scuba diving and paragliding – plus, of course, the waters are some of the cleanest and clearest in the Mediterranean.

The Costa Brava boasts one of Europe's greatest concentrations of blue-flag beaches, an international standard awarded for the cleanliness of the water and coast and quality of facilities.

WALKING

Throughout the Costa Brava and the foothills, you're spoilt for choice in the number and type of **walks** you can try. A network of signposted trails, following a clearly defined **footpath** (*sender*), crisscrosses the region. Split into three categories according to their length, the routes are colour-coded: parallel horizontal yellow and white lines for short local paths; green and white lines for medium-distance paths; and red and white lines for the very long trails. The two major long-distance routes touching on the Costa Brava are the **GR92**, which runs along the French border to Portbou before cutting south to Barcelona; and the **GR11**, which runs east from Andorra to a trailhead on the Cap de Creus headland. Local tourist offices stock free leaflets and maps outlining dozens of walks in their area.

The Camí de Ronda

Among the loveliest routes is the **Camí de Ronda**, made up of old coastguards' and farmers' trails that hug the coast-line. Meaning "patrol walk", it originally referred to any coastal path but now means – in the Costa Brava region, at any rate – the long-distance coastal route linking these paths into one trail.

In the bad old days of the tourist boom, the paths were built over or simply allowed to crumble into the sea, but now the Catalan government is gradually restoring them: it will soon be possible to walk the entire coast from the French border to Blanes. For now, the path is intermittent and varies from a single-file dirt track to wide, paved sections on the edges of towns. Parts cut across well-used beaches or follow a road for a short distance, while others snake over desolate headlands and can be quite arduous, although they're often the best – or only – way to reach some of the more isolated coves. You'll also sometimes find yourself on parts of the GR92, which cuts in and out of the Camí de Ronda.

CYCLING

Long-distance **cyclists** will enjoy the **Ruta del Carrilet**, which follows the old railway line from Olot to Girona and on to Sant Feliu de Guíxols through rolling countryside.

Eventually, it will connect Olot with the mountains, enabling you to cycle from the Pyrenees to the Mediterranean. You can rent a bike at several points along the way; tourist offices in Girona, Olot and Sant Feliu de Guíxols have details. There's also a network of good off-road tracks, indicated by red signs with a bike symbol, and some footpaths – marked on the rambler sign by a small bike symbol – are open to cyclists.

**Beware of cycling on even minor roads,
since motorists are often oblivious to bikes.**

GOLF

Voted by the International Association of Golf Tour Operators as the best emerging **golf** holiday destination in 2000, the Costa Brava staged the 2000 Spanish Open at the demanding PGA Catalunya course, designed by Neil Coles. The region boasts nine top-class courses and a further eight pitch-and-putt courses. You don't have to become a member, but you will need to one of a club in your own country; a round is expensive, at about €60 for eighteen holes in high season. The best way to get around both issues is to take advantage of one of the **golf packages** offered by tour operators and some hotels.

Golf courses

PGA Golf de Catalunya Caldes de Malavella ⓣ 972 472 577, ⓦ www.pgacatalunya.com.

Club de Golf Girona Sant Julià de Ramis ⓣ 972 171 641, ⓦ www.golfgirona.es.

Empordà Golf Club Gualta ⓣ 972 760 450, ⓦ www.empordagolfclub.es.

Club de Golf Costa Brava Santa Cristina d'Aro ⓣ 972 837 150, ⓦ www.golfcostabrava.com.

Torremirona Golf Club Navata
ⓣ 972 553 737, ⓦ www
.torremirona.com.

Golf Serres de Pals Pals
ⓣ 972 637 375, ⓦ www
.golfserresdepals.com.

Club de Golf Pals Pals ⓣ 972
636 006, ⓦ www.6tems.com
/golfpals.

Peralada Golf Club Peralada
ⓣ 972 538 287, ⓦ www
.golfperalada.com.

Club de Golf d'Aro-Masnou
Platja d'Aro ⓣ 972 816 727,
ⓔ golfdaromasnou@retemail
.es.

DIVING AND SNORKELLING

Numerous **diving** schools offer a range of services from beginners' courses to boat excursions and equipment rental. The main areas of interest are around the Illes Medes Maritime Reserve, famous for its fauna and coral beds, and the tiny inlets of the Cap de Creus and the coves near Begur and Palafrugell, where there are over three hundred species of fish, including barracuda and sea horses, drifting among coral and shipwrecks. Always dive with a school (all closed Nov–Easter) registered with the local Association of Diving Centres (ⓦ www.costabrava.org/guisub). A single dive will **cost** around €40, which includes equipment; a six-dive week's pass is €135, a ten-dive voucher €220. A six-day beginners' course is €360.

Many schools also organize **snorkelling** excursions to the many hard-to-reach coves. With your own gear, you could head for easier-to-reach inlets in the southern Baix Empordà and northern Alt Empordà.

WATERSPORTS

Windsurfing is very popular, and there are plenty of oper-ators renting equipment (around €18/hr) and running courses (€25/hr). Summer is relatively calm, but pay keen attention as squalls can sweep windsurfers out to sea. Most towns have **sailing** clubs, and the area runs a number of competitive events, the most famous being Palamós's impressive Christmas Race of big yachts. In most resorts, watersports possibilities include **jet-skiing** (around €12 for 15min), **water-skiing** (roughly the same), being dragged behind a boat on a giant **banana** (about €6) as well as a more sedate **pedalo** (around €3.60/hr). **Parasailing** costs around €36/hr.

One of the best ways to explore coves is by **kayak**, which cost about €15 for half a day (plus a large deposit). A handful of operators can also rent you a small **inflatable** or rigid **motorboat** for about €24/hr.

AERIAL SPORTS

In Empuriabrava is one of Spain's best **skydiving** centres, offering tandem jumps and a range of courses (see p.280). **Sightseeing flights** over the rocky shoreline or the volcanoes of La Garrotxa airport, bookable through local operators (prices vary according to route and number of passengers). There are **ultralight** clubs in Empuriabrava and L'Escala (around €36 for 30min), or you could try **ballooning** in Platja d'Aro (see p.159) or La Garrotxa (see p.97) for about €120: two balloonists do all the work, while you just enjoy the ride.

HORSE RIDING

Both the coast and the hinterland have a long tradition of **horse riding**, and the better stables keep well-cared-for Spanish and Arabian breeds. The tough choice is whether to plump for La Garrotxa or to try one of the few beachside riding spots, primarily around L'Estartit and Pals (see p.249). Half a day's excursion will cost about €50.

Shopping

I f you take advantage of all the shopping on offer, your finances are going to take a battering: Girona, Olot, Palamós, Platja d'Aro and Cadaqués will all leave a healthy dent in your credit card.

Catalans are very image-conscious, so **clothes** and **shoe** shops are well abreast of fashion. The area's artistic tradition translates into good **jewellery** on sale, as well as a thriving trade in modern **arts and crafts**. La Bisbal is the capital of the region's **ceramics** industry, selling distinctive earthenware plates, tiles and pottery. During the summer, some towns stage open-air **medieval crafts** fairs, the best being in Peratallada and Castell d'Aro, while Torroella de Montgrí hosts an enjoyable **world market**, featuring handmade and fair-trade products.

Markets

Very much a feature of normal life, the bustling weekly **markets**, selling everything from fruit to clothes, are good for picking up bargains. Those in Girona, Palamós and Palafrugell are the biggest and best.

Monday Cadaqués, Olot, Torroella de Montgrí.
Tuesday Besalú, Girona, Lloret de Mar, Palamós, Pals, Verges.
Wednesday Banyoles, Begur, Llançà, Sant Antoni de Calonge, Sant Pere Pescador.

Thursday Calonge, L'Estartit, Figueres, Tossa de Mar.
Friday La Bisbal, Platja d'Aro, Port de la Selva, Portbou.
Saturday Empuriabrava, Girona.
Sunday L'Escala, Palafrugell, Roses, Sant Feliu de Guíxols.

Directory

ADDRESSES Abbreviations follow a standard format: c/Balmes 9 is no. 9 on Carrer (street) Balmes; Pl Catalunya 21 is no. 21 on Plaça (square) Catalunya; Ctra is Carretera (highway); Avgda is Avinguda (avenue). Plaça Catalunya 21, 5-2, means Flat 2 on the 5th floor at no. 21 Plaça Catalunya. S/n means *sense número* ("no number"). Ctra Barcelona km2,3 means that the address is 2.3km along the Barcelona road beyond the town.

CONTRACEPTIVES Widely available in pharmacies, bars and supermarkets.

ELECTRICITY The current is 220v AC, with standard European-style two-pin plugs. British equipment will need an adaptor, while North American equipment will need an adaptor and a 220-to-110 transformer. ⓦ www.kropla.com has details.

EMERGENCY NUMBERS Medical, fire & police ⓣ 112; local police ⓣ 092; national police ⓣ 091.

TIME Spain is 1hr ahead of London and Dublin, 6hr ahead of New York and 9hr behind Sydney. Clocks go forward by 1hr on the last Sunday in March and back 1hr on the last Sunday in October.

TIPPING Give about 5 percent for taxis and restaurants, about €0.15 in a café and €1 for a hotel porter. Tipping is uncommon in bars unless you're being served on a terrace. A *menú del día* normally includes service (look for *Servei (no) inclós* – "Service is (not) included"), but it's polite to leave a small tip as well.

THE GUIDE

Girona

ocal writer Josep Pla called **GIRONA** a "small and delicate city" – a fitting epithet for this compact provincial capital that has a history as vivid as its delightful old quarter and a culinary tradition as lively as its nightlife. National polls consistently rate it as the most desirable place to live in Spain. Having undergone a huge transformation in recent years, Girona has been able to modernize itself while keeping its historical and cultural heritage intact, and the pride Gironins take in their city is palpable.

The **Barri Vell** (Old Quarter) rises from the bustling **Rambla** on the east bank of the Riu Onyar through the atmospheric streets of **El Call**, the beautifully preserved medieval Jewish quarter, to the towering **cathedral**. Still partly protected by medieval walls, the Barri Vell boasts some outstanding **museums** and is teeming with shops, bars and restaurants. On the west bank of the river is the attractive nineteenth-century **Mercadal** district, home to lively shopping streets and squares.

Some history

Iberians had populated the area since the fifth century BC, but Girona was founded in the first century AD, when the

Romans established a fort, Gerunda, on the Via Augusta road between Rome and southern Spain. After the Romans, Girona was ruled briefly by **Visigoths**, **Moors** and then **Charlemagne**. For six hundred years, Girona was an important centre of **Jewish** learning, a role erased by the expulsion of the Jews from Spain in 1492.

By the fifteenth century, Girona's population numbered some eight thousand, marking a period of prosperity which lasted two centuries, until the city was hit by the effects of Spain's constant battling with nearby **France**. Tenacious defence of sieges by Napoleon's troops in 1808 and 1809 earned the city the title of "Immortal".

Industrial revolution and cultural growth, begun in the nineteenth century, were curtailed by the **Spanish Civil War** and the years of neglect and repression under **Franco**'s dictatorship. The return of **democracy** in 1975 marked the beginning of the city's rise to capital of the richest province in Spain. The Barri Vell was restored to its former glory, a university was founded in 1993 and a thriving cultural scene has been re-established on a rich tradition, creating a renewed sense of confidence which is evident today in every part of the city.

Arrival and information

Girona airport (☎972 186 600) lies some 13km south; the only transport into town is a taxi (around €15). From **Barcelona airport**, buses and trains (every 20min) run to Barcelona Sants station, from where dozens of trains serve Girona (takes 1hr 30min; last train 9.20pm); there are also plenty of buses from Barcelona's Estació del Nord bus station – take metro line 1 from Sants to Arc de Triomf – to

Girona (takes 1hr 30min; last bus 8.30pm). From **Perpignan airport**, shuttle buses and taxis cover the 5km to the train station, from where there are services to Girona, direct or changing in Portbou (takes 1hr 40min; last train 7.30pm).

Girona's **train station** (℡972 207 093) is on Carretera Barcelona in the new part of the city, about twenty minutes' walk southwest of the old town. Behind the train station on Plaça Espanya, the **bus station** (℡972 212 319) has frequent services to Barcelona, the coast and inland towns.

By **road**, Girona is easily accessed off the A7 *autopista* and the toll-free N-II, and stands at the hub of routes from around the region.

INFORMATION

The main **tourist office** is very central at Rambla Llibertat 1 (Mon–Fri 8am–8pm, Sat 8am–2pm & 4–8pm, Sun 9am–2pm; ℡972 226 575, ⓦwww.ajuntament.gi); staff are very helpful, and stock excellent maps, literature and accommodation lists. There's also an **information stand** in the train station (Mon–Sat 10am–8pm, Sun 10am–2pm), and another in the arrivals hall of the airport (July–Oct Mon, Tues & Thurs–Sun 9am–9pm, Wed 3–9pm).

The **Punt de Benvinguda** (Welcome Point) at c/Berenguer Carnicer 3 (Mon–Sat 10am–8pm, Sun

---

MUSEUM PASS

Girona's museum pass (*multi-entrada Girona Museus*) covers entry to all of the city's museums (apart from the Museu del Cinema) for €4.80, a saving of up to €6 on the individual charges. You can buy it at the Punt de Benvinguda or any museum.

GIRONA

0 — 150 m

N

RESTAURANTS, CAFÉS & BARS

Aleshores	V
L'Antiga	e
L'Arcada	c
Arts	b
El Balcó	Z
Le Bistrot	X
Boira	W
Café Royal	N
Cal Ros	P
Casa de l'Abat	U
Casa Marieta	H
Cipresaia	d
El Cercle	I
Creperie Bretonne	Q
Cul de la Lleona	G
Granja Mora	A
Lagunak	

Riu Galligant

Torre Gironella

Museu Arqueològic

PASSEIG ARQUEOLÒGIC

Catedral

Museu d'Art

Convent de Sant Domènec

PL. SANT DOMÈNEC

Sant Nicolau

PLAÇA SANT PERE

PEDRET

BELLAIRE

Banys Àrabs

P

PL. DE LA CATEDRAL

CUNDARO

FORÇA

CALLE

Bonastruc ça Porta

2

3

R

T

BALLESTERIES

Museu d'Història

Sant Feliu

CALDERERS

Q

PALAMÓS

PALAFRUGELL

PONT DE PEDRET

Riu Onyar

Punt de Benvinguda

i

JOSÉ CANALEJAS

PONT DE ST. AGUSTÍ

PONT DE MANUEL

S

PL.

BERENGUER CARNICER

RAMON FOLCH

PONT DE PEDRA

FRAL DEL BESTIAR

P

CARRETERA N II

Parc de la Devesa

PASSEIG DE LA DEVESA

P

AVDA. DE FRANÇA

Riu Ter

Fontana d'Or

CORT-REIAL

PL. OLI

G

H

I

J

K

L

M

N

A B C D E & F

La Llibreria	a
Museu del Vi	L
Nummulit	Y
Particular	D
El Pati Verd	g
La Penyora	f
Platea	S
La Polenta	K
Pol Nord	B
Primo Piatto	C
L'Spaghetteria de Cocolino	E
Tapa't	R
La Terra	O
Via	T
Zanpanzar	F
	J

ACCOMMODATION

Alberg de Joventut	6
Barri Vell	2
Bellmirall	3
Carlemany	11
Coll	5
Condal	9
Costabella	1
Europa	10
Fornells Park	12
Melià Confort	13
Peninsular	8
Ultonia	4
Viladomat	7

Universitat

Palau dels Agullana

See Inset

Diputació

Fontana

Convent de Sant Josep

ESCALES DE LA LLEBRE

PL. SANT JOSEP

CORT-REIAL

PL. OLI

CIUTADANS

PEIXETERIES VELLES

FERRERIES VELLES

MERCADERS

Ajuntament

PUJADA DEL REI MARTÍ

MOU DEL TEATRE

Antic Convent de la Mercé

CAPUTXINS

Jardins de la Muralla

PONT DE SANT AGUSTÍ

Riu Onyar

ARGENTERIA

RAMBLA LLIBERTAT

PL. GENERAL MARVÀ

PONT DE PEDRA

Jardí de l'Infancia

INDEPENDÈNCIA

MERCADAL

ANSELM CLAVÉ

NORD

HORTES

S. Susanna

SANTA CLARA

PLAÇA CATALUNYA

PL. S. SUSANNA

Museu del Cinema

GINESTA

PL. POMPEU FABRA

F. EIXIMENIS

GRAN VIA JAUME I

PLAÇA JOSEP PLA

PL. DE LA CONSTITUCIÓ

Casa Batlle

CRISTÓFOL GROBER

AVDA. SANT FRANCESC

N-II

Casa Gispert Saüch

PL. HOSPITAL

GRAN VIA JAUME

GIRONA

▲ Train & Bus Stations

63

10am–2pm; winter Mon–Sat closes 5pm; Ⓣ972 211 678), also run by the local tourist board, offers a free reservation service for hotels, restaurants, taxis and guided tours. You can also check your **email** here.

A mini-train makes a circuit around the old town (every 30min: summer daily 10am–2pm & 4–9pm; winter Sat & Sun 10am–2pm & 4–6pm; €2.75), setting off from the corner of the Pont de Pedra with c/Santa Clara. Buy tickets from the driver.

Accommodation

The few **hotels** and **hostals** in the Barri Vell are comfortable and reasonably priced, although upmarket places tend to be further out. If you have transport, it's worth considering **turisme rural** houses in small outlying towns. Another option is a self-catering **apartment**: Apartaments Barri Vell, c/Bellmirall 4 (Ⓣ972 223 583; ❶), has large, atmospheric suites of well-equipped rooms at knockdown prices in a twelfth-century building very near the cathedral.

HOTELS

Hostal Bellmirall

c/Bellmirall 3 Ⓣ972 204 009.

Closed Jan & Feb. No credit cards.

This fascinating *hostal*, with seven en-suite rooms, is housed in a fifteenth-century building on a fourteenth-century Barri Vell street. Their breakfasts are the best in town. ❸

Hotel Carlemany

Pl Miquel Santaló Ⓣ972 211 212, Ⓕ972 214 994, Ⓦwww.carlemany.es.

A modern four-star hotel in the heart of the residential district about twenty minutes' walk south of the Barri Vell, with an exceptionally good restaurant. ⑥

Hostal Coll

c/Hortes 24 ⓣ 972 203 086.
A very simple *hostal* near c/Sta Clara, two minutes from the Rambla, with eight rooms, all en suite. ②

Hotel Condal

c/Joan Maragall 10 ⓣ 972 204 462.
Simple, friendly place with quiet rooms in a modern apartment block five minutes' walk south of the Rambla. ②

Hotel Costabella

Avgda França 61 ⓣ 972 202 524, ⓕ 972 202 203.
Comfortable place with a pool, done down by its location, 2km north of the city on the main road opposite a hospital. ⑥

Hotel Europa

c/Juli Garreta 21 ⓣ 972 202 750.
A minute's walk east of the train station, this unassuming two-star hotel well off the tourist trail represents good value. ③

Hotel Fornells Park

N-II km719, Fornells de la Selva ⓣ 972 476 125, ⓕ 972 476 579.
A pleasant hotel with a pool and good restaurant, 3km south on the Barcelona road – a relaxing base for touring the area. ⑤

Hotel Melià Confort Girona

Ctra Barcelona 112 ⓣ 972 400 500, ⓕ 972 243 233, ⓔ melia .confort.girona@solmelia.es.
An uninspiring location above a hypermarket between the Barcelona road and the railway track 1km from the centre does no justice to this plush – and soundproofed – hotel. ⑥

Hotel Peninsular

c/Nou 1–3 ⓣ 972 203 800.
Pleasant place – far cheerier than it first appears – on a pedestrianized street. Rooms on higher floors are brighter, but all are comfortable and have decent-sized bathrooms and TV. ③

ACCOMMODATION

Hotel Ultonia

Av Jaume I, 22 ☏ 972 203 850,
🖷 972 203 334,
✉ hotel.ultonia@husa.es.
Attractive hotel near Plaça
Independència with attentive
service, large rooms with air
conditioning, and modern
bathrooms. Some on higher
floors have spacious
balconies. ❻

Pensió Viladomat

c/Ciutadans 5 ☏ 972 203 176.
An unpromising entrance
leads to a very friendly *pensió*
with lovely, airy rooms.
Considering its in the Barri
Vell, it's a bargain, especially
as the spacious rooms, mostly
en suites, have been
refurbished to hotel standard.
❷

HOSTEL

Alberg de Joventut

c/Ciutadans 9 ☏ 972 218 003,
🖷 972 212 023,
✉ alberg_girona@tujuca.com.
Very upmarket hostel with
TV and computer rooms, and
rooms sleeping two to eight.

Its location in the Barri Vell
is very enticing, but those
over 30 (who don't get a
discount) could get the same
value for money at a *pensió*.
Curfew 11pm. ❶

TURISME RURAL

Els Arbres

Mas Falgars, Bescanó ☏ 972
440 020.
Large house 7km west of
Girona, with a lovely garden
(plus pool); B&B, half or
full board in four spacious
rooms. ❷

Cal Rellotger

Can Toni Manescal, Fornells de
la Selva ☏ 972 476 117, 🖷 972
476 735, ✉ graner@infonegocio
.com.
Inviting self-catering house
6km south of Girona rented
out whole, featuring a garden
and three large doubles. ❶

Can Pinyarol

c/Mosca 3, Juià ⓣ 972 490 258.
Imposing, attractive three-storey place (rented whole)
with four bedrooms and
sleeping eleven, in a small
village 8km northeast. ❸

Mas Grau

Can Cendra, Bescanó ⓣ 608
791 287.
Ten minutes' drive west of
Girona, this lovely, rambling
old farmhouse in the woods
offers self-catering for up to
fourteen – the bigger the
group, the lower the per-person cost. ❶

Mas de la Roda

c/Creu 31, Bordis ⓣ & ⓕ 972
490 052, ⓦ www.come.to
/masdelaroda.
Four huge rooms offered
individually for B&B or half
board in an imposing stone
house ten minutes' drive
northeast, with organic meals
cooked by the French-speaking owner. ❸

Mas Saló

Sant Martí Vell ⓣ 972 490 201.
A big old house sleeping up
to eight, set in pleasant
gardens with a pool about
9km northeast. The doubles
are large and airy with wood
furniture, and the house is
rented whole. ❸

The Barri Vell

Focal point of Girona is its compact **Barri Vell** (Old
Quarter), one of the most beautiful old quarters of any
Spanish city, which rises from the bustling **Rambla
Llibertat** through tiny streets to the towering **cathedral**.
The enthralling **Museu d'Art** and **Museu d'Història** are
top draws, while the old **city walls** can be walked in their
entirety.

Girona was for many centuries one of Spain's most important centres of Hebrew learning; **El Call**, the Jewish quarter within the Barri Vell, is second to none for its atmosphere and state of preservation. At its heart stands the **Bonastruc ça Porta** cultural centre and museum. Below the cathedral, the **Església de Sant Feliu** is a short walk from the enchanting **Banys Arabs** and **Museu Arqueológic**.

RAMBLA LLIBERTAT AND AROUND

Hub of the city is the **Rambla Llibertat**, a small pedestrianized avenue shaded by plane trees that defines the western boundary of the old town. The Rambla is the perfect setting for a meal or a drink at a café, and a good reference point for walks around the Barri Vell; the best time to see it is in the early evening when it throngs with people taking the *passeig* ("stroll").

For reviews of Rambla cafés and restaurants, see pp.81–85.

Adjoining the Rambla to the north are the shopping streets of **c/Argenteria** and **c/Ballesteries**, while reaching east to c/Ciutadans are narrow passageways that were once home to various guilds – as suggested by names like c/Peixateries Velles (Old Fishmongers' Street).

A short walk from the south end of the Rambla lies the arched **Plaça del Vi**, once the site of the wine market and now home to the austere fifteenth-century **Ajuntament** (Town Hall). On the northeastern corner of the Plaça del Vi, about three metres up the wall, is a tiny carving of an impish head – *En Banyeta*, supposedly a medieval usurer who was turned to stone and now watches over the citizens to make sure they pay their taxes. Legend has it that if you rub noses with him, all your debts will be cancelled.

Along Carrer Ciutadans

The narrow, fourteenth-century **Carrer Ciutadans** runs from Plaça del Vi to Plaça de l'Oli. This was where the wealthy built their houses, the most striking of which is the **Fontana d'Or**, near its northern end and now an arts centre. Broad Romanesque arches support its ornate Gothic superstructure, while the picturesque courtyard is one of the few patios in the city visible to the public.

Just past here, an impressive stone stairway, the **Pujada de Sant Domènec**, climbs up to the right. Beside it, a curved archway joins the two parts of the plain facade of the Baroque **Palau dels Agullana**, a mansion built between the fourteenth and eighteenth centuries; you'll see the unusual perspectives of this corner in dozens of paintings and arty photos all around town. Alongside the Palau dels Agullana is the **Plaça de l'Oli**, site of the old oil market and now lined with bars and restaurants.

EL CALL

Heading north from Plaça de l'Oli, you come to the bars and antiques shops of the slender **Placeta del Correu Vell**, site of one of the Roman city gates, now long-gone.

North from here runs the high-walled **Carrer de la Força**, originally part of the Via Augusta connecting Iberia with the rest of Europe. It formed the core of the Roman town and steadily increased in importance as the city grew, to become the heart of **El Call**, the Jewish Quarter. At its height, between the twelfth and fifteenth centuries, this short, steeply climbing street was home to a synagogue, ritual baths, school and Jewish butcher's, although none survive today. Now the street houses private apartments, interspersed with restaurants and galleries and two of Girona's best museums.

GIRONA'S JEWISH HISTORY

El Call, or the Jewish Quarter, is the best-preserved such area in western Europe, and although there are no Jews living there today, the new Centre Bonastruc ça Porta (see below) is leading to a resurgence in interest in the city's Jewish past.

The first documents relating to Jews in Girona date from 890, when some twenty families settled near the cathedral. Carrer de la Força became the centre of the community, which numbered over three hundred – five percent of the city's population – at its height in the thirteenth to fifteenth centuries. This period saw the quarter become a prestigious centre of Jewish learning, thanks largely to the rabbi of Girona, Nahmànides. A city within a city, it had a mayor responsible to the king, who provided protection in return for payment, and was independent of the city government.

From the eleventh century onwards, though, Jews suffered persecution. In 1391, a mob killed about forty of the Call's residents, and the rest had to be locked up in the Torre Gironella for their own protection. The Call became a ghetto: the city authorities forced Jews to wear distinctive clothing on the few occasions they were allowed outside the district and prohibited them from having doors or windows opening on to Carrer de la Força. The decline of the community culminated in the expulsion of all Jews from Spain in 1492. Those who departed were forced to sell their property, while those who converted to Christianity in order to stay ended up facing the full brunt of the Inquisition.

Centre Bonastruc ça Porta

c/St Llorenç 1. Mon–Sat 10am–8pm, Sun 10am–3pm; Nov–April Mon–Sat closes 6pm. Museum €1.80.

Hidden behind tall wooden doors about halfway up Carrer de la Força is the **Centre Bonastruc ça Porta**, a museum and cultural centre dedicated to the history of Girona's Jews, with an associated research institute and library. The complex – about a dozen houses in the area where the synagogue is thought to have stood – is named after **Nahmànides** (known in Catalan as Bonastruc ça Porta), founder of the mystical Cabbalist school of Judaism and born in Girona in 1194. A doctor, philosopher and poet, Nahmànides became the rabbi of Girona and subsequently Grand Rabbi of Catalonia; he wrote the earliest example of Cabbalist poetry in Spain as well as a large number of educational tracts directed at both Christians and Jews.

The **museum** begins with panels giving lively and informative insight into Girona's Jewish history and the daily life of the community; a detailed model shows how the quarter would have looked in the thirteenth century. To the right, a darkened room houses *steles*, or **Hebrew tombstones**, many used as building materials after 1492 and since recovered. The underlit floor depicts the ancient "Bou d'Or" (Golden Calf) Jewish cemetery, which stood to the north of the city on the Montjuïc hill and which was the main source of the tombstones.

Stairs lead up to a temporary exhibition area adorned with a large modern bronze **sculpture** of Christopher Columbus, commemorating Jewish learning in such areas as astronomy and navigation that helped him to reach the Americas. Doors lead to a **patio** with a large marble Star of David set into the floor. These patios played an important part in the daily life of the quarter: since Jews weren't allowed to overlook Carrer de la Força they created levels of courtyards and gardens within buildings.

Museu d'Història de la Ciutat

c/Força 27. Tues–Sat 10am–2pm & 5–7pm, Sun 10am–2pm. €1.25.
Near the northern end of c/Força is the absorbing **Museu**

d'Història de la Ciutat (Museum of the City's History), which occupies the former eighteenth-century Capuchin Monèstir de Sant Antoni, itself built on a Gothic site dating from at least 1447.

The grisly yet rather touching Capuchin **cemetery** is one of only three of its kind in the world. After death, the bodies of the monks were preserved and left in a seated position in niches around the wall for two years until they mummified, whereupon they were dressed and displayed for purposes of meditation and reflection.

The rest of the museum has few English notes, but much is self-explanatory and there are enough videos and work-ing models to keep you interested. Downstairs is a **chronology** of the city's development, featuring old elec-tric street lights (Girona was the first city in Spain to have them, in 1886). **Prehistoric** settlement and the **Roman** and **Visigoth** presence in the area are explained on the first floor by models, charts and a wide range of finds. The sec-ond level explains the countless **sieges** and battles with French and Spanish troops, with scale layouts, documents and old uniforms. The history of the **sardana** dance occu-pies the third floor, as does an interesting depiction of the story of the **city walls**.

THE CATHEDRAL

Pl de la Catedral. July–Sept Tues–Sat 10am–8pm, Sun 10am–2pm; March–June Tues–Sat 10am–2pm & 4–7pm, Sun 10am–2pm; Oct–Feb Tues–Sat 10am–2pm & 4–6pm. Cathedral free, Museu Capitular €3.

The northern end of c/Força opens onto **Plaça de la Catedral**, where stand the double towers of the four-teenth-century **Portal de Sobreportes**, a gate first built by the Romans in the third century (you can see the origi-nal stones at the base of the gate).

From the square, one of the largest Rococo staircases in Europe – an imposing flight of ninety steps, from 1690 – leads up to the **cathedral** (a gentler road to the right of the steps leads to the cathedral's south door), which occupies what has been a place of worship since Roman times. The first cathedral replaced a Moorish mosque in 1038, and the building evolved over the centuries: most of the current limestone structure dates from the fourteenth and fifteenth centuries but a few earlier parts survive, including the eleventh-century north tower and the Romanesque cloisters.

At the top of the stairs is the ornate **west facade**, built between the fourteenth and eighteenth centuries; its sturdy Gothic bell tower and intricate Baroque high niches combine to create an oddly harmonious whole. Later additions are the 1960s statues in the niches, and the bronze angel atop the belfry, cast in 1968 to replace the seventeenth-century original.

Inside, the over-riding impression is of sheer size: at just under 23m, this is the broadest Gothic **nave** in the world, second only to the 25m-wide Baroque nave of St Peter's in Rome. Originally intended to contain three naves, a controversial decision of 1417 to follow the plans of Guillermo Bofill and build just one aisle was initially opposed on safety grounds, work only proceeding after a panel of architects had re-examined Bofill's designs.

Notable throughout are the fourteenth- to sixteenth-century **stained-glass windows** depicting the story of St George and the Ascension, some of the earliest examples in Catalonia, and the fourteenth-century embossed silver canopy over the **high altar** with its highly detailed gilded silver reredos. Behind stands the marble "Charlemagne's Chair", dating from the eleventh century. Legend has it that if a man and a woman sit on it together, they'll be married within a year, but if a single man sits on it alone, he'll stay

THE CATHEDRAL ●

single; it's said that novices were made to sit in the chair as
an extra guarantee of chastity.

Museu Capitular

Inside the cathedral, high wooden doors opposite the main
entrance lead to the **Museu Capitular**, a rather overpow-
ering display of elaborate goldwork. Its few outstanding
pieces include alabaster statues reminiscent of Chaucerian
characters and a beautiful tenth-century illuminated manu-
script of the *Beatus*.

The highlight is in the final room, where hangs the stunning eleventh-century **Tapis de la Creació** (Tapestry of
the Creation), which originated in Italy; the earliest record
of its being in Girona dates from 1538. At its centre is a circle within a circle, depicting the Pantocrator surrounded by
a dove, the angels of light and darkness, Adam and Eve and
the acts of creation. The top edge of the border has figures
symbolizing the year (a man holding a wheel) and the seasons (men harvesting, keeping warm, planting and carrying
a scythe).

The twelfth-century cloisters, part of the Romanesque
church, are reached through the museum.

MUSEU D'ART

Pujada de la Catedral 12. Mon–Sat 10am–7pm, Sun 10am–2pm;
Oct–Feb Mon–Sat closes 6pm. €1.80.

Alongside the cathedral stands the **Museu d'Art**, a collection of Catalan art in the lofty former Bishop's Palace. A
leaflet in English, and notes held in some rooms, provide
good descriptions of the key exhibits.

The first upper floor, devoted to **Romanesque and**

WALKING THE CITY WALLS

The walk around Girona's fourteenth- and fifteenth-century city walls – which stand in a semicircle between the cathedral and the river – takes about an hour, although climbing down at various points to explore could turn it into a half-day jaunt. The walls are studded with towers, all of which are clearly labelled.

The best route begins through the arch between the cathedral and the Museu d'Art. Follow c/del Bisbe Cartañà round to the left and pass through the gateway into the tiered greenery of the Jardins de la Francesa. Look on the buttresses to the right of the cathedral's apse for the only gargoyle with a human face: legend has it that she was a witch who used to throw stones at passing religious processions and was turned to stone herself. Steps in the lowest terrace of the garden lead to the walkway along the walls. Passing over the eighteenth-century Portal de Sant Cristòfol brings you to steps branching down to the Jardins dels Alemanys, a lovely, shaded garden amid the ruins of a seventeenth-century barracks.

After another section on the wall, steps after the Torre del Telègraf o del Llamp – with its spiral staircase leading up to fabulous views – let you pass through the Portal de la Reina gateway to the twelfth-century Torre Gironella, partly destroyed by Napoleon's troops in the 1809 siege.

A small gate leads on to a long, straight section punctuated by round towers. The first, the Torre de Sant Domènec, was originally defensive – a medieval toilet is set into the wall beside it – then a water tower, and now provides great views. From here, the walls descend, eventually reaching steep stone steps that lead down to street level by the southeast corner of Plaça Catalunya.

Gothic art, houses an exceptional tenth-century portable altar from Sant Pere de Rodes, one of the very few still preserved in Europe, and a minutely detailed twelfth-century

MUSEU D'ART

crossbeam from the church at Cruïlles. Of great curiosity value are the unique fourteenth-century stencils used to make the cathedral's stained-glass windows. The second and third floors house elaborate fourteenth- to eighteenth-century **religious art**, most interesting of which is the altarpiece from Segueró, consisting of wooden panels painted with biblical scenes. Also on the third floor is ceramic work by Modernist architect **Rafael Masó** (see p.80). The top floors cover works by nineteenth- and twentieth-century **Catalan Impressionists**, notably the landscapes of Joaquim Vayreda and the scenes of Girona by Santiago Rusiñol.

Carrer del Rei Martí, which descends northwards from Plaça Catedral, suffered constant flooding until the medieval residents raised the street to balcony level. The original front doors are now underground.

BANYS ARABS

c/Ferran el Catòlic. April–Sept Mon–Sat 10am–7pm, Sun 10am–2pm; Oct–March Tues–Sun 10am–2pm. €1.25; audioguide €2.50 extra.

Just north of the cathedral, the **Banys Arabs** – not a true Arab baths, but a twelfth-century Romanesque building based on Moorish design – is one of the best-preserved medieval bathhouses in Spain. The scene, so it's said, of hot-blooded medieval frolics, the building was closed down in the fifteenth century, taken over in 1617 by a Capuchin convent, and restored in 1929 by Modernist architects Rafael Masó and Emili Blanc.

An excellent free leaflet guides you along, starting with the grand *apodyterium* (changing-room), with niches in the walls for clothes. The route leads through the dark, stone-vaulted *frigidarium* into the large *tepidarium*, featuring seating around the walls. A door leads on to the remains of the plunge pool and *caldarium*, where parts of the underfloor heating system are visible. Next door is the furnace, and a flight of stairs up to the roof and green-tiled cupola.

ESGLÉSIA DE SANT FELIU

Pl Sant Feliu. July–Sept Tues–Sat 10am–8pm, Sun 10am–2pm;
March–June Tues–Sat 10am–2pm & 4–7pm, Sun 10am–2pm;
Oct–Feb Tues–Sat 10am–2pm & 4–6pm.

At the top of Pujada Sant Feliu, 50m west of Plaça de la Catedral, is the side door of the gloomy fourteenth- to seventeenth-century Gothic **Església de Sant Feliu**. Its truncated **tower**, a distinctive feature of Girona's skyline, was struck by lightning in 1581 and never repaired. In the left wing of the transept lie the **tombs of Sant Narcís**, patron saint of Girona – a wooden thirteenth-century one, supposedly containing the saint's remains, and an elaborate Gothic one dated 1328, depicting scenes from his life. Either side of the high altar are eight second- to fourth-century **sarcophagi** – probably from the Roman necropolis that stood on this site – most of them Christian, although two older ones show lion-hunting and Pluto abducting Proserpine.

At the foot of the church's front steps is El Cul de la Lleona (The Lioness's Rear), a copy of a twelfth-century statue of a lioness climbing a pillar. Myth has it that if a visitor kisses the animal's backside, they'll return to Girona. Some steps make it easier for you.

MUSEU ARQUEOLÒGIC

Monèstir de Sant Pere de Galligants, Pl Sta Llúcia. Tues–Sat 10am–2pm & 4–6pm, Sun 10am–2pm. €1.80.

The **Museu Arqueològic** is sited in a twelfth-century

Benedictine monastery just north of the tiny Riu Galligants; the facade incorporates an arched doorway thought to predate the rest of the building by up to a century. Inside are three long naves with a wide transept, and small cloisters. The museum has few English notes, so you might want to shell out €1.50 for the English guidebook.

The first room houses exhibits from **prehistoric** eras and includes a model of silos discovered at Mas Castellar, near Empúries, showing how wheat was stored in pot-shaped cavities dug into the soil. Off this room an interesting display chronicles **Iberian** culture and includes objects from the **Greek** colonies at Empúries and Roses. In a small room adjoining the transept is a largely intact **Roman mosaic** depicting a chariot race, discovered in 1876 in a Roman villa on the outskirts of Girona. In the same room is the Macau Collection, donated by the family of a local archeologist, which includes an elaborate fourth-century Roman **sarcophagus** dubbed "The Seasons", discovered in 1847 in Empúries.

Mercadal

West of the Riu Onyar and connected to the Barri Vell by footbridges – as well as, further south, the wide, stone Pont de Pedra – lies the nineteenth-century **Mercadal** quarter, housing the stylish commercial areas of Carrer Santa Clara and **Plaça Independència**. Nearby is the **Museu del Cinema**, an interactive history of moving images.

PLAÇA INDEPENDÈNCIA AND AROUND

Sited prominently on the western bank of the river is the bar- and restaurant-lined **Plaça Independència**, with its heroic bronze statue cast in 1894 depicting the defenders of Girona. Running parallel to the river south of the square is the bustling nineteenth-century shopping street **Carrer Santa Clara**, with its waist-high street lamps.

Most interesting of the narrow pedestrian bridges across the Onyar is the **Pont de les Peixateries** (Fishmongers' Bridge), along c/Santa Clara, built in iron and wood by the Gustave Eiffel company in 1877. It's also good for views of the backs of the houses giving onto the Onyar.

Towering plane trees northwest of Plaça Independència, across the busy Giratori del Rellotge roundabout, mark the Parc de la Devesa, scene of Girona's colourful Tuesday and Saturday markets.

MUSEU DEL CINEMA

c/Sèquia 1. Tues–Sat 10am–8pm, Sun 11am–3pm. €3.

Off the southern end of c/Santa Clara is the **Museu del Cinema**, built around the private collection of Tomás Mallol, an award-winning local film-maker, with just the right mix of hands-on exhibits and information. After a short introductory film, in Catalan only but fairly self-explanatory, you take the lift to the third floor and work your way down through the themed levels, which feature imaginative displays of the origins of projected images in different cultures and the development of cinema. There's a section on how cartoons are made, plus an educational area for kids. The shop is full of memorabilia.

A MODERNIST TRAIL

Just as Barcelona has its tradition of Modernist architects with the likes of Gaudí, Girona has Rafael Masó i Valentí. Born here in 1880, Masó studied in Barcelona then returned to become active in Girona's public and cultural life, twice being voted city councillor; he died in 1935. This walk, setting off from the Barri Vell, takes in his most interesting buildings.

Casa Masó, c/Ballesteries 29, is the house in which Masó was born and which he remodelled between 1911 and 1919, giving it an odd mix of new and traditional styles; the Modernist curlicues and undulating window-frames and door-way appear almost uncomfortably superimposed on the rather louring structure. Five minutes' walk south is Saguer, c/Argenteria 29, a pharmacy designed by Masó in 1908.

Cross the Pont Sant Agustí outside Saguer to get to Plaça Independència. Follow c/Santa Clara left (south) to the Pont de Pedra bridge, and 100m to the right (west) on c/Nou is the tiny c/Fontanilles; the Casa Batlle (1910), influenced by Glasgow

Eating

For a relatively small city, Girona has an extraordinarily wide choice of **restaurants** to suit most budgets. The pavement cafés on the Rambla are fine enough, but for a proper meal, you're better off in the Barri Vell, Plaça Independència, or c/Pedret, fifteen minutes' walk north of the Rambla. **Vegetarians** are also well catered for. Details of **opening hours** are on pp.34–35.

There's a full menu reader, in Catalan and English, on pp.363–367.

architects such as Charles Rennie Mackintosh, takes up this end of the block, crowned by stylized owls in green and white tiles. Down to the western end of c/Nou and 100m left on Gran Via is the Banco Santander; walk past it and cross the road to view the blue and white tiles of the irregular corner house Casa Gispert Saüch (1921), incorporating wrought iron on its balconies and blending traditional materials with contemporary styles.

Walk down the short c/Alvarez de Castro beside the house and then right for the triangular Plaça Marquès de Camps. Some 200m left (west) is Masó's most imaginative building. Built as a flour mill in 1911, the Farinera Teixidor, Ctra Sta Eugènia 42, fuses turrets, wrought iron, ceramics and glass in a castle-like creation. It now houses the offices of the *El Punt* newspaper, where you'll find a café-restaurant (daily 8am–midnight) serving an inexpensive *menú del día*. Final port of call, further west on the same street at no. 19, is the Casa Punxa, built in 1922, whose simple, vertical facades contrast with an elaborate green-tiled spired dome.

CAFÉS

L'Antiga
Pl del Vi 5.
Winter closed Mon.
In an old terraced building beneath the arches, popular for coffee, cakes, great breakfasts and delicious, thick hot chocolate.

Arts
Rambla Llibertat 33.
Backing onto the river, this trendy café, with one of the Rambla's friendliest terraces, serves good coffee and snacks.

El Cercle
c/Ciutadans 8.
Closed Mon.
A bohemian-chic café that attracts a mixed arty and trendy crowd for the temporary exhibitions adorning its stone walls.

EATING

Granja Mora

Cort Reial 18.

Closed Mon.

A city institution since 1939, this cheerfully jumbled milk bar serves excellent homemade cakes and pastries.

La Llibreria

c/Ciutadans 8.

Tasty snacks are served in this small, friendly café inside a cavernous bookshop.

Tapa't

Cort Reial 1.

Winter closed Mon.

Small, cheerful tapas bar with a wide selection of dishes at any time of day. Equally pleasant for afternoon coffee.

RESTAURANTS

L'Arcada

Rambla Llibertat 38.

Grab a drink on the terrace then try the excellent Italian cuisine in the relaxed upper-floor restaurant; top choices are mussels with onion and cheese or pasta with pepper and ham. Moderate.

El Balcó

c/Hortes 16.

Closed Sun.

Welcoming little Argentinian restaurant on a pedestrianized street west of c/Santa Clara. Try the *matahambre* ("hunger-killer") – a filling meat roll – or a huge steak. Moderate.

Le Bistrot

Pujada de St Domènec 4.

One of Girona's best eateries, featuring 1890s decor. At lunchtime you can get an extensive *menú del día* for €12, while evenings are à la carte. Go for the imaginative *pà amb tomàquet* meals, crêpes – plenty of them vegetarian – or the grilled meat and *mar i muntanya* dishes. Inexpensive.

Boira

Pl Independència 17.

Traditional Catalan cooking with a modern slant in a lovely setting backing onto the river. A very reasonable *menú del dia* costs €9. Try the cod cannelloni in onion sauce or double-cooked duck with pears in red wine. Moderate.

Cal Ros
Cort Reial 9.
Closed Sun eve & Mon.

This old-fashioned restaurant under the arches serves some of the city's finest Catalan fare. Known for its rice and cod dishes, it also offers some fabulous desserts, notably curd mousse with blackcurrant sorbet. Moderate.

Casa Marieta
Pl Independència 5.
Closed Sun eve & Mon.

One of the oldest restaurants in Girona, with a high, vaulted ceiling, serving traditionally cooked local meat and fish and filling stews. Try the very good *pica-pica* starter. Moderate.

Cipresaia
c/General Fournàs 2.
Closed Mon.

Comfortable old-world restaurant at the foot of c/Força, with lovely

Mediterranean cuisine, including very good fresh fish and tasty *Entrecot de Girona* in anchovy sauce. Expensive.

La Creperie Bretonne
Cort Reial 14.
Closed Sun.

An anarchic warren of small, extravagantly decorated rooms, with an excellent selection of crêpes and Breton cider and a wide choice for vegetarians. Inexpensive.

El Cul de la Lleona
c/Calderers 8.
Closed Sun & Mon.

Small, welcoming joint serving up a cuisine combining subtle Moroccan influences with chunky Catalan flavours. Especially good are the salads with orange and rosewater dressing, while the Arab pastries and mint tea are deliciously sinful. Budget.

Lagunak
c/Pedret 136 ☎ 972 412 291.
Daily 8–11.30pm.

Towards the north end of c/Pedret, this popular, plush

RESTAURANTS

Basque place serves enormous portions of superb meat and fish. Expensive.

El Museu del Vi
Cort Reial 8.
Closed Mon & early Sept.
Favoured by a lively young crowd, this old-fashioned eatery offers a good, filling selection of meals from *pà amb tomàquet* and tapas to plentiful meat dishes. Budget.

El Pati Verd
Pl Miquel Santaló ⊤ 972 211 212.
Closed Sun.
A sumptuous restaurant in *Hotel Carlemany*, rapidly gaining a reputation for superb cooking based on creative variations of traditional local cuisine. Expensive.

La Penyora
c/Nou del Teatre 3.
Closed Sun.
Very popular little place that is unusual in offering two *menús del dia*, one for carnivores and one for vegetarians. Budget.

La Polenta
Cort Reial 6.
Mon–Fri 1–4pm.
Lunchtime veggie joint serving a small range and a very good *menú del dia* for €6. Budget.

Pol Nord
c/Pedret 120 ⊤ 972 200 927.
Closed Sun.
One of the most popular and prestigious restaurants on the street, serving Catalan cuisine with a creative slant, including some delicious *mar i muntanya* dishes. Expensive.

Primo Piatto
c/Pedret 132.
Closed Mon.
Excellent Italian cuisine in a labyrinthine *masia* divided into two; the ground-floor area is slightly less pricey. Inexpensive.

L'Spaghetteria de Cocolino
c/Alemany 3.
Closed Sun.
Warm decor in a small restaurant near the cathedral, with a huge variety of pasta

dishes and delicious desserts. Moderate.

Zanpanzar
Cort Reial 10–12.
Tues–Sun noon–11.30pm.
Out front is an atmospheric bar with excellent Basque-style tapas (keep the toothpicks: they charge you by the number left on your plate). At the back the restaurant serves succulent meat and fish dishes, top choices being sea perch with green pepper, and cider-roast lamb. Moderate.

Drinking and nightlife

Girona's **nightlife** is good and varied – and late. People tend to sit and chat at the pavement cafés before dinner, only moving on to the **bars** after midnight.

Aleshores
Pl Independència 4.
House music in a long, narrow, packed bar with a dance floor at the end.

Café Royal
Pl Independència 1.
Daily 9am–3am.
Relaxing bar that's good for breakfasts and an afternoon tipple. Quieter than the nearby competition after dark.

La Casa de l'Abat
c/Galligants s/n.
Closed Sun.
Opposite the Museu Arqueològic in the sixteenth-century Bishop's House, this atmospheric bar offers live world music (including tango and jazz), and serves delicious snacks.

Nummulit
c/Nord 7.
A lively, fun bar behind c/Sta Clara popular with gays that plays mainly 1980s music to a

mixed crowd and wide age range.

Particular
c/Pedret 76.
A friendly little bar in a 600-year-old lime kiln, with hip-hop, drum 'n' bass and *mestissatge* (a mix of ethnic and modern beats).

Platea
c/Real de Fontclara 6.
A large DJ bar behind Plaça Independència with a big dance floor, playing an eclectic selection from salsa to rock to a mainly studenty clientele.

La Sala del Cel
c/Pedret 118.
Daily 11pm–6am.
A huge multi-level club in an old *masia* – mainly house, with some chillout rooms and terraces. Visiting and resident DJs put it on the club circuit for locals and the Barcelona crowd.

La Terra
c/Ballesteries 21.
A pleasant, colourfully tiled bar overlooking the river, hosting a vaguely hip crowd.

Via
c/Pedret 72.
Daily 11pm–5.30am.
At the southern end of Pedret, this lively joint has a stark house bar downstairs and vibrant salsa bar upstairs.

Shopping

With more **shops** per person than any other city in Spain, stylish, affluent Girona is the ideal place to take your credit card for a spin. In the Barri Vell, carrers Ballesteries, Cort Reial, Mercaders, Argenteria, Ciutadans and the Rambla have modern **clothes** boutiques and **antiques** emporia jostling with fair-trade shops and designer furniture. Over in Mercadal, try carrers Santa Clara and Nou and Plaça

Independència for less esoteric establishments, Spanish chains and more traditional clothes shops. Further south, there's some good shopping to be had around the *Hotel Carlemany* in the classy clothes and **food** outlets on carrers Joan Maragall, Rutlla, Creu and Migdia. Best of Girona's excellent *pastisseries* is Faure, on c/Argenteria – try *Mosques de Girona* (chocolates in the shape of flies to commemorate the defeat of the French in 1285; see p.347) and the tasty local *xuxos*, long, sugary doughnuts overflowing with custard.

Ambrosia, c/Carreras Peralta 4, in a fifteenth-century building near Plaça del Vi, only sells products made in monasteries and convents; top buys include the natural honey and exquisite sweets.

Listings

Banks Most banks have branches and ATMs on Rambla Llibertat, Gran Via and c/St Francesc.

Bike rental Decathlon, Mas Grí commercial estate (☎ 972 417 663), on the Ctra Barcelona 2km south of the centre.

Books and maps Ulysus, c/Ballesteries 29, has a good selection of local maps. The English Bookshop is at c/Rutlla 22.

Car rental Most agencies are in or near the train station and at the airport; try Avis ☎ 972 206 933, or Europcar ☎ 972 209 946.

Hospital Dr Trueta Hospital (☎ 972 202 700) is on Ctra de França north of the centre.

Internet Planet Bar, c/Alegria 4; or the Punt de Benvinguda office (see p.61).

Laundry Bugaderia El Sol, c/Ballesteries 4; Bugaderia Ninfi, c/Juli Garreta 44.

Pharmacy Most central is Saguer, c/Argenteria 29.

Police The Policia Municipal are in the Ajuntament ☏ 092.

Post office Main branch at the northern end of Gran Via on the corner with Plaça Independència. There are *estancs* everywhere.

Taxis At the train and bus stations, and Plaça Independència. Giro-Taxi (☏ 972 222 323) has taxis for the disabled.

Inland from Girona

The region **inland from Girona** is deepest Catalonia, where medieval cities and hilltop villages gaze towards jagged mountain peaks and muted jade and terracotta tones stand in cool contrast to the turquoise and cobalt colours of the coast. Very few non-Spanish tourists find their way here, yet the area offers an excellent base away from the bustle of the resorts.

Map 1 at the back of the book covers
the area inland from Girona.

North of Girona as the altitude gently rises towards the foothills of the Pyrenees, the town of **Banyoles** sits on a small, fertile plain, dominated by its distinctive figure-of-eight lake fed by underground streams. The prehistoric **Coves de Serinyà** caverns are set among evergreen oaks nearby. Neighbouring **Besalú** is famous for its disjointed eleventh-century bridge and warren of ancient streets. High in the mountains further west, the stunning **Parc Natural de La Garrotxa** is ideal country for rambling, horse riding or even ballooning over the dormant volcanoes of the region. At the heart of the park lie the county town of **Olot** and nearby medieval village of **Santa Pau**.

Banyoles and around

Surrounded by hills, the busy market town of **Banyoles** clusters around its medieval main square but is more famous for its lake, a favourite for Sunday morning rambles or rowing. The oldest human remains in Catalonia were found in the Paleolithic **Coves de Serinyà** to the north, while the medieval streets of **Besalú** shelter one of only three medieval Jewish ritual baths surviving in the world.

BANYOLES

BANYOLES, 20km north of Girona, is widely known for its **lake**, or *estany*. The venue for the rowing events in the 1992 Olympics, it's a pleasant place for an excursion afloat and has a lovely perimeter walk. The town, a good fifteen-minute walk east of the lake, is surprisingly dreary, focused around the medieval porticoed **Plaça Major**, home to shops, galleries and pavement cafés. Banyoles' Wednesday market has been held in the Plaça Major since the thirteenth century.

Nearby is the small Plaça de la Font, where the fourteenth-century Pia Almoina, or almshouses, at no. 11 host the **Museu Arqueològic** (July & Aug Tues–Sat 11am–1.30pm & 4–6.30pm, Sun 10.30am–2pm; rest of year Tues–Sun 10.30am–1.30pm & 4–6.30pm; €3). Grouped around an attractive Gothic courtyard, the museum displays local finds, including medieval ceramics.

Estany de Banyoles

Banyoles' charm lies in its lake, the **Estany de Banyoles**, reached by a clearly signposted main road from the town centre. Fed by underground streams, the lake is up to 62m deep in parts and is surrounded by seven *estanyols*, or ponds, including the Estanyol Can Sisó, which inexplicably turns red in the winter, and the Estanyol Nou ("new"), which appeared overnight in 1978. Half-hour **boat trips** (March–Dec Tues–Sun 10am–7pm; €6) leave every hour from the eastern shore, where you can also rent **rowing boats** (€3.60/hr). You can take the plunge at designated **swimming** areas.

A mini-train runs hourly (daily 10am–7pm; €3.60) from Plaça Major to the more populated east side of the lake.

The perimeter has a clearly marked **footpath** (8km) that rarely gets busy, which you can also follow by bike: rent from Las Vegas, Passeig Draga 2, near the mini-train stop. The path takes you past *pesqueres*, ornate private fishing and bathing huts which reach out into the water at the end of rickety walkways, and the eerie *estanyols*. A third of the way round, walking clockwise – at the further point of the lake from the hotels and restaurants – you come to the lovely twelfth-century **Església de Santa Maria**, a waterside church with low, sculpted capitals around the door. Some 3km further, before coming full circle, you'll see a detour signposted to the **Mirador** ("Belvedere"), a climb of roughly 500m rewarded by fabulous views over the lake. Better still is the walk 300m on from the Mirador to the evocative **Puig de Sant Martirià**, the ruins of a minuscule chapel amidst an olive grove.

Practicalities

Girona–Olot **buses** stop on Passeig de l'Indústria near the main crossroads, at the entrance to the old town. The

BANYOLES

91

tourist office is on the same road at no. 25 (June–Aug Mon–Sat 10am–2pm & 5–7pm, Sun 10am–1pm; rest of year Mon–Fri 10am–2pm & 5–7pm, Sat 10am–1pm; ⊤ 972 575 573, ⓌÔwww.plaestany.org).

The best **place to stay** is on the lake. *Hotel Mirallac*, Pg Darder 50 (⊤ 972 571 045; ⑥), has large rooms with lake views, while a more economical option is the cosy *Fonda La Paz*, Ponent 18 (⊤ 972 570 432; ②) in a sidestreet off the lake, which also has a good restaurant. In town, a smart *Alberg de Joventut*, c/Migdia 10 (⊤ 972 575 454, Ⓕ 972 576 747; ①), offers good dorms a short walk south of Plaça Major. Best **campsite** is the small *El Llac* (⊤ 972 570 305, Ⓔ e.llac@retemail.es), near the Església de Santa Maria.

There are several **cafés** and **restaurants** on the eastern shore, the best, apart from *Fonda La Paz*, being the popular *La Masia*, a huge place with a pleasant terrace but – aside from its good *menú del dia* at €8.50 – expensive. In town, the atmospheric *La Cisterna*, c/Alvarez de Castro 36 (closed Mon), serves tasty Catalan cuisine, while the slightly cheaper *El Capitell*, Pl Major 14 (closed Mon) specializes in cod and grilled meats. The best **bars** are under the arches in Plaça Major or on the lakeside near the *Hotel Mirallac*, where some stay open until 2am.

COVES DE SERINYÀ

July–Sept daily 11am–7pm; March–June Tues–Fri 10am–4pm, Sat & Sun 11am–6pm; Oct–Feb Tues–Fri 10am–3pm, Sat & Sun 11am–5pm. €1.50.

Some 3km north of Banyoles, a small signpost on the right marks a sharp turn-off to the **COVES DE SERINYÀ**, atmospheric Paleolithic limestone caves. The site – rarely crowded – is immaculately laid out around a footpath through oaks and silver birches. Excavations have turned up over thirty thousand objects, including evidence of human habitation alongside remains of lions, panthers, hyenas and elephants.

In the summer, there are on-site displays of flint-napping, dye-making and leather-cutting.

Two caves are accessible at present. The **Cova d'Arbreda**, a working dig beneath a steel roof, overlooks the narrow valley. Finds here date from between 100,000 and 15,000 years ago, the most significant being flint from southern France; as local flint was too brittle for use as tools, the nomadic cave-dwellers would travel hundreds of kilometres north each year to find it before returning here to work it. A 200,000-year-old tooth, the oldest human remain in Catalonia (now on display in Barcelona) was found at the Cova de Mollet, at the foot of the slope. The numinous **Cova de Reclau Viver** at the end of the path has preserved more of its original shape. Finds, including Bronze Age funeral urns, date back 40,000 years and there is evidence of domestic animals being kept here some seven thousand years ago.

BESALÚ

About 16km northwest of Banyoles, the stunning medieval bridge of the town of **BESALÚ** suddenly rears up in front. Occupied by Romans, Visigoths, Franks, Moors and the French, Besalú was declared a site of national historical interest in 1966; most of what survives dates from a 200-year period of independence between the tenth and the twelfth centuries when it was the capital of a principality ruled by the dynasty of Guillem el Vellós (William the Hairy).

The Town

Two minutes' walk west of the main road is the enchanting sixteenth-century porticoed **Plaça Llibertat**, where you'll find a couple of cafés and some small shops selling local produce.

Plaça Llibertat has been the site of Besalú's Tuesday market since medieval times.

Just off the square is the twelfth-century **Miqvé** (daily 10am–2pm & 4–7pm; €0.60; key from tourist office), one of only three medieval Jewish ritual purification bathhouses left in the world, where men and women would bathe before religious study and marriage, and women would also bathe after childbirth and menstruation. Little more than a high-ceilinged room with steps down to where the pool once was, the building nonetheless exudes an atmosphere of calm spirituality.

Another minute's walk brings you to the town's eleventh-century pedestrian **toll bridge**. Built in an L-shape, its foundations governed by the position of the rocks in the river, the stone bridge – destroyed and rebuilt many times, most recently in the Spanish Civil War – gives an idea of Besalú's importance: it is overpoweringly large in comparison with the diminutive size of the town today.

Southwest of Plaça Llibertat, a narrow street leads to the fan-shaped expanse of the Pla de Sant Pere, dominated by the Benedictine **Monèstir de Sant Pere**, founded in 977, of which only the eleventh-century church is still standing. The imposing facade is crowned by a simple Romanesque belfry, while inside, the narrow nave is remarkable for the semicircular ambulatory. The tiny c/Ganganell leads 100m northwest to the architectural mishmash of the twelfth-century **Església de Sant Vicenç**. Extensively rebuilt over the centuries, its simple Romanesque facade and main door contrast with an ornate thirteenth-century rose window and intricately carved Gothic side door.

The torching of the Església de Sant Vicenç during the Spanish Civil War uncovered a Moorish rock-crystal vase containing coins, now on display in Girona's Museu d'Art.

Practicalities

Buses stop on the main C150 road, a short walk from Plaça Llibertat, where you'll find the **tourist office** under the arches at no. 21 (daily 10am–2pm & 4–7pm; ℡ 972 591 240, ⓦ www.6tems.com/besalu). Best bet for **parking** is on the main road.

Accommodation in town is limited to the comfortable en-suite rooms of the friendly *Fonda Venencia*, c/Major 6 (℡ 972 591 257; ❶), and the charming, old-fashioned *Habitacions Marià*, Pl Llibertat 7 (℡ 972 590 106; ❷). The agreeably dated nineteenth-century *Hotel Siques* is on the main road outside town, Av Lluís Companys 6–8 (℡ 972 590 110; ❸). The lovely hilltop hamlet of **Beuda**, 5km north, holds a couple of excellent **turisme rural** houses: with four antique-furnished, en-suite doubles, the seventeenth-century *Mas Salvanera* mansion (℡ 972 590 975, ⓕ 972 590 863, ⓦ www.salvanera.com; ❸), offers near-hotel quality, while the equally beautiful *Can Maholà* (℡ 972 590 162, ⓦ www.beuda.com/mahola; ❹) has two spacious stone houses sleeping four and eight.

Cort Reial, Pl Llibertat 14, has a good-value **restaurant** and snack bar. The *menú del dia* at *Can Quei*, Pl St Vicenç 4, is €8.50 or €12, that at *Can Siques* in *Hotel Siques* €15. *Pont Vell*, c/Pont Vell 28, by the bridge, charges €30 for an outstanding modern take on traditional Catalan cuisine,

BESALÚ

while atmospheric *Els Fogons de Can Llaudes*, Pla de St Pere 6, serves more traditional fare in an eleventh-century former chapel. Plaça Llibertat has reasonable **bars**, including the friendly, late-opening *Miqwahs*.

The fast C260 links Besalú with Figueres, 28km east.

Parc Natural de La Garrotxa

West of Besalú stretches the **PARC NATURAL DE LA GARROTXA**, which dips and climbs through a landscape of dormant **volcanoes** moulded into lush, rolling hills by more than ten thousand years of erosion. The north of the park is dominated by the lovely city of **Olot**, set amid fertile scenery perfect for rambling and flanked by two villages: **Castellfollit de la Roca**, to the northeast, perched precariously above a basalt precipice and, to the southeast, the enchanting **Santa Pau**, dominated by an imposing semi-ruined castle and starting point for some spectacular walks. Marked footpaths set out on crisscrossing tracks through the ancient **Fageda d'en Jordà** beech wood to the wildest volcanoes, classified as dormant even though they haven't erupted in over eleven thousand years.

CASTELLFOLLIT DE LA ROCA

The medieval village of **CASTELLFOLLIT DE LA ROCA**, 14km west of Besalú, stares down from the edge of

ACTIVITIES IN THE GARROTXA PARK

The tourist offices in Olot (see p.102) and Santa Pau (see p.103), as well as the Casal dels Volcans in Olot (see p.100), have details of walking itineraries in the Garrotxa Park lasting from thirty minutes to six hours. We've also put together a walking route, on p.101. Other activities include the breathtaking early-morning balloon ride over the volcanoes (€120); the price includes cava and cake on board and a hearty breakfast after you land. Reserve through Vol de Coloms in Santa Pau (☎ 972 680 255, ⓦ www.garrotxa.com/voldecoloms). More affordable is a 4x4 journey to areas that are otherwise inaccessible (reserve at the Santa Pau office, c/Major 24, ☎ 972 680 078; €15–48). For horse riding (€14/hr), try Hipica Les Forques, Ctra Olot–Sta Pau km7 (☎ 972 680 358), or Camping La Fageda, nearby at km3.8 (☎ 909 702 821). Hipica Les Forques also runs horse-drawn carriage excursions (€5) and mini-train rides around the woods and volcanoes (daily 10am–1pm & 3–6pm; €5.50). The Area Recreativa de Xenacs, 3km south of Olot in Les Preses (☎ 972 195 087), organizes walks, archery and mountain biking, and also has a good restaurant.

a sheer precipice 60m above the Fluvià river. Sadly, it fails to live up to its location, although it's worth wandering through the narrow streets to the viewing platform above the chasm. The *Pensió Ca La Paula*, Pl St Roc 3 (☎ 972 294 032; ❷) is very pleasant, with comfortable **rooms** and a good **bar** and **restaurant**. A worthwhile detour runs 3km west to the charming village of Sant Joan de les Fonts, from where signposts lead you across a medieval stone bridge to the *Columnes basaltiques*, a soaring cliff of perfectly symmetrical basalt columns doused by a waterfall.

CASTELLFOLLIT DE LA ROCA

OLOT

The outskirts of the county town of **OLOT** are an unprepossessing modern sprawl concealing a very pretty old quarter. Described as conservative with a radical undertone – or trendy with traditional roots – Olot's labyrinthine **Barri Vell** is a hive of avant-garde art galleries, churches, Modernist architecture and frenzied shopping huddled at the base of the squat **Montsacopa** volcano; just out of town is the fascinating **Casal dels Volcans** information centre.

Established in 872, Olot was under the sway of the unpopular abbots of Ripoll until earthquakes in 1427 and 1428 almost completely destroyed the town. The townspeople seized their chance and rebuilt everything 1km east to escape the abbots' clutches. A late-nineteenth century renaissance – thanks mainly to a burgeoning industry in religious images – went hand in hand with a flourishing cultural scene and the **Olot School** of painters, who created an Impressionist style using sombre, volcanic colours in contrast to the bright Mediterranean palette of other Catalan schools.

The Barri Vell

The bustling **Barri Vell** hosts some inviting sights. Southwest of the simple Plaça Major, the eighteenth-century **Església de Sant Esteve**, built on the site of a tenth-century church, dominates the skyline from its perch at the top of a flight of sweeping steps. Rebuilt after the earthquakes and successively renovated, it has an uncluttered facade marked by empty niches where statues of saints stood until their destruction in the Spanish Civil War. Highlight of its lofty interior is the Baroque *Verge del Roser* wooden altarpiece.

OLOT

◄ Montsacopa Volcano

C. DE LA VERGE DEL PORTAL
C. DE L'AIGUA
C. DE LA CENDRADA
C. DELS VALLS NOUS
C. DE LA VERGE DEL PORTAL
C. MAJOR
PTGE. DEL TURA
C. BAIX DEL TURA
C. ALT DEL TURA
Nostra Dona del Tura
PLAÇA DE CAMPDENMÀS
C. DE LA PARRA
C. FERRARONS LLIBERADA
C. D'ALFONS V
C. DELS SASTRES
C. ALT DE LA MADUIXA
C. DELS CIVILLERS
CRO. DE SANT ANTONI
C. DE SANT FRANCESC
PLAÇA DE SANT FRANCESC
C. DE SANT ASSÍS
C. ESGLEIERS
C. DE LA MADUIXA
C. BAIX DE FERRARONS
C. NOU DE ST. ANTONI
C. BONAIRE
Plaça Major
C. SERRA I GINESTA
C. SERRA I GINESTA
C. BISBE LORENZANA
Bus Station
C. DE SANT ROC
C. CARNISSERIES
C. DELS
C. MAJOR
C. BELLAIRE
C. DEL PATI DE LA PRESÓ VELLA
C. DE SANT ROC
PLAÇA MORA
C. MACARNAU
Sant Esteve
C. OM
C. FONTFREDA
C. DE SANT ESTEVE
C. DE SANT TOMÀS
C. ANTONI LLOPIS
C. DE L'HOSPICI
Museu Comarcal de la Garrotxa
C. DEL RENGLE
C. MARIA VAYREDA
C. FONTANELLA
PLAÇA RECTOR FERRER
C. AMARGURA
C. JOAQUIM VAYREDA
C. DE SANT RAFEL
C. DELS DOLORS
C. DR FÀBREGAS
C. DE SANT FERRIOL
RG. BISBE GUILLAMET
C. DE SANT FERMIN
C. MULLERAS
C. P. GALWEY
C. PARE ROCA
Plaça Clarà
C. PANYO
C. BISBE VILANOVA
N

ACCOMMODATION
Alberg de Joventut 2
Borrell 3
Narmar 1

CAFÉ, BARS & RESTAURANTS
Bruixes i Maduixes C
Bar 6T7 B
Cocodrilo D
El Cornet H
La Deu E
Ramon F
Il Ritrovo I
S'Beisl G
Vanil A

0   200 m

1010

◄ Casal dels Volcans, 2, 3 & E

99

Marked trail no. 17 leads from Sant Esteve along a
pleasant path to the top of the Montsacopa volcano
(takes 15min). On the edge of the wooded summit crater
stands the picturesque eighteenth-century Ermita de
Sant Francesc chapel. The views are superb.

Some 400m east, the easily overlooked **Església Nostra
Dona del Tura**, first mentioned in 872, hides behind a
twentieth-century facade but houses a small twelfth-century
wooden sculpture of the *Verge del Tura*, patron saint of
the town. The interesting **Museu Comarcal de la Garrotxa**
is at c/Hospici 8 (Mon & Wed–Sat 11am–2pm & 4–7pm,
Sun 11am–2pm; €1.20). Its initial rooms chronicle the
region's history, but the best exhibits are works by the Olot
School of painters, notably Joaquim Vayreda's evocative
landscapes. Sculpture ranges from the simplicity of Josep
Clarà's life models to contemporary abstract works in metal.

Casal dels Volcans

July–Sept Mon & Wed–Sat 10am–2pm & 5–7pm, Sun 11am–2pm;
rest of year Mon & Wed–Sat 10am–2pm & 4–6pm, Sun 11am–2pm;
ⓦ www.agtat.es. Exhibition €1.80.
Southwest of the Barri Vell, the quiet, nineteenth-century
Plaça Clarà leads into the broad Passeig Barcelona for the
ten-minute walk to the landscaped **Parc Nou**. In the centre of the park is a lovely Italianate mansion housing the
Casal dels Volcans information centre. Its fascinating
exhibition displays photos and models chronicling the
region's turbulent geological history, including perfectly
formed natural basalt columns, and even a floor-shaking
simulation of an earthquake. The Casal also provides excellent maps and walking tours of the Parc Natural de La
Garrotxa.

A VOLCANO WALK

The Casal dels Volcans (see opposite) can give details of well-signposted walking routes through the park. We've put together a circular walk starting and finishing in Santa Pau that is a combination of two of these (nos. 1 & 4); it takes a good 5hr but is easily manageable, although the final few metres up to the Santa Margarida volcano are a bit of a scramble. Trails are marked with a black number beside a symbol of two ramblers in a coloured square, which also shows the next stop and final destination.

From Santa Pau, set off from the car park by the bridge into the old town, and follow trail 4 signs to Santa Margarida along the river for about 30min, when you'll pass the Volcà de la Roca Negra on your left. After the Collellmir farmhouse, the route joins up with trail 1, which leads for 30min up to the crater of the Volcà de Santa Margarida. At the summit, inside the grassy caldera, a wooded landscape frames a tiny chapel (no access) in the heart of the hollow. Cross the caldera and head down the other side of the volcano, following trail 1 to Croscat, for about 45min to the Area de Santa Margarida; here you'll find the Lava campsite and, opposite, the Santa Margarida café, where you can get a drink or a filling meal.

From the café, it's about another 1hr 15min to Can Passavent, skirting the base of the Volcà de Croscat. A further 45min brings you to the Area de Can Serra (also accessible by car, signposted off the Olot–Santa Pau road). Here you can either rent a horse-drawn carriage through the dense beech woods of La Fageda d'en Jordà (1hr round trip; €5), or follow the rough, twisting trail 1, which takes about 30min to emerge into the open, leading to the medieval chapel of Sant Miquel de Sa Cot, a popular picnic spot. The path eventually brings you back to where you left trail 4 at the foot of the Santa Margarida volcano, for the easy river walk back to Santa Pau.

OLOT

Practicalities

Regular **buses** from Girona, Figueres, Barcelona, Lloret de Mar and outlying villages pull in at the bus station on c/Bisbe Lorenzana, opposite the helpful **tourist office** at no. 15 (Mon–Fri 9am–2pm & 3–7pm, Sat 10am–2pm & 5–7pm, Sun 11am–2pm; ☏972 260 141, ⓦwww.citolot .com). There are **taxi** stands on Plaça Clarà and at the bus station. All the main **banks** have ATMs in the Barri Vell; the Puigvert **pharmacy** is at Plaça Major 1; and the **police station** is on Plaça Can Joanetes (☏972 279 133).

Places to stay range from the beautiful mansion housing the *Alberg de Joventut*, Pg Barcelona 15 (☏972 264 200, ⓔalberg_olot@tujuca.com; ❶; closed Sept), with basic dorms and a midnight curfew, to the central *Pensió Narmar*, c/St Roc 1 (☏972 269 807; ❶) offering modern en-suite rooms (although it can get noisy on weekend nights). The outwardly nondescript *Hotel Borrell*, two minutes' walk south of Plaça Clarà at c/Nònit Escubós 8 (☏972 269 275, ⓕ972 270 408; ❸), houses the most comfortable air-conditioned rooms in town.

Olot's **restaurants** rely on Catalan cuisine or *cuina volcànica*. The best are *Ramon*, Pl Clarà 4; the much-respected *La Deu*, Ctra La Deu; and *El Cornet*, c/Serra Ginesta 17 (closed Mon), which also makes tasty pasta and pizzas. *S'Beisl*, Pl Almoina 1 (Mon–Sat 9am–11pm) makes Basque tapas, while for superb Italian food try *Il Ritrovo della Dolce Vita*, Ctra Barcelona 1. Plenty of Barri Vell **bars** have terraces; good choices include the slightly hippyish *Bruixes i Maduixes*, c/Bonaire 14; *Cocodrilo*, a laid-back cocktail bar beside *Pensió Narmar*; and the livelier *Vanil* and *Bar 6T7*, both on tiny Carrer dels Sastres.

SANTA PAU

SANTA PAU's defensive perimeter of windowless house-walls hides a beautifully preserved medieval core. Despite wars, occupation and earthquakes, the village has remained largely unchanged since the thirteenth century, while the restoration that has been done has maintained the original feel of the village. Today, Santa Pau rarely gets too busy, except possibly for Catalans enjoying a long Sunday lunch in one of the village's good restaurants.

The cobbled old quarter clusters around two adjacent squares, featuring low wooden balconies decked in flowers. The porticoed thirteenth-century **Plaça Major** is an irregular triangle built on sloping ground, which gives it an enjoyably anarchic air. Scene of the Monday market since 1297 (originally livestock, and now local crafts and fruit and veg), it's dominated by the enormous Romanesque **Església de Santa Maria**, rebuilt in the fifteenth century. The thirteenth- to eighteenth-century **castle**, an angular, crumbling edifice, once the baronial seat of the region, rises over the small **Placeta dels Balls**, once the castle moat.

Practicalities

The **tourist office**, Pl Major 1 (Mon & Wed–Sat noon–5pm, Sun noon–3pm; ☎972 680 349), is a mine of information on walking routes and local history. In town, **accommodation** and **food** are available at the pricey *Cal Sastre* (☎972 680 049; ❹) on Placeta dels Balls, which serves filling mountain fare and has seven old-fashioned guest rooms. The atmospheric *Can Menció* (☎972 680 014; ❷), on Plaça Major, is a bar which doubles as village shop and rents out cheerful rooms; their huge sandwiches are especially welcome after a long walk.

Idyllic **turisme rurals** include the eighteenth-century

mansion of *Prat de la Plaça*, Pla de La Cot 65 in Santa Pau (℡972 680 509; ❷), rented whole, or the spacious rooms of the tenth-century *Can Jou* in the neighbouring hamlet of St Jaume de Llierca (℡972 190 263, ✉canjou@turismerural .net; ❶). The large *Mas El Carré*, with a pool, lies 2km east in Els Arcs (℡972 680 487; ❷), or there's the secluded twelfth-century *Rectoria de la Miana* further southeast in St Ferriol (℡972 590 397; ❷).

The best **campsites** are off the Ctra Olot–Sța Pau: *Camping Lava*, km7 (℡972 680 358, ✉tourturistic@ garrotxa.com), which also has log cabins, and *Mas Patxet*, km11 (℡972 680 066).

The road from Olot to Santa Pau
continues 25km east to Banyoles.

La Selva

I f anywhere fits the popular conception of the Costa Brava, it's **La Selva**, the region occupying the southernmost portion of the coast. The towns here were among the first in the country to be adapted for tourism and the area bore the brunt of the pre-regulation construction excesses. High-rise blocks were flung up on the site of fishermen's cottages and wealthy mansions alike, and a mock Spanish culture was touted to sunseeking tourists. Things are changing, though, and the region's three major

THE CAMÍ DE RONDA

Much of the La Selva coastline is too sheer for a footpath, and the only part of the Camí de Ronda (see p.49) is a 500m section heading northeast from Lloret de Mar's Platja Gran; the continuation of this stretch is steadily being restored. An alternative is to follow the well-signposted GR92 long-distance trail, which swoops into all three main towns before heading back inland by anything up to 750m into the pine woods; where possible, it approaches the sea, most notably between Fenals and Lloret, for short stretches between Lloret and Tossa, and partly on the corniche road between Tossa and Sant Feliu de Guíxols.

towns have something to offer most visitors – if only a couple of hours' pottering among the still-beautiful coves and gardens that pepper the rocky shoreline.

Map 1 at the back of the book covers the La Selva region.

The thriving fishing port of **Blanes** marks the southern limit of the Costa Brava, a high-rise tourist resort tacked onto the original old town and harbour. Tackier still, neighbouring **Lloret de Mar** – crammed with clubs and nightlife – also boasts an absorbing history and some tranquil scenery. Further along the coast, **Tossa de Mar** mercifully escaped the worst of development fever; the only medieval walled town on Catalonia's coast, Tossa was a haven for artists in the 1930s, and is still imbued with a bohemian ambience which leavens the tiresome over-commercialization of much of this area.

Blanes

The jagged Sa Palomera headland jutting out from the beach divides **BLANES** neatly in half and offers a succinct glimpse of two distinct facets of the region. To the south stretches the long swath of sand and high-rise blocks of the modern **S'Abanell** suburb, while to the north, the **old town**'s low-rise buildings and small, curving beach and promenade culminate in the bustle of the fishing port.

ARRIVAL AND INFORMATION

The GI512 **road** connects Blanes with Lloret, Tossa and the coastal towns to the north, and also links up with the

BLANES FIREWORKS COMPETITION

In the last full week of July, during Blanes' Festa Major, Sa Palomera is the setting for one of the most spectacular free fireworks displays in Spain. First held in 1906, the awe-inspiring feast of noise and colour now attracts pyrotechnics teams from all over the world and thousands of spectators who pack the beach and promenade. Shows start nightly at 10.30pm, with most vantage points filling up long beforehand. The best views are from the sea, with the backdrop of the old town: boat operators (who normally ply between resorts) offer excursions from S'Abanell beach or neighbouring Lloret de Mar to view the displays – get tickets (€8) and information from the beach stands.

N-II, 3km southwest, and the A7 *autopista*, 10km northwest. The scenic but expensive A19 *autopista* from Barcelona ends a little northwest of Blanes.

The handy seafront **bus station** is on Plaça Catalunya, opposite Sa Palomera and very near the **tourist office** at no. 21 (Mon–Sat 9am–8pm; ☎972 330 348, ⊛ www.blanes.net), which hands out useful maps and a good free leaflet on walks around the town. The **train station** is 2km southwest (☎972 331 827), with services from Barcelona (every 30min) and Girona (every 2hr); half-hourly shuttle buses (free with a train ticket) run to Plaça Catalunya. Taxis (☎972 330 037) wait at Plaça Catalunya and the station; the ride between the two costs about €7.

Several operators run regular boat services (Easter–Oct daily 9am–5.30pm) between Blanes and Tossa de Mar (and beyond), stopping at all main beaches. See p.27 for more.

BLANES

BLANES 0   200 m

ACCOMMODATION

Beverly Park	1
Boix Mar	6
Hostal Doll	4
Esplendid	2
Pi-Mar	5
San Antonio	3

CAFÉS, BARS & RESTAURANTS

L'Activa	G
Anchor	B
Casa Oliveras	C
Cava Nit	J
Inti Huasi	H
Marisqueria El Port	D
Marítim	E
Mascotte	I
Paparazzi	A
Sant Jordi	F

ACCOMMODATION

The few **hotels** in the old town are atmospheric, but those at the more tourist-oriented S'Abanell are bigger; the ones set back from the sea offer better value. There's a wide choice of **apartments** and **villas**, almost exclusively in S'Abanell; Finques Gironès, c/Raval 31 (℡972 330 594, ℻972 337 329, ⓦwww.fincas-girones.com), is the largest agency.

Most of the **campsites** are generic. *Reina Maris*, at Paratge dels Olivers (℡972 331 531; closed Oct–April), is ten minutes' walk from the beach, but well shaded and with a pool. *S'Abanell*, Avgda Villa de Madrid 7–9 (℡972 331 809, ⓦwww.sabanell.com), is a stroll from the sea in the

BLANES

centre of S'Abanell and convenient for shops and restaurants, but can get crowded.

Beverly Park

c/Mercé Rodoreda s/n,
S'Abanell ☎ 972 352 426,
ⓕ 972 330 110,
ⓦ www.hotelbeverlypark.com.
Closed Nov–March.
Plush hotel in a quiet area of
S'Abanell with modern en-
suite rooms – good for
relaxing around the pool or
working out in the gym after
a fine buffet breakfast. ❺

Boix Mar

c/Enric Morera 3, S'Abanell
☎ 972 330 276, ⓕ 972 351 898,
ⓦ www.publintur.es/hboixmar.
Closed Nov–March.
Smart family-run three-star
with pool, jacuzzi, minigolf
and tennis courts, two streets
back from the seafront.
Rooms are bright, en suite
and cheerfully decorated. ❹

BLANES

Hostal Doll

Pg Pau Casals 70–71 ☎ 972 330 008.

Friendly budget *hostal* at the quieter, port end of the old town, with good, but slightly gloomy, en-suite rooms. ❷

Esplendid

Av Mediterrani 17, S'Abanell ☎ 972 336 561, ☎ 972 337 949, ⓦ www.gib.es/esplendid. Closed Nov.

Plush place complete with tennis and swimming pool three streets back from the beach in the heart of the nightlife area, with quiet, spacious rooms. ❺

Pi-Mar

Pg de S'Abanell 8, S'Abanell ☎ 972 352 817, ☎ 972 330 110, ⓦ www.hotelpimar.com. Closed Nov–April.

The best of S'Abanell's seafront options: a smart restaurant with modern rooms, most with sea view, and a good terrace bar. ❹

San Antonio

Pg del Mar 63 ☎ 972 331 150, ☎ 972 330 226. Closed Nov–Feb.

Pleasant, good-value two-star on the old-town seafront, with simple but comfortable en-suite rooms boasting good views of the sands and fishing port. ❹

THE TOWN

Climbing the **Sa Palomera** rock presents great views over the two sides of Blanes; take the stone steps which lead up from the small spit of sand at the start of the promenade. South lie the three packed kilometres of **Platja S'Abanell**, lined by hotels and apartment blocks. North is the **old town**, which retains its low buildings and medieval streets, fronted by the sedate **Platja de Blanes**, which ends at the **port**. On the steep hillsides above town is the **Jardí Botànic Mar i Murtra**, a short walk from the town's best beach, **Cala Sant Francesc**.

BLANES

The old town

Running northeast from Sa Palomera to the port, the sandy, gently shelving **Platja de Blanes**, the town's main beach, gets a lot less crowded than the hotel-heavy S'Abanell. Framing it, the **promenade** – site of the Monday market – changes halfway along from a sun-soaked boulevard with restaurant terraces to a shaded stretch of public gardens, before culminating in the workaday **port**, which comes alive for the late-afternoon fish auction.

Overlooking Blanes is the sixteenth-century Castell de Sant Joan (no access). The tiring climb up from the port (1.3km), on a turn-off from the Mar i Murtra road, rewards you with sea views amid cicadas and the scent of eucalyptus.

Parallel to the promenade, one street in, the sheltered **Passeig de Dintre** is home every morning to a lively fruit and veg **market**. From here, the medieval **Carrer Ample** leads left (northwest) inland; this has been a busy shopping street for centuries, and an ornately tiled fishmongery dating from 1861 still plies its trade at no. 9. An impressive fifteenth-century Gothic **fountain** decorated with gargoyles emerges from a wall on the right-hand side of the street; it's been sliced in two by the buildings, indicating that it was probably once the centrepiece of a long-gone square amidst a much grander c/Ample.

Feeding right (northeast) off c/Ample, Carrer Nou leads to the fourteenth-century **Església Parroquial i Palau dels Vecomtes de Cabrera** (the Parish Church and Palace of the Viscounts of Cabrera). Largely destroyed by French troops in the seventeenth century, it was restored in the eighteenth century, but all that remains of the original structure is the crenellated fourteenth-century facade, with a high arched doorway and towering square belfry. The interior is very simple, with a plain vaulted ceiling.

Jardí Botànic Mar i Murtra

Pg Karl Faust 9. April–Oct daily 9am–6pm; Nov–March Mon–Fri 10am–5pm, Sat & Sun 10am–2pm. €2.25.

On a headland 1km northeast of the port, the **Jardí Botànic Mar i Murtra** – founded in 1924 by German industrialist Karl Faust on the site of an eighteenth-century garden – offers a pleasurable afternoon wandering on hilly paths amid the flora, looking out over the turquoise sea. **Bus** #3 (every 15min) runs from the bus station to the gardens, via the promenade and the port (takes 15min). On foot, the steep climb is signed along Carrer Esperança. Parking is very limited.

From the entrance, a well-signposted **path** leads you through themed areas based on climatic or geographical areas. The **Subtropical garden**, which includes a rambling cactus collection, leads into the **Temperate garden**, featuring bamboo groves and towering Chilean palms. The loveliest is the **Mediterranean garden**, where olives and tamarisks flow down to the belvederes at the cliff edge, from the largest of which, steps climb through an avenue of cypresses to a small square framed by orange trees, bearing a tiled fountain decorated with Goethe's poem *Where the Oranges Blossom*. Dotted around are areas of **poisonous**, **medicinal** and **aromatic plants**.

Blanes' finest beach, the sheltered horseshoe bay of Cala Sant Francesc, lies 15 minutes' walk along the road past the gardens' bus stop. The tranquil, unspoilt cove shelves gently and its crystalline waters are great for swimming.

S'Abanell

South of Sa Palomera, the modern **S'Abanell** suburb – a 1960s residential and tourist development – is a bit of a sprawl, but it's saved by the glittering sands of **Platja S'Abanell**, which, despite the hotel crowds, has some quieter areas a few hundred metres out of the centre. As you'd expect, there's a huge range of **watersports** on offer from beach stands, from water-skiing to parasailing.

EATING

Most **restaurants** are generic outlets clustered around S'Abanell; with a couple of exceptions, the promenade in Blanes offers similarly nondescript fare. The old town is a different story, and some excellent meals are to be had in the narrow streets away from the beach.

L'Activa
c/Theolongio Bacchio 5.
Closed Tues.
Set in a brightly lit renovated medieval building, this plush upstairs restaurant, specializing in locally caught seafood and grilled meats, has a *pastisseria* downstairs serving mouthwatering cakes. Expensive.

Casa Oliveras
Pg Cortils i Vieta 8.
Daily 8–11pm.
An imaginative blend of Catalan and Latin American food served in antique-decorated rooms, or on the rooftop terrace, of this plant-festooned old building on the promenade. Moderate.

Cava Nit
c/Forn 5.
Daily 8pm–midnight.
A wide variety of tasty sweet and savoury crêpes, plus Catalan-style pizzas. The platters of cheeses, pâtés and *embotits* are very filling, and there's plenty of choice for vegetarians. Inexpensive.

BLANES

Inti Huasi

c/Forn 13.

Mon, Tues & Thurs–Sun 8–11pm.

Friendly, lively place serving an eclectic mix of Mexican and Latin American food. Budget.

Marisqueria El Port

Port Pesquer.

Closed Sun eve.

Tucked away behind the fish market, this down-to-earth eatery with outside tables serves excellent fresh fish, seafood and tapas. Budget.

Paparazzi

c/Camadasa 7.

Closed Wed.

Superb, warmly decorated Italian–Argentinian restaurant behind the seafront, serving creative and generously portioned dishes. Inexpensive.

DRINKING AND NIGHTLIFE

Blanes offers two distinct types of **nightlife**. The old town offers great laid-back bars and terrace cafés on and around the promenade, while S'Abanell offers a number of stylish late-night bars and clubs in between its anonymous tourist haunts.

Anchor

c/S'Auguer 4.

Closed Mon.

Small, friendly bar, run by an Englishwoman and set in an old backstreet fisherman's cottage. Subtly lit and with a lively but intimate feel, it's usually packed with locals; few visitors stumble across it.

Maritim

c/Vila de Paris 2.

A late-night magnet in S'Abanell, playing a wide range of music from Spanish pop to house. One or two other bars in the same short street are also worth checking out, but don't bother arriving before 1am.

Mascotte

c/Forn 4.

Closed Mon.

A favourite after-dinner haunt in the middle of the old town with a penchant for

1980s and 1990s music and an excellent range of rums.

Sant Jordi
Pg S'Abanell 33.
Daily 9pm–3am.
Imagine a public baths designed by Gaudí and then turned into a salsa dancehall and you've got this curious institution. One of the oldest and most stylish clubs in Blanes, its tiled pillars and garish mural only add to its undeniable charm.

LISTINGS

Banks Major banks, all with ATMs, are around Rambla Joaquim Ruyra in the old town and Avgda Vila de Madrid in S'Abanell.
Hospital c/Sebastiá Llorens, on the Lloret road at the nortwestern entrance to Blanes ☎ 972 331 027.

Moped rental Mopeds to Rent, Edifici Lotus, c/Olivers, Els Pins ☎ 972 350 951.
Pharmacy Adell, c/Muralla 34, in the old town; Baltasar, Avgda Vila de Madrid 17, in S'Abanell.
Police Av Joan Carles I, 120 ☎ 092.

Lloret de Mar

LLORET DE MAR, 6km northeast of Blanes, is like a dissolute uncle: you know you should be shocked, but you can't help feeling a sneaking affection. On one hand is the gaudy over-commercialization that has made Lloret a byword for all things cheap and nasty, while on the other – underneath the tack – beats a two-thousand-year-old heart. Lloret boasts high-rise monstrosities alongside characterful mansions, and a town centre with one of Europe's highest

LLORET DE MAR

Castell d'en Plaja

LLORET DE MAR

CAFÉS, BARS & RESTAURANTS

L'Arrosseria de Fenals	C
Bumper's	I
Can Tarrades	L
Colossos	G
Gran Café Latino	K
Hula Hula	E
Jamaica Tavern	M
La Lonja	N
Marechiaro	D
Stones	J
Tropics	H
El Trull	A
Zoom	B
Zorba	F

ACCOMMODATION

Aquarium	2
Guitart Rosa	1
Hostal La Habana	7
Marsol	6
Pensió Reina Isabel	8
Hostal Santa Cristina	4
Santa Marta	3
Vila de Mar	5

Centre Cultural Verdaguer

Bus Station

Platja de Lloret

Tossa de Mar & A

J, Fenals & Blanes

Cala Banys

200 m

116

LLORET'S FESTA MAJOR

Lloret's colourful Festa Major – held between July 24 and 26 every year, with live music, *sardanes* and sports – has a very local feel. The most spectacular event is the religious procession by boat from the main beach to the Ermita de Santa Cristina. At the *Ball de les Almorratxes*, in front of the Ajuntament, couples dance in a mock fight over an Arab-style jar (the *almorratxa*), recalling a local legend where a Moorish man wished to dance with a Christian woman who refused him. At the end of the dance, the woman throws the jar to the ground; if it smashes, it's said that she'll marry within the year.

concentrations of clubs crowded around a tiny but colourful fifteenth-century church. Fanning out from Lloret's charming **old town** are some of the prettiest – and most crowded – **beaches** on the Costa Brava. Southwest, the modern suburb of **Fenals** is mostly taken up with holiday homes, while the surprisingly tranquil **Jardins de Santa Clotilde** offer pleasant respite from sun and sea.

After Iberian and Roman settlement, Lloret's first period of growth was between 1812 and 1868, when over 120 oceangoing ships were built in its dockyards, and local traders arrived back from the Americas with cocoa, molasses, tobacco, mahogany and cotton. Many townspeople made their fortunes in the Caribbean or Latin America in the nineteenth and early twentieth centuries before returning to settle. The next boom came in the 1950s with the arrival of Spanish holiday-makers, and three decades of unchecked high-rise development. These days controls are more stringent and there's a sense of renewed pride in the way grand old buildings are being cared for.

LLORET DE MAR

ARRIVAL AND INFORMATION

The GI682 coastal **road** links Lloret with Blanes to the southwest and Tossa de Mar to the northeast. From Girona, exit either the A7 or N-II to head into Lloret via the GI680; coming from Barcelona and the south, you'd do better on the A19 motorway to Blanes. Within Lloret, there's a large underground **car park** on Plaça Pere Torrent, just off the main avenue leading down to the seafront.

Buses pull in to the huge **bus station** (⊕972 365 788) on Carretera Blanes at the entrance to the town; you can also get buses to the outlying beaches from here. **Trains** go as far as Blanes (see p.106), from where regular buses connect to Lloret. Tickets for the **boat** service (see p.27) which connects local beaches are available from stands on the promenade.

The helpful and well-stocked seafront **tourist office** is in the town hall at Pl de la Vila 1 (June–Sept Mon–Sat 9am–9pm, Sun 10am–2pm; rest of year Mon–Sat 9am–1pm & 4–8pm; ⊕972 364 735, ⓦwww.lloret.org), with a desk at the bus station (Easter–Sept Mon–Sat 9am–9pm, Sun 10am–2pm). The unofficial **website** ⓦwww.lloretdemar.net has plenty of useful information.

ACCOMMODATION

Though Lloret has more **hotel** beds than Barcelona, the vast majority are block-booked by agents; you should be sure to reserve a room before you arrive. To book **apartments**, contact Lloveras, Pl de la Torre 1 (⊕972 370 475, ⓕ972 370 425), or Albamar & Almirall, Pg Agustí Font 20 (⊕972 364 823, ⓕ972 370 816, ⓦwww.albamar-almirall.com), which rents large seafront apartments sleeping two to eight.

Campsites are way out of town, only really accessible with your own transport. Quiet, shady *Canyelles* (℡ 972 364 504, ℻ 972 368 506; closed Nov–March) is 5km north at Platja Canyelles, with good amenities. Well-equipped *Santa Elena-Ciutat*, about 3km southwest of Lloret on the main Blanes road (℡ 972 364 009, ℻ 972 367 954; closed Nov–March), also has mobile homes and cabins for rent.

Aquarium
c/Pere Codina i Mont s/n ℡ 972 366 395, ℻ 972 367 504.
Closed Nov–Feb.
Sumptuous hotel four blocks in from Fenals beach, excellent for families, featuring large pools and supervised indoor and outdoor kids' play areas as well as a gym and bars. Balconied, en-suite rooms are comfortable and spacious. ❺

Guitart Rosa
c/St Pere 67 ℡ 972 365 100, ℻ 972 363 002,
Ⓦ www.guitarthotels.com.
This late nineteenth-century colonial mansion, in the heart of the old town and set in its own shaded grounds around a pool, is sheer indulgence at a reasonable price. Some of the airy rooms are in the original house, others in the similarly attractive modern annexe; all

are comfortably furnished and have balconies. ❻

Hostal La Habana
c/Les Taronges 11 ℡ 972 367 707, ℻ 972 372 024.
Closed Nov–Feb.
A friendly, smart family-run pension, with small but comfortable rooms – some en suite – and a good restaurant. ❷

Marsol
Pg Jacint Verdaguer 7 ℡ 972 365 754, ℻ 972 372 205.
One of the better-value hotels on Lloret's seafront, with a pool and sauna. The rooms are on the small side but well furnished, and some have sea views. ❺

Pensió Reina Isabel
c/Vall de Venecia 12 ℡ 972 364 121, ℻ 972 369 978.
Closed Nov–Feb.

LLORET DE MAR

Quirky old-town place popular with backpackers, with a hundred-year-old magnolia growing in the middle of the bar (every year or so, the owners saw another bit out of the ceiling to allow it to grow). All the bright, airy rooms are well maintained, and some are en suite. ❷

Hostal Santa Cristina
Ermita Sta Cristina 7 ⓣ 972 364 934.
Closed Nov–Feb.
Charming *hostal* in the grounds of the Ermita Santa Cristina 4km south of Lloret overlooking two coves, with sparse en-suite rooms, sumptuous faded sitting-rooms and a good-value restaurant. ❸

Santa Marta
Platja de Sta Cristina ⓣ 972 364 904, ⓕ 972 369 280, ⓔ hstamarta@grn.es.

Set in extensive grounds above Cala Santa Cristina, this plush four-star hotel has access to the beach and pool, tennis courts and one of its excellent restaurants via a winding path through the pines. All the sumptuous rooms have excellent sea views and come with air conditioning, satellite TV and balcony. ❾

Vila del Mar
c/de la Vila 55 ⓣ 972 349 292, ⓕ 972 371 168, ⓦ www.hotelviladelmar.com.
Closed Dec & Jan.
Compact, welcoming four-star hotel just back from the seafront and smartly decorated in an eighteenth-century style. The comfortable, quiet en-suite rooms – with air conditioning – are a welcome haven from the old town streets. ❽

THE TOWN AND AROUND

The best way to appreciate Lloret is to take a walk through the **old town**'s maze of narrow pedestrian streets: nowhere is the town's diversity more evident than around **Carrer**

Vila and **Plaça Església**. A bakery, confectioner's and butcher jostle with tattoo parlours, tearooms and dance clubs; all-day English breakfasts are as common as *pà amb tomàquet*. Holding court on Plaça Església is the late-Gothic **Església Parroquial**, originally heavily fortified, with brick walls capped by brightly coloured tiles on its ornate domed roof, a style that was to influence Modernist architects. Inside, look out for the elaborately gilded sixteenth-century altarpieces, which survived a fire during the Civil War, and the seven enormous, sombre paintings of the Passion by an unknown, late sixteenth-century artist.

The Rally Catalunya Costa Brava, held every April as part of the World Rally Car Championship, starts and finishes at the southwestern end of Lloret's promenade, a spot marked with a plaque and the handprints of past winners.

Centre Cultural Verdaguer

Pg Camprodón i Arrieta 1. June–Sept daily 10am–8pm; Oct–May Tues–Sat 10am–2pm & 4–6pm, Sun 10am–2pm. Free.

On the café-lined **Passeig de les Palmeres** promenade, 50m from Plaça Església – site of Lloret's old shipyards – is the **Centre Cultural Verdaguer**, an eclectic historical museum set in the former home of the Garriga family, Indianos who grew wealthy in Cuba before returning home to Lloret. The **ground floor** is taken up with a display of model ships, crafted from South American hardwood rescued from local Indiano houses that were torn down to make way for hotels. The most alluring exhibits in the **upstairs rooms** are the collection of satirical 1930s sketches by local artist Joan Llaverias i Labró, depicting fable-like animals, and the photographs of old Lloret before the tourist boom. The **top floor** is a re-creation of how the

INDIANO ARCHITECTURE

In several Costa Brava towns, you'll come across a style of architecture brought back from the Americas by locals who had emigrated in the nineteenth century. On returning, these Indianos or Americanos – the terms are used interchangeably – used their new-found wealth to build sumptuous mansions in a striking blend of Spanish-colonial style with traditional Catalan architecture and newfangled Modernist influences. The most common pattern was to build on the seafront facing inland, as it was considered vulgar to face the sea. As was the case in the Centre Cultural Verdaguer, the back garden (which often became the front entrance, as modern generations reoriented their houses to overlook the beach) featured a palm tree standing below a colonnaded verandah, which led into a solid, traditionally styled building. The interiors usually display the elaborate flowing lines of Modernism and the use of traditional tiles and wrought iron in contemporary patterns; one of the best examples is *Hotel Diana* in Tossa de Mar (see p.131). Many of Lloret's Indiano houses were pulled down in the 1960s to make space for hotels, but examples survive in places, with more in Tossa de Mar, Sant Feliu de Guíxols, Begur and Olot.

house might have looked in its heyday, its sturdy Indiano furnishings marrying traditional Catalan styles with Modernist and colonial influences.

The main beaches

Lloret's elevation to tourist stardom was thanks to its sweeping main beach, **Platja de Lloret**, which stretches the length of the town and is capped at either end by strings of tiny coves. Its beauty was its downfall, though, and it now gets extremely crowded with rows of basting bodies; the

LLORET DE MAR

southern end is more family-oriented than the northern end. Its southwestern point is marked by a rock topped by a bronze statue of the **Dona Marinera** (Sailor's Wife). Local legend has it that if you stare at the same spot on the horizon as the statue, and touch her right foot, you'll be granted a wish. The footpath to the Dona Marinera statue leads 100m past the rock to the tiny Cala Banys, with a minuscule beach overlooked by the terraces of relaxing *Cala Banys* bar (daily 10am–3am).

Clinging to the rocks at the northeastern end of Lloret's beach is the private **Castell d'en Plaja**, a turreted folly built in the 1930s for Narcís Plaja, an industrialist from Girona, that adds a touch of exotic fakery to the skyline. The **Camí de Ronda** (see p.49) winds 500m past the castle along the shoreline, from where paths dive down to a string of relatively uncrowded coves, offering great snorkelling among the rocks.

The overflow suburb of **Fenals** lies 500m southwest of the town centre, with a beach similar to Lloret's; the far southwestern corner, framed by pines, is much less frenetic than the hotel-lined strip nearer Lloret.

Jardins de Santa Clotilde and around

Ctra Blanes km9.3. Tues–Sun 10am–1pm & 4–8pm. €3.

Some 3km southwest of Lloret on the Blanes road, a signposted turning leads to the **Jardins de Santa Clotilde**, private gardens that were opened to the public in 1997. First laid out a hundred years ago in Modernist style, with terraces around a central square, they offer a cooling break amid fountains and statues and offer some inspiring views of the sea through avenues of tall cypresses and pines. Visitor numbers are limited to fifty at a time, although if you go in the early afternoon when everyone's at the beach, you're likely to have the place to yourself, even in August. The gardens overlook the peaceful **Cala Boadella**, divided in two by a rocky outcrop; the south side – popular with families – is mixed nude and clothed, while the north side is entirely nude.

A kilometre further on are signs to the eighteenth-century **Ermita de Santa Cristina**, which stands on the site of a much earlier church in a peaceful, shaded clifftop garden overlooking the sea. Only occasionally open for weddings and the annual procession (see p.117), the chapel is worth visiting for its tranquil gardens, laced with paths winding down through groves of evergreen oaks, pines and olives to the two sheltered coves below; both beaches are sandy and get very much less crowded than those nearer Lloret.

Cala Canyelles and Cala Morisca

Northeast of Lloret are a couple of delightful coves worth investigating. Some 5km along the road towards Tossa de Mar, a signposted turning leads down to **Cala Canyelles**, a long, attractive beach with a small fishing quay. The very good *El Trull* seafood restaurant (see opposite) and nearby campsite (see p.119) mean that the sandy, sheltered bay does get busy, but still not on the scale of Lloret. **Cala Morisca** is reachable only by a fairly arduous hour-long walk from Cala Canyelles, following the signposted GR92 path through the pines and then down a gully. Though rarely empty, the beach is a just reward: its tiny rock-strewn shore is almost virgin and the waters are excellent for snorkelling.

EATING

Lloret is crammed with fast-food places, but you'll also find some good **restaurants** in and around the old town.

L'Arrosseria de Fenals
Pg Ferran Agulló 14, Fenals.
Daily noon–midnight; closed
Nov–March.
Welcoming restaurant near
Fenals beach, with a shaded
terrace and plenty for
carnivores and vegetarians
alike. Starters are particularly
tasty, the best being cream of
pea soup with lemon sorbet
and superb apple vichyssoise.
Inexpensive.

Can Tarrades
Pl Espanya 7, Lloret.
Nov–March closed Mon–Thurs.
Bright, tasteful place with
excellent Catalan cooking;
try the seafood or grilled
meat specialities. The
tempting starters, especially
the *escalivada*, are among the
best in town. Moderate.

La Lonja
c/St Cristòfol 2, Lloret.
Oct–March closed Mon–Thurs.
Down-to-earth restaurant
serving solid Catalan fare,
especially seafood; the *menú
del dia* is €7.25. Also worth
trying is the excellent range
of tapas. Budget.

Marechiaro
c/St Pere 48, Lloret.
Oct–March closed Mon–Thurs.
Set a few streets back from
the sea, this extremely good
Italian restaurant has a quiet,
welcoming interior garden
and serves large, appetising
pizzas and a tasty range of
grilled meats and fresh pasta.
Inexpensive.

El Trull
Cala Canyelles.
An excellent restaurant with a
large terrace overlooking this
beach 5km out of town (see
opposite). The varied menu
includes seafood, meat, pizzas
and *pà amb tomàquet*, and
takes in a daily seafood special
at up to €42 a dish.
Moderate to Expensive.

Zorba
c/Carme 2, Lloret.
Daily 1pm–midnight; closed
Nov–March.
With a cool blue and white
interior terrace, this amiable
restaurant serves top-notch
Greek food. The leek and
feta pie and stuffed tomatoes
are outstanding. Inexpensive.

LLORET DE MAR

DRINKING AND NIGHTLIFE

Lloret's **nightlife** is legendary, with over thirty clubs and countless bars catering for a mixed crowd from beery Brits to cool Catalans. However this isn't a heavy-duty, Ibiza-style clubbers' haunt; the choice will satisfy most tastes – and Lloret doesn't take itself too seriously. **Bars** are found mainly in the old town around c/Vila and c/Carme. Most **clubs** are grouped further west along Avgda Just Marlés and charge €8–10 admission (drinks cost the same again), but there are plenty of very visible touts handing out free or discount passes.

The daiquiri cocktail was invented by a Lloret man, Constantí Ribalaigua Vert, who emigrated to Cuba in 1899 at the age of 11. In *Islands in the Stream*, Hemingway refers to evenings spent in Havana drinking Constantí's "double daiquiris".

Bumper's

Pl del Carme 4.

Daily 9.30pm–5.30am;
Nov–March closed Sun–Thurs.

Three areas – two indoors with large dance floors – that are very popular with a young crowd looking for Caribbean, salsa, swing and pop. The garden bar, featuring palms, glass dance floor and tropical fish, is great for chilling with a cocktail.

Colossos

Avgda Just Marlés 38.

Daily 9pm–6am; Nov–March closed Sun–Thurs.

Two dance floors, four bars and famous foam parties (every Mon in summer). The playlist is mainly house, hard house and trance, alongside a large quota of Top 40 and 1980s pop.

Gran Café Latino

Pl Espanya 3.

Daily 9pm–6am; Nov–March closed Sun–Thurs.

A sumptuous mansion converted into a stylish salsa bar, with a medium-sized dance floor downstairs (usually packed) and a quieter gallery bar upstairs.

Hula Hula
c/Carme 34.

May–Oct daily 8pm–6am;
Nov–April Fri & Sat 10pm–6am.

Done up as a Polynesian fishing village, complete with bamboo, papier-mâché gods and fishing nets, this friendly bar serves extravagant cocktails, while Latino, salsa and Spanish pop pull in a wide range of ages and nationalities.

Jamaica Tavern
c/Venècia 49.

Daily 5pm–3am.

Opened in 1972 by a die-hard Bob Marley fan and now run by him and his son, this lively bar plays reggae to a clued-up crowd of all ages, as well as serving Red Stripe beer and a wide variety of Jamaican rums.

Stones
c/Sta Caterina 11.

Daily 9pm–5am; Nov–March closed Sun–Thurs.

Genial bar with a large dance floor, playing very loud 1960s and 1970s rock classics for a broad cross section of locals and tourists.

Tropics
Avgda Just Marlès 36.

Daily 9pm–6am; Nov–March closed Sun–Thurs.

Tropical decor spreading over five bars and two dance floors, with the most spectacular lights and sound system in town. The resident DJ was formerly in Ibiza, and visiting DJs give the place a Balearic feel, although the catholic music policy takes in house, trance, mellow, swing, hip-hop, pop and classic rock.

Zoom
c/Ponent s/n.

Daily 10pm–3am; Nov–March closed Sun–Thurs.

Lloret's sole house-only bar, a stylish factory-chic underground warehouse with no seating. Chillout rules until 1am, after which the DJ cranks things up.

LLORET DE MAR

127

LISTINGS

Banks All the major banks have ATMs on the promenade and c/Vila.

Bicycle rental CROM, Av Alegries 12 (☎ 972 365 412), rents quad and mountain bikes.

Car rental Avis, c/Enric Granados 24 (☎ 972 373 023); Europcar, Avgda Vila de Blanes (☎ 972 363 366).

Moped rental World of the Bike, Valentí Almirall 5 (☎ 972 363 770); Mopets to Rent, Pla de Carbonell 23 (☎ 972 366 162).

Police c/Verge de Loreto 3 ☎ 092.

Taxis Ranks in front of the town hall and at the bus station (☎ 972 364 803), and in Fenals on the corner of Avgda Amèrica and c/Macià Doménech (☎ 972 365 177).

Tossa de Mar

From Lloret, the road snakes 13km northeast with just a few glimpses of the sea to the medieval walled town of **TOSSA DE MAR**, popular as an artists' retreat in the 1930s: Marc Chagall visited, and dubbed it "The Blue Paradise" for the clarity of sea and sky. Despite being one of the first towns in Spain to be adapted for tourism, Tossa saw development on a much more human scale than some of its neighbours, restricted by its setting – hemmed in by the sea on one side and the Cadiretes mountains on the other – and has retained a mildly bohemian air.

What sets the place apart is its unique **Vila Vella** (Old Town), on the Cap de Tossa headland at the southern tip of the town. In 1186, Abbot Ramon de Berga allowed local mountain farming communities to occupy the Cap de Tossa; he ordered construction of the walls, determined the

St. Feliu de Guíxols, Lloret de Mar ▲

TOSSA DE MAR

Bus Station

AV. FERRAN AGULLÓ
AV. FERRAN AGULLÓ

MIRAMAR

ACCOMMODATION

Pensió Can Tort	6
Pensió Cap d'Or	8
Capri	5
Hotel Diana	4
Hotel Neptuno	1
Gran Hotel Reymar	7
Pensió Roqueta Mar	3
Hotel Tonet	2

GIVEROLA
SANT VICENÇ
GIVEROLA
TOMÀS BARBER
SANT SEBASTIÀ
POLA
MARIA AUXILIADORA
A

Vila Vitalis

AVINGUDA DEL PELEGRÍ
MARIA AUXILIADORA
BERNATS
PLAÇA DE L'ANTIC HOSPITAL DE SANT MIQUEL
CURT
NOU
POLA
NOU
AV. COSTA BRAVA

LA GUARDIA
AMETLLERS
PAU MOREU
LA GUARDIA
ROSA RISSECH
TARULL
TORRENT D'EN BOU
SANT ANTONI
NOU
FRANCESC MAS I ROS
DOCTOR TRUETA
DR. TRUETA
JOSEP PLA
SANT MIQUEL
POU DE LA VILA

Església de Sant Vicenç

DELS TAPERS
ROSA RISSECH
ESGLÉSIA
ESGLÉSIA
ESGLÉSIA
P. LOLA BECH
P. FRANCESC SERRA
POU DE LA VILA
PLAÇA ESGLÉSIA
SANT TELM
PLAÇA D'ESPANYA
DEL MAR
PASSEIG DEL MAR

DE LES FLORS
SANT JOSEP
VILA NOVA
SOCORS
Capella de Socors
PASSEIG DEL MAR

CLOS
PESCADORS
AIGÜERES
DEL PONT VELL
ROQUETA
CODOLAR
PORTAL
ESTOLY
SOCORS

Platja Es Codolor ◄

Torre de les Hores
PLAÇA D'ARMES
DEL TINT
PORTAL

Platja Gran

Museu Municipal
VILA VELLA

Ava Gardner Statue

▼ Lighthouse

N

0   100 m

Mar Menuda & ▶

CAFÉS, BARS & RESTAURANTS

Bahía	J
Bar 17	I
Bounty	C
Can Tonet	D
Castell Vell	K
Ely	A
Pizzeria La Grotta	G
La Lluna	L
Mediterraneo	E
Es Molí	B
Sa Cova d'es Congre	H
Trinquet	F

TOSSA DE MAR

129

size of houses within (four arms wide and six arms long), and established the town's laws, including the curious edict requiring adulterers to run naked through the streets while being beaten by the other residents. The walls and towers that still encircle the Vila Vella date from a rebuilding in 1387.

Neighbouring is the pretty eighteenth-century **Vila Nova** (New Town), and although there are some lovely **beaches** within easy reach, more impressive still are the strings of **coves** to the south and, especially, the north of town.

ARRIVAL AND INFORMATION

Road access into Tossa is picturesque: from Girona, you approach on the GI681, while the only two other ways are from the north or south along the pretty GI682 corniche road. There are free **car parks** five minutes' walk from the centre, and a fee-paying car park at the main beach. **Buses** from Blanes train station, Girona and Barcelona arrive at Tossa's **bus station** (☎972 340 108) on Avinguda Pelegrí, at the entrance to the town.

The modern Ajuntament, very near the bus station, houses the **tourist office**, Avgda del Pelegrí 25 (Easter–Sept Mon–Sat 9am–8pm, Sun 10am–2pm; Oct–March Mon–Sat 10am–1pm & 4–7pm, Sun 10am–2pm; ☎972 340 108, ⓦwww.tossademar.com). **Boats** (see p.27) to and from Blanes, Lloret, St Feliu and Palamós stop off at Platja Gran.

ACCOMMODATION

There's a broad range of **hotels** and **pensions** in the Vila Vella. Most **apartments** are in the Vila Nova; the seafront *Apartaments Mar Menuda*, c/Mar Menuda s/n (☎972 340

179; ❷; closed Oct–April) offers comfortable, modern six-person units with balconies, rented by the week. Best of the **campsites** sprinkled either side of Tossa (no public transport) are the well-equipped *Cala Llevador*, 3km south (℡ 972 340 314, ⓦ www.calallevado.com; closed Oct–April), and the plush *Pola*, in a pretty cove 4km north off the corniche road (℡ 972 341 050; closed Nov–April); pitches are more expensive the closer you get to the sea.

Pensió Cap d'Or
Pg del Mar 1 ℡ & ℻ 972 340 081.
Closed Nov–March.
Excellent-value, family-run place nestling under the walls of the Vila Vella. Delicious breakfasts, included in the rates, are served overlooking the sea, and the airy rooms have tranquil views of the beach. ❸

Pensió Can Tort
c/Pescadors 1 ℡ 972 341 185.
Closed Nov–March.
In the heart of the restaurant area, this very friendly *pensió* occupies a lovely nineteenth-century building. Rooms are simple but very large, and all en suite. ❸

Capri
Pg del Mar 17 ℡ 972 340 358, ℻ 972 341 552.
Closed Nov–March.
Comfortable and good value, right on the beach in the Vila Nova. Most of the large, well-furnished rooms have balconies with sea views. ❸

Hotel Diana
Pl Espanya 6 ℡ 972 341 886, ℻ 972 341 103.
Closed Nov–March.
Stunning two-star hotel on the promenade, occupying a Modernist mansion built by an Indiano (see p.122) in the nineteenth century, and featuring some superb architectural features, especially in the lounge and dining room. ❺

Hotel Neptuno
c/La Guardia 52 ℡ 972 340 143, ℻ 972 341 933.
Closed Nov–March.
Peaceful rustic-style hotel five

minutes' walk from the beach, set around its own gardens and swimming pool. **4**

Gran Hotel Reymar

Platja de Mar Menuda s/n
Ⓣ 972 340 312, Ⓕ 972 341 504.
Closed Nov–March.

Sumptuous beachfront hotel across the cove from the Vila Vella, with numerous restaurants, terraces, a pool and a gym. Most bedrooms have lovely views of the sweep of the bay. **8**

Pensió Roqueta Mar

c/Roqueta 2 Ⓣ 972 340 082.
Closed Nov–April.

Some way back from the beach in the Vila Nova, so very quiet. Service is friendly, the restaurant is good and the rooms, though small, are cool and en suite. **3**

Hotel Tonet

Pl Església s/n Ⓣ 972 340 237.
This friendly family-run place opposite the church is also one of the very few to stay open all year, and boasts a good, economical restaurant. The old-fashioned rooms are en suite, comfortably furnished and welcoming. **3**

THE TOWN

Focal point of Tossa is its walled **Vila Vella**, protecting the wide sweep of the **Platja Gran** below. Outside the medieval walls, the streets and squares of the **Vila Nova** fade into the low-key modern town – separated from the Vila Nova by a riverbed – to encircle the beach, culminating in the **Mar Menuda** at the northernmost end.

Avinguda Costa Brava, a shopping street heading inland from the beach alongside the river, hosts Tossa's market every Thursday.

Vila Nova and around

Central point of the Vila Nova is the pedestrianized **Plaça Espanya**, a favourite meeting-point for the locals, who remain oblivious to the crowds of trinket-hunting tourists around them. Bordering on Plaça Espanya, the whitewashed **Capella de Socors**, consecrated in 1593 and enlarged in the eighteenth century, remains tiny, a charming building with a narrow stone doorway giving onto the simple nave. A stroll southwest on **Plaça Església** is the larger **Església Parroquial de Sant Vicenç**, originally located in Vila Vella but rebuilt here in 1755 as Tossa developed out of its original core on the promontory. A relatively simple Gothic structure with a very plain altarpiece, it stands out for its beautiful Romanesque font and the sombre painting by Xavier Espinola commemorating the arrival in the bay of Sant Ramon de Penyafort, Tossa's co-patron saint.

Tucked away amid modern houses on Avinguda Pelegrí, next to the tourist office some 250m northwest of Plaça Església, lies the **Vila Vitalis**, a Roman villa dating from the first century BC. As excavation work is still ongoing, it can only be visited on guided tours (Easter–Sept Tues 10am; €2.25); however, since all the finds are on display in the Museu Municipal, you're better off heading there.

East of the Vila Nova, several short streets lead to the pedestrianized **Passeig del Mar**, lined with restaurants, which frames the **Platja Gran**. Very much the domain of the body beautiful, this main beach is ideal for lounging in the sun or swimming lazily in the clear, gently shelving waters.

Mar Menuda

The small Avinguda Sant Ramon de Penyafort hugs the shoreline northeast around the bay to **Mar Menuda**. The beach here, popular with divers and cluttered with fishing boats, is remarkable for the natural cross of pink feldspar visible in the granite rock framing the cove. Legend has it that this is where Sant Ramon de Penyafort gave a dying man his absolution in 1235, upon which a flash of lightning marked the stone with the sign of the cross.

At Mar Menuda, Andrea's, c/St Ramon Penyafort 11 (☏ 670 288 718, ⓦ www.andreas-diving.com) and Mar Menuda, on the beach (☏ 689 785 168), both offer guided dives and courses with English-speaking instructors.

Vila Vella

The main entrance to the **Vila Vella** is through the **Torre de les Hores**, a fortified gateway with a plaque commemorating the town charter granted by Abbot Ramon de Berga, into the shaded **Plaça de les Armes**. A maze of tiny, flower-bedecked streets swarms up from here between the quarter's whitewashed houses to a squat nineteenth-century **lighthouse** on the pine-clad summit of the headland, from where a path leads down northwards to the Platja Gran past a **statue of Ava Gardner**, who visited Tossa on a film-shoot in 1950, and the remains of the original medieval church. Views of the bay from the ruined walls are spectacular. A flight of steps beside the Torre de les Hores, accessed from the Plaça de les Armes, leads up to a short walkable section of the ramparts, which give good views over the town.

Museu Municipal

Pl Roig i Soler 1. Tues–Sun: June–Sept 10am–10pm; Oct–May 10am–1pm & 3–6pm. €2.25.

Adjacent to the Plaça de les Armes is the **Museu Municipal**, housed in the eighteenth-century former governor's residence. It was opened in 1935, as a museum of contemporary art, and owes much to the community of artists and writers – including Marc Chagall, Georges André Klein, André Masson and Oswald Petersen – who spent their summers in Tossa in the 1930s. The museum was enlarged recently, and now displays works of art alongside exhibits chronicling the town's history. The imaginatively displayed **Roman mosaic** from the Vila Vitalis, depicting the householder, dominates the ground floor. Upstairs, look out for a subtly lit selection of delicate seventeenth- and eighteenth-century glassware. Pride of place goes to donations from **Marc Chagall**, on the second floor, which include his haunting *Celestial Violinist*, exemplifying his ethereal style, and a collection of letters and unconventional sketches.

South of the Museu Municipal, through a small arch, a path leads down to Platja Es Codolar, a tiny, sheltered cove with room for sunbathing between fishing boats pulled up onto the beach.

EATING

Tossa's **restaurants** are located primarily around the entrance to Vila Vella or on the seafront; many of the latter serve a bit of everything to cater for all tastes, with varying degrees of success, but there are one or two exceptions, listed below.

Bahía
Pg del Mar 19.
Closed Nov–Jan.
A busy restaurant on the promenade, justly famous for its superb seafood and a favourite with Catalans for Sunday lunch – which usually consists of cannelloni or prawns for starters followed by a chunk of grilled meat or fish. Moderate.

Can Tonet
Pl Església 2.
Another local favourite,

opened in 1900, that serves very tasty Catalan dishes, mainly grilled meats, fish and *pà amb tomàquet*. Inexpensive.

Castell Vell
c/Abat Oliva 1.
Closed Nov–Feb.

One of the best Vila Vella options, tucked away behind the Torre de les Hores, with a welcoming pergola-covered terrace and an art gallery inside. The mixed platters of the day's catch are superb. Expensive.

Pizzeria La Grotta
Passatge Xixanet 1.
Closed Nov–March.

This pleasant restaurant in a Vila Nova side street cooks the best pizzas in town – wood-fired, of course – while the generous portions of pasta are excellent. Inexpensive.

La Lluna
c/Abat Oliva s/n.
Closed Nov–March.

Great restaurant, serving only tapas and set in an atmospheric old building in one of the Vila Vella's narrow climbing streets. Cobble together a meal from the selection chalked on a board, and wash it all down with a local wine. Excellent value for money. Budget.

Es Molí
c/Tarull 5.

Set in an enticing courtyard amid orange trees, fountains and a nineteenth-century windmill, this large restaurant serves superb seafood and a small but choice menu of grilled meats and fish. Expensive.

Sa Cova d'es Congre
Pg del Mar 43.
April–Oct daily 1–11.30pm.

One of the best on the waterfront, dishing up a varied menu. Friendly service and generous portions of tasty food, ranging from seafood, *torrades* and meat to pizzas, salads and *plats combinats*. Inexpensive.

TOSSA DE MAR

DRINKING AND NIGHTLIFE

Tossa's low-key **nightlife** is a world away from the over-the-top hedonism of its neighbours. The action revolves around the numerous terrace **bars** in the Vila Vella and on the seafront, and a few late-night bars and **clubs** around c/Sant Josep in the Vila Nova.

Bar 17
c/Espolt 9.

Closed Nov–March.

On the corner of c/St Josep, this very ordinary-looking place, which usually stays open much later than is permitted, plays an eclectic selection of music.

Bounty
c/Església 1.

April–Oct daily 10pm–5am.

A reggae bar popular with locals and visitors, just round the corner from c/St Josep.

Ely
c/Pola s/n.

April–Oct daily 10pm–6am.

A club with the innocent, relaxed air of a village disco, playing an odd hotchpotch of music spanning at least forty years and so drawing in a diverse clientele.

Mediterraneo
c/Sant Josep 11.

Closed Nov–March.

Small, very friendly bar run by a British couple, playing rock old and new. It's popular with both locals and visitors as first stop on the after-dinner circuit.

Trinquet
c/Sant Josep 9.

Closed Nov–March.

Odd place, mainly catering for a younger crowd, with dripping chandeliers and 1990s pop in the spacious front area, and a pleasant tree-festooned terrace at the back.

LISTINGS

Banks Major banks with ATMs
are in the pedestrianized streets
of the Vila Nova, or on Avgda
Costa Brava.
Hospital CAP Casa del Mar, Av
Catalunya s/n ☎ 972 341 828.
Pharmacy Antiga, c/St Telm 27
in the Vila Nova; Castelló,
Avgda Ferran Agulló 12, about

200m from the tourist office.
Police c/Església 4 ☎ 092.
Post office Two minutes from
the tourist office at the junction
of c/Bernats and c/Maria
Auxiliadora.
Taxis At the bus station ☎ 972
340 549.

SOUTH OF TOSSA DE MAR

The winding GI682 road running south and north of Tossa
leads to some of the prettiest coves in La Selva, boasting the
typical characteristics of Costa Brava **beaches**: small,
framed by pine-clad hills and with crystalline turquoise
waters. Few are easily accessible, and so most don't get too
crowded. Several **buses** a day serve these beaches from
Tossa's bus station, but access is much more practical with
your own transport.

Some 3km south of Tossa are **Cala Llevador**, a sandy
little cove at the end of a straight track off the main road,
and **Platja Llorell**, a larger affair with watersports and
xiringuitos. Both can get busy, especially since the first is
dominated by a campsite. A shore-hugging footpath that
connects the two leads on to a couple of idyllic beaches not
directly accessible from the GI682. **Cala d'en Carles** is a
sandy cove with canoes and windsurfing equipment for
rent, while the even tinier **Cala Figuera** is completely
untouched and is very popular for nude bathing. About
4.5km south of Tossa, a turning off the GI682 leads down a
winding road to the small sandy beach at **Platja Porto Pi**,

with good watersports facilities, a couple of *xiringuitos* – and a fraction of the crowds attracted to Platja Llorell.

NORTH OF TOSSA DE MAR

The GI682 **corniche road north** from Tossa to Sant Feliu de Guíxols (see p.143) is one of the most spectacular drives in the western Mediterranean. It winds for 22km around 365 curves through lush pine and cork woods, providing sudden glimpses of thrusting headlands and tiny coves down below. Belvederes along the way give views of the most beautiful stretches, while small impromptu parking areas and abrupt turn-offs mark paths or roads down to the most accessible **beaches**. Two **buses** a day – morning and afternoon – run from Tossa to Sant Feliu de Guíxols, stopping by the main beach approaches.

The first easily accessible beach is the deep inlet of **Cala Bona**, 3km from Tossa, where trees grow almost to the water's edge (best access is a footpath from the parking area as the road climbs up the north side of the inlet). Pass by the busy Cala Pola and Cala Giverola in favour of the stunning **Cala Futadera**, 6km from Tossa (park at the belvedere just after signs to Cala Giverola and walk down). Futadera is a small cove with no facilities, and is wonderfully tranquil; the shallow, rock-strewn waters – ideal for snorkelling – run the gamut of all shades of blue and green. Just beyond Futadera, a detour off the corniche leads inland up to the nineteenth-century Ermita de Sant Grau, from where the views along the rugged coastline are spectacular.

Cala Salions is worth bypassing to reach the unspoilt **Platja Vallpresona**, 16km from Tossa (a footpath heads down from a bend in the road where you'll usually see cars parked). The cove is well worth the half-hour hike, its gently shelving waters framed by pines and sheltered by rocks; the beach is entirely nudist.

A sharp signposted turning about 2km further on the corniche road leads down a narrow, eucalyptus-lined track to a car park alongside a good-value restaurant and bar, *Senyor Ramon*. The long sweep of the sandy **Platja del Senyor Ramon**, which rarely gets crowded (expect some nude bathing), is at the bottom of steps leading from the parking area.

The next two beaches, **Platja de Canyet** and the larger **Platja dels Canyerets**, 1km further on, are built-up and get very busy. The few remaining beaches from here to Sant Feliu de Guíxols (see p.143), 5km northeast, are only accessible by sea, although the road continues to hug the cliff-edge for most of the way.

The Baix Empordà
– south

Retaining the charm which the La Selva coast to the south has largely lost, the indented shoreline of the **Baix Empordà** is the stretch of coast which prompted local writer Ferran Agulló to coin the term Costa Brava ("Rugged Coast") in the early 1900s. The **southern** part of the region is characterized by the vivid turquoises and greens of idyllic pine-clad coves strung out along the shore, broken only by long stretches of golden sandy beaches. Sophisticated towns and villages nestle by the water's edge or remain aloof inland, unblighted by mass tourism.

**Map 0 at the back of the book covers
the whole Baix Empordà region.**

Separated from La Selva not only by a serpentine cliff-hugging road but also by a leap in perception is the genteel fishing port of **Sant Feliu de Guíxols**, with its neighbour **S'Agaró**, founded in the 1930s as a Modernist utopia for the rich and famous.

THE CAMÍ DE RONDA

The Baix Empordà has led the way in restoring and marking out its section of the Camí de Ronda (see p.49): little of it had been built on, and large sections follow the GR92, which hugs the coast at this point. The trail is very varied in this region, with easy stretches well above the sea interspersed with parts along beaches and even through towns. Some sections are much tougher – invariably coinciding with the least accessible coves – but it's possible to follow the Camí de Ronda for virtually the length of the coastline here.

The section from Platja de Sant Pol (see p.148) to Platja d'Aro's main beach and on to Platgeta de l'Ermita (see p.167) is fairly easy. A more arduous stretch links from Platja de Can Cristus to Sant Antoni de Calonge (see p.169), after which the trail runs along the beach at Palamós to continue through yet more demanding sections to Calella de Palafrugell (p.191). The path runs intermittently through the town, before continuing to Llafranc (p.199) and the Far de Sant Sebastià lighthouse. Toughest of all is the final stretch running inland along the GR92 from the lighthouse to Cala Pedrosa (p.204) and along the cliff-edge as far as Tamariu.

Many coastal towns in the Baix Empordà developed as the maritime extension of older inland settlements. The Catalan system of inheritance dictated that the best land be bequeathed to the older children, the younger ones getting the least fertile tracts along the coastal strip. When tourism took hold, the latter suddenly found themselves wealthy by simply selling their land, while their older siblings were left working the fields. Parallels of the rivalry this created can be seen in the relationship between sedate inland towns and thriving coastal upstarts – none more so than bustling **Platja d'Aro**, which has come to eclipse in size and clout its medieval neighbour **Castell d'Aro**. A similar reversal is underway in **Sant Antoni de Calonge**, which is beginning to overshadow the village of **Calonge** that spawned it.

An exception to the rule is the market town of **Palafrugell**, which has maintained its parental position at the hub of its three beautiful coastal offshoots – **Calella de Palafrugell**, **Llafranc** and **Tamariu**. Meanwhile, **Palamós**, with its busy fishing port and thriving commercial centre, has all the feel of a thriving Catalan county town, making the most of its seaside location without letting the Mediterranean rule its fate.

Sant Feliu de Guíxols

A working fishing port and one-time cork manufacturing town 38km southeast of Girona, **SANT FELIU DE GUÍXOLS** is the faded grand-dame of the Costa Brava. There's a lot of old money here, plus a striking blend of Indiano and Moorish-style architecture and restaurants that are famous throughout Catalonia for their quality – yet the town lacks a certain spark. The genteel hotels fringing neighbouring **Platja de Sant Pol** and the opulent residential enclave of **S'Agaró** do little to lighten the tone.

April's impressive Catifa de Flors ("Carpet of Flowers"), to celebrate Corpus Christi, sees the Passeig del Mar decorated with thousands of flower petals arranged in bright patterns.

ARRIVAL AND INFORMATION

Buses from Girona via the C250 stop on Plaça del Monèstir in front of the **tourist office** (Easter–Oct daily

10am–2pm & 4–8pm; Nov–March Mon–Sat 10am–1pm & 4–7pm, Sun 10am–2pm; ☎972 820 051, ⓦwww.guixols .net). The spectacular GI682 corniche road north of Tossa de Mar (see p.128) enters town by the bullring, while the southbound C253 arrives at the northeast end of the beach. There's metered **parking** on the seafront and car parks near the tourist office. **Boats** arrive on the beach from all points south as far as Blanes and north as far as Palamós.

ACCOMMODATION

Accommodation is expensive but generally quiet; if you want a beachfront room, head 1500m north to Platja de Sant Pol. The best choice of **apartments** is at Villa Costa Brava, Ctra Girona 52 (☎972 327 070, ⓕ972 326 940). **Campers** have a good option in *Camping Sant Pol*, Ctra Palamós (☎972 327 269, ⓦwww.campingsantpol.com; ❶; closed Dec–Feb), right on the beach and with plenty of shade.

Hotel Barcarola
Platja de Sant Pol s/n ☎972 326 932, ⓕ972 820 197, ⓦwww.barcarola.com.
Smart, comfortable beach hotel with a range of rooms and apartments with balcony or terrace, also with exceptionally good-value winter breaks. ❻

Hostal Buxó
c/Major 18 ☎972 320 187.
Closed Nov–Feb.
In the heart of the old town,

this family *hostal* has been around since 1931 and boasts a very good timber-beamed restaurant. ❸

Curhotel Hipócrates
Ctra St Pol 229 ☎972 320 662, ⓕ972 323 804.
Closed Nov–Jan.
Plush health spa above the town with anti-stress and beauty treatments and programmes for weight loss and quitting smoking. The rooms are bright and

THE BAIX EMPORDÀ – SOUTH

sumptuous, perhaps to compensate for the ascetic cures. **7**

Hotel Plaça

Pl Mercat 22 ⓣ 972 325 155, ⓕ 972 821 321, ⓦ www.hotelplaza.org.
Modern hotel in the lively market square with a relaxing rooftop terrace and air-conditioned rooms. The pleasant family who own it take pride in the smallest detail. **5**

Hotel Sant Pol

Platja de Sant Pol s/n ⓣ 972 321 070, ⓕ 972 822 378,

ⓦ www.hotelsantpol.com.
Closed Nov.
Friendly, family-run seafront hotel, with an excellent restaurant and large, modern balconied rooms, some featuring jacuzzis. **4**

Hotel Tulipán

c/Joan Maragall 28 ⓣ 972 323 251, ⓦ www.hotel.tulipan.com.
Closed Nov–March.
Congenial, laid-back town-centre hotel that is excellent value as well as being gay-friendly. The spacious bedrooms are sparsely furnished but all en suite. **3**

THE TOWN

The charming nineteenth-century **Passeig del Mar** prom-enade separates the narrow streets and squares of the town from the wide sweep of the **beach**. Framed by the Sant Elm headland to the south and the Fortim headland to the north, the **Platja de Sant Feliu** is ideal for lazing, with diving and sailing as stand-bys. Set back from the sea, the lively **Rambla Vidal** leads to a jumble of backstreets and the bustling **Plaça del Mercat**, while the town's history is reflected in the different ages and styles of its lovely **Benedictine monastery**, with its Romanesque Porta Ferrada facade.

SANT FELIU DE GUÍXOLS

The beachfront

Nowhere is Sant Feliu's old-world style more apparent than on the wide **Passeig del Mar** and the mansions lining it, the most beautiful of which is the ornate Modernist **Casa Patxot** on the corner of Rambla Portalet, built in 1920 and now home to a bank. Opposite it is the **Casino dels Nois** social centre and café, built in 1899 in Moorish style with brightly coloured swooping arches and windows; it's now the favourite haunt of elderly domino players and office workers lingering over afternoon coffee.

The English-speaking owner of Piscis, Ctra Girona 97–103 (℡ 972 326 958), offers diving courses, while Club Nàutic Sant Feliu (℡ 972 321 700), in the Port Nàutic at the north end of the beach, organizes sailing. Day Sail (℡ 972 323 307) offers a full, luxurious day on board a ketch with crew, buffet and drinks for between three and six people at €54 to €90 each.

Across the road from Passeig del Mar, genteel, shaded gardens line the **Platja de Sant Feliu**, a wide, sheltered bay with coarse sand and gently shelving water, good for families and not usually crowded. Separating the pleasure beach from the unsightly fishing port further north is the **Fortim** headland, reached by a wide footpath.

The town centre

The broad pedestrianized shopping avenue of **Rambla Vidal** strikes off from Passeig del Mar into the town, with a small grid of old and new commercial streets branching off it on either side at right angles. A warren of lanes with small shops, restaurants and bars connects the side streets, occasionally opening out into a square, the most lively being the eighteenth-century **Plaça del Mercat**, 100m southwest of Rambla Vidal, with a covered daily **market**.

Sant Feliu's weekly fair, held since the fifteenth century, takes place every Sunday in Plaça del Mercat and along the promenade.

The monastery

The ruins of Sant Feliu's tenth-century **monastery**, beside the tourist office a few metres west of Plaça del Mercat, are fascinating, with centuries of haphazard additions and extensions jostling for attention. The outer parts of the site are open to the elements, but a gate next to the tourist office leads into a **church** and **museum** within what remains of the building.

The most prominent feature is the **Porta Ferrada**, a horseshoe-arched Romanesque facade which dates from the ninth and tenth centuries. Either side of it, the original church's semicircular **Torre del Fum** and rectangular **Torre del Corn**, from the same era, create curiously dis-

FESTIVAL INTERNACIONAL DE LA PORTA FERRADA

From July to September every year, Sant Feliu hosts the Festival Internacional de la Porta Ferrada, with music, theatre and dance in all styles performed by artists from all over the world. Performances are staged in the Teatre Municipal or the Monastery Church, while a range of free open-air concerts takes place on the seafront and in patios and gardens around town. The tourist office has full information and tickets (€8–30).

SANT FELIU DE GUÍXOLS

similar bookends. Later Baroque additions can be seen in the typically ornate **Arc de Sant Benet**, built in 1747, standing alone in front of the monastery.

Inside the **church**, the broad Gothic nave and three polygonal apses, crowned by beautifully intricate keystones, were built in the fourteenth and fifteenth centuries on the site of an earlier Romanesque construction. Within the monastery, the **Museu de la Vila** (Town Museum; June–Sept Tues–Sun 11am–2pm & 6–9pm; Oct–May Tues–Sun 11am–2pm & 5–8pm; €3.60), has an interesting exhibition on Sant Feliu's cork industry, as well as archeological finds discovered in the monastery, including fourteenth-century ceramics and seventeenth-century stained glass.

Platja de Sant Pol

Separating Sant Feliu from the S'Agaró headland (see p.151) to the north of the town is the sweeping **Platja de Sant Pol**, reached by the GIV6622 road from Sant Feliu's fishing port or by a turn-off from the uninspiring Avgda Platja d'Aro connecting Sant Feliu with Platja d'Aro. As wide as it's deep, the crescent-shaped, sandy bay offers good swimming in its protected waters, while a string of smart hotels and restaurants along the uncluttered seafront makes it an ideal, relaxing place to base yourself for a stay.

A mini-train sets off from the promenade (Wed–Fri & Sun 6.30pm; €3.60) for an hour-long circuit, taking in Platja de Sant Pol and the views from the Ermita de Sant Elm overlooking the town.

EATING

People come from miles around to dine at Sant Feliu's outstanding **restaurants**. Modern and individual styles of cuisine flourish alongside traditional Catalan fare to offer a generous choice of good food at a wide range of prices. The seafood restaurants, especially, are expensive but most serve a reasonably priced and delicious *menú del dia* at lunchtime.

Bahía
Pg del Mar 17–18.

One of the oldest and most famous seafood restaurants in the area, with a plush summer terrace, succulent traditional dishes and an especially good *pica-pica* menu for starters. The *menú del dia* at €10.80 is excellent value. Moderate.

Can Claver
c/Joan Maragall 18.
Oct–Easter closed Sun eve.

A nineteenth-century town house is the setting for this friendly restaurant serving Catalan fare and good paella and *fideuà*. The *menú del dia* is great value at €7.50. Inexpensive.

Casa Buxó
c/Major 18.
Closed Nov–Feb.

This busy locals' restaurant serves extremely good Catalan home cooking in comfortable dark-wood surroundings. Moderate.

Cau del Pescador
c/St Domènec 11.
Closed Tues and Jan.

Atmospheric restaurant in an old fisherman's house serving terrific fish and seafood caught locally. The *menú del dia* at €10.20 is a snip. Moderate.

La Cava
c/Joan Maragall 11.
Tues–Sun 6–11pm.

Down-to-earth old-town restaurant, with tasty tapas and an eclectic range of exotic dishes including curry, couscous and savoury pastry dishes. Good veggie options too. Inexpensive.

SANT FELIU DE GUÍXOLS

El Dorado Petit
Rambla Vidal 23.
Closed Wed and Nov.
A legendary Art Deco Mediterranean restaurant founded in 1971 by a local man, who subsequently set up similar restaurants in Barcelona and New York. The food is superb and based around imaginative and succulent variations on local seafood and fresh fish dishes. Eating à la carte is expensive, but the *menú del dia* is only €10.80. Expensive.

El Gallo
c/Especiers 13.
Daily noon–11pm; Oct–June closed Sun eve & Mon.
Atmospheric stone-walled tavern near the market, with a great selection of over fifty tapas from seafood to veggie choices. Budget.

La Taverna del Mar
Pg de Sant Pol 11.
Closed Tues and Dec.
With a fabulous terrace overlooking the beach at Platja de Sant Pol, this 1930s restaurant has a top-notch seafood platter and lobster stew. Expensive.

DRINKING AND NIGHTLIFE

Between June and September, terrace **bars** are set out on the south side of the beach, but this apart, the abiding feeling is that Sant Feliu's young people head off to Platja d'Aro, 5km north, for entertainment, especially later in the evening. The small *Alan's Bar*, c/St Llorenç 28 (closed Mon) is run by a friendly Catalan–French couple now that Geordie Alan has retired, and caters for a broad age range and a rather arty clientele. The owners – who are jazz and blues fans – play a lively selection of music. A fixation with Friesian cows marks the decor in the lively *Lawyer*, c/St Domènec s/n (closed Mon), which is somewhere between a pub and an upmarket eatery serving tasty snacks. The liveliest nightspot is the open-air *Palm Beach* **club**, c/President Irla 1 (June–Sept daily midnight–6am), where a roster of DJs keeps the young crowd happy with ambient, jungle, techno house and trip-hop.

LISTINGS

Banks The main banks have branches with ATMs in the shopping streets and on the promenade.
Hospital Creu Roja, Ctra Palamós s/n ⓣ 972 822 222.
Internet Loading, Pl Sant Joan 17

(Mon–Sat 10am–1pm & 4–8pm).
Police c/Callao s/n ⓣ 972 820 933.
Post office c/Girona 15, one street back from the seafront.
Taxis Stand on the Pg del Mar ⓣ 972 320 934.

An easy excursion inland from Sant Feliu is to the charming hilltop village of Romanyà de la Selva (see p.175), located on the minor GI661 off the main C250 Girona road.

S'AGARÓ

The dreary main road of shops and restaurants linking Sant Feliu de Guíxols with Platja d'Aro gives little idea of the attractive Modernist architecture and peaceful setting of **S'AGARÓ**. Tucked away on a headland 2km northeast of St Feliu, S'Agaró was created in the 1920s by Josep Ensesa Gubert as a community of seaside villas for the wealthy, and the design of all the mansions was entrusted to **Rafael Masó**, the architect responsible for many of Girona's most attractive buildings (see box p.80). An inn, **Hostal de La Gavina**, originally intended for guests of residents, quickly found itself playing host to the likes of Charlie Chaplin,

S'AGARÓ

Orson Welles, Bogart and Bacall, Ava Gardner and Frank Sinatra, becoming the Costa Brava's first five-star hotel.

S'Agaró is still somewhat elitist, and only residents can take cars in (visitors must park in the free area outside and pass the gatehouse on foot), but a wander through the quiet streets is a pleasure. The most impressive building, **Senya Blanca**, belongs to the Ensesa family and boasts a Greek temple-like summerhouse on the cliff-edge, which can be seen from the Camí de Ronda footpath passing below (see box). A short, signposted stroll inland from here leads to the tiny **church**, consecrated in 1943 and dominated by its high atrium vestibule, built using Gothic arches salvaged from Girona's ruined Sant Francesc convent.

During July and August, S'Agaró's church hosts a classical music festival; get tickets (€12) from Platja d'Aro's tourist office.

S'Agaró's handful of superb **beaches** rarely get crowded. Loveliest is **Cala Sa Conca**, reached by footpath (see box) or by car from the C253 Palamós road at a turning to the east just before the Port Nàutic in Platja d'Aro. The gently curving beach – popular with thong-clad sun-worshippers – is cleft by a craggy outcrop: the northern side is less busy and better for snorkelling, the bigger southern side prime swimming territory.

To **stay** in sheer luxury, you can't beat the sumptuous *Hostal de La Gavina* (☏ 972 321 100, ☏ 972 321 573, ✉ gavina @iponet.es; ❾; closed Nov–March), replete with oak beams and light stone. A byword in Spain for opulence, it's also famous for the quality of its **restaurant** and the splendour of its surroundings and facilities, including the huge pool on the low cliff-edge.

S'AGARÓ

THE CAMÍ DE RONDA AT S'AGARÓ

A restored section of the Camí de Ronda footpath begins at the north side of Platja de Sant Pol and skirts the shoreline at S'Agaró. The round trip of 2km, returning on any of several routes branching off through S'Agaró town, can take as little as half an hour; or you could easily stop off for a swim or carry on walking along the beach to Platja d'Aro (see p.154), 3km further north. It's feasible, although tricky in parts, to walk from Platja de Sant Pol all the way to Palamós (about 9km in total), returning by bus.

From Platja de Sant Pol, the wide trail leads below the *Hostal de La Gavina* above the water's edge to a set of steps up to the belvedere on the Punta d'en Pau, a tiered bank of stone seats offering lazy views out to sea. From here, the path almost turns full circle at the deep inlet of Cala del Barco before passing below the imposing stone walls and arches of the Senya Blanca summerhouse. After steps known as the Escales de la Gacela – which lead off the trail into S'Agaró – you come to a set of steps descending tortuously to the secluded Cala Pedrosa. The path continues to another belvedere at the foot of a broad flight of steps dedicated to Rafael Masó – which lead up to S'Agaró's church – after which a straighter section of the Camí de Ronda leads to the wonderful Cala Sa Conca (see opposite).

As an alternative to retracing your steps to Platja de Sant Pol, you could climb a flight of steps in the southwest corner of Cala Sa Conca beach, which lead through the streets of S'Agaró to the church at the head of the Rafael Masó steps. Platja d'Aro lies beyond Cala Sa Conca, but the way is blocked by a canal; you'll need to make a detour 300m inland to a crossing-point on the main road and back again on the other side of the canal (takes 15min) to reach Platja d'Aro's beach.

S'AGARÓ

Platja d'Aro and around

PLATJA D'ARO comprises a neon strip of bars and shops running parallel to, but hidden from, 3km of busy sandy beach: if you're looking for somewhere quiet or picturesque, then this isn't the place for you. What Platja d'Aro does offer is excellent **nightlife**, a beautiful **beach**, some account-draining shopping and an odd mishmash of high-rise apartments and bustling main drag separated by three blocks of leafy Mediterranean suburbia. Framing the straight sands are a string of delightful **coves**, where you can find a contrasting semblance of solitude even in the height of summer. Inland from Platja d'Aro, the parent town of **Castell d'Aro** – in striking contrast to its wayward child – hides a tiny and charming medieval heart.

ARRIVAL AND INFORMATION

Platja d'Aro lies on the C253 **road** from Sant Feliu de Guíxols; exiting the A7 *autopista*, you'll enter on the C250 Girona–Sant Feliu road, from where a signposted turning leads to the town centre. There's a huge **car park** in Plaça Europa, off the Avgda Castell d'Aro, with overflow parking available in nearby Masia Bas by the main roundabout, except during the weekly **market** (Fri 9am–2pm). The main **bus station** is just off the Carretera de Sant Feliu, 500m west of the centre, from where it's a fifteen-minute walk – or a €3 taxi-ride – into town. **Boats** arrive on the beach from all points south as far as Blanes and from Palamós to the north.

The smart **tourist office**, c/Cinto Verdaguer 4 (daily: June–Sept 8am–10pm; Oct–May 9am–1pm & 4–7pm;

❶ & Palamós   Cala Rovira

CAFÉS, BARS & RESTAURANTS

Alhambra	E
Ambar	L
Aradi	G
Assac Bar	J
Atico	H
Big Rock	B
Els Cinc Pebres	K
Maddox	M
Mas Marcó	A
900 House Bar	F
Palapa	C
La Pizza	D
Villa Elena	I

ACCOMMODATION

Bell Repós	3
Can Japet	2
Columbus	7
Cosmopolita	6
Costa Brava	8
Els Pins	4
Planamar	5
San Jorge	1

PLAÇA DE LA SARDANA

AV. CAVALL BERNAT

PTGE. ERICONS

TRAV. CAVALL BERNAT

PUNTA ROCOSA

El Cavall Bernat

200 m
0

VICTOR CATALÀ

GAZEL

MUNTANYA

PUIG S'AGOTA

VICENÇ BOU

DEL NORD

ESGLÉSIA

PEP VENTURA

PONENT

PESCADORS

J. MARAGALL

ESGLÉSIA

ESGLÉSIA

ALEGRIA

NSTRA. SRA. DEL CARME

DE LA RIERA

MANNÀ

MSN CINTO VERDAGUER

CELI MAR

CIUTAT DE PALOL

PASSEIG MARÍTIM

DE LES ESCOLES

CASTELL D'ARO

PINEDA

DEL MAR

PINEDA DEL MAR

LLEIDA

PLAÇA D'EN MARTÍ BAS

MIRAMAR

PLAÇA D'EUROPA

J. BAS

AV. S'AGARÓ

LLEVANT

DE LA PAU

ONZE DE SETEMBRE

PLAÇA CATALUNYA

NSTRA. SRA. DE FANALS

NSTRA. SRA. DE MONTSERRAT

RAFEL CASANOVES

COSTA BRAVA

BARCELONA

DE BRUSSEL·LES

JULI GARRETA

STRASBURG

SIENA

AV. DE LUXEMBURG

DR FLEMING

NSTRA. SRA. DE FANALS

PTGE. VALÈNCIA

VALÈNCIA

PLAÇA DEL DR JOSEP TRUETA

JOSEP M. VILA

Platja Gran

Platja d'Aro

PLATJA D'ARO

❶ A & Castell d'Aro   B   A

❷ C, Bus Station & S'Agaró   Port Nàutic

PLATJA D'ARO AND AROUND

Ⓣ972 817 179, ⓌWww.platjadaro.com), which serves Platja d'Aro, S'Agaró and Castell d'Aro, occupies the ground floor of the Ajuntament, and offers good accommodation and events listings and some interesting guided walking tours of Ciutat de Palol (see p.161) and Castell d'Aro. In summer, an **information point** (July & Aug daily 10am–1pm & 5–9pm) is open on the Avinguda Castell d'Aro opposite the *Valldaro* campsite, 1km north of the centre.

ACCOMMODATION

It's advisable to choose **accommodation** well away from the noisy nightlife. You'd do best plumping for a place on the seafront, where there are no cars and barely any late-night bars, or in the residential areas parallel to it, rather than on the main drag. The estate agency Finques Platja d'Aro, Avgda S'Agaró 78 (Ⓣ & Ⓕ972 819 656, ⓌWww.finquesplatjadaro.com), deals in holiday **apartment** rentals. The more luxurious **campsites** are on the roads along the seafront or inland to Castell d'Aro, although there are a couple of good ones by the beach on the outskirts of town.

Bell Repós

c/Verge del Carme 18 Ⓣ972 817 100, Ⓕ972 816 933.
Closed Oct–May.
Very close to the centre and beach, this family-run hotel is separated from a quiet side road by its own inviting garden. Most of the airy rooms give onto the garden and have balconies; there are discount offers in June and September. ❸

Can Japet

Avgda Cavall Bernat 50 Ⓣ972 817 366, Ⓕ972 819 151.
This charming hotel on the main drag was founded at the end of the nineteenth century as an inn for cart drivers transporting cork between Sant Feliu and Girona. The rooms are small but comfortable and surprisingly quiet as they give onto an inner courtyard, and

the restaurant is renowned for its excellent traditional cooking. ❸

Columbus

Pg Marítim 100 ⓣ 972 817 166, ⓕ 972 817 503, ⓦ www.eurocolumbus.com.
Closed mid-Nov to Easter; open at Christmas.

A century-old seafront hotel set in gardens with its own tennis courts and pool, where guests are offered a free beginners' diving lesson. ❼

Cosmopolita

c/Pinar del Mar 1 ⓣ 972 817 350, ⓕ 972 817 450, ⓔ hotelcosmopolita@teleline.es.
Closed mid-Nov to Easter; open at Christmas.

The large rooms at this friendly seafront hotel have decent-sized balconies, although it's advisable to ask for a seafront room as the street-view ones can get noisy at night. ❻

Costa Brava

Punta d'en Ramis 17 ⓣ 972 817 308, ⓕ 972 826 348, ⓔ aromar@grn.es.
Closed Nov–Feb.

Originally founded in the 1920s as a restaurant, this was the Baix Empordà's first beach hotel, perched on a low cliff, and retains its oak-beam and marble-balustrade charm. ❻

Els Pins

c/Verge del Carme 34 ⓣ 972 817 219, ⓕ 972 817 546, ⓔ hotel_els_pins@cambrescat.es.
Closed Nov–Feb.

A well-cared-for establishment built around a small shaded courtyard and with a sheltered pool. All the comfortable bedrooms have balconies giving onto the courtyard. ❻

Planamar

Pg del Mar 84 ⓣ 972 817 177, ⓕ 972 825 662, ⓔ HotelPlanamar@yahoo.com.
Closed Oct–March.

Situated at the quieter end of the beach, this family hotel, which has a great rooftop sun terrace complete with gym, jacuzzi and swimming pool, is excellent value for money. ❹

San Jorge

Ctra Palamós 107 ⓣ 972 652 311,

PLATJA D'ARO AND AROUND

(F) 972 652 576, (e) hotelsanjorge
@hoteles-silken.com.
Closed Dec & Jan.
On a low headland
overlooking two tiny coves
(see p.167), this plush and
friendly hotel with its clifftop
garden and pool is 1km north
of town on the Palamós road.
Nearly all the modern,
comfortable rooms overlook
the sea and have balconies, air
conditioning and sumptuous
bathrooms. ❾

CAMPSITES

Cala Sa Cova

Avgda Cavall Bernat 150 (T) 972
818 234, (w) www.sacova.net.
Closed Oct–Easter.
This small, welcoming site is
right on the beach at the tiny
cove of the same name and
about five minutes' walk
north of the centre. The
pitches are well shaded and
the facilities are fairly
modern.

Mas Sant Josep

Ctra de Sta Cristina a Platja
d'Aro km2 (T) 972 835 108,
(w) www.msantjosep.com.
Closed Jan.
This smart, well-shaded
campsite is centred around a
nineteenth-century *masía* and
a huge swimming pool on
the old main road between
Castell d'Aro and Santa
Cristina d'Aro, 3km west of
the centre. The facilities are
excellent and include shops,
tennis courts, bars and a
restaurant.

Riembau

Apt de Correus 181 (T) 972 817
123, (F) 972 825 210,
(w) www.riembau.com.
Closed Oct–March.
A huge site on the outskirts
of the town, 1.5km
southwest, with every facility
imaginable, including gym,
swimming pools, minigolf,
restaurants and a helicopter
excursion service (the last
also available to non-
residents).

THE TOWN

Platja d'Aro is focused around two fairly distinct areas. On the one hand, the **beach** and outlying coves define daytime activities, while the shops, bars and restaurants of the main drag formed by **Avinguda S'Agaró** and **Avinguda Cavall Bernat**, lying parallel to the seafront and separated from it by shaded suburban houses and apartments, come alive after dark. At the north end of town, Platja d'Aro's Roman past is evident in the few salvaged remains of the **Ciutat de Palol** villa.

Until recently, Avinguda S'Agaró was known as Avinguda Sant Feliu, a name you might still see used.

PLATJA D'ARO ACTIVITIES

Thrill-seekers in Platja d'Aro will enjoy a helicopter flight along the spectacular shoreline with Turisvol, at *Camping Riembau* (☎ 972 817 123), while more leisurely thrills are to be had with a balloon ride over the Baix Empordà by L'Empordanet (☎ 972 641 550); both cost around €110. Several operators along the seafront and in the Port Nàutic offer watersports such as jet-skiing, water-skiing and parasailing, while the Escola Municipal de Vela (☎ 972 816 777), in the port, is the place for windsurfing and kayak rental. Divers have several options, including Amfos Sub d'Aro, Avgda Cavall Bernat 4 (☎ 972 825 389), which runs courses (from €48) and offer equipment rental. Aquadiver, Ctra Circumval.lació (☎ 972 818 732), is a water park on the northwestern edge of town with slides and chutes. The eighteen-hole Golf d'Aro golf course (☎ 972 826 900) is set on the Mas Nou hill overlooking the coast, while Pitch & Putt Platja d'Aro, in Les Suredes (☎ 972 819 820), is 1.5km west of town on the road to Castell d'Aro.

PLATJA D'ARO AND AROUND

Platja Gran

The three-kilometre **Platja Gran** is framed along almost its entire length by an uneven toothy grin of high-rise blocks, interspersed with some older low-rise buildings and backed by a pedestrianized promenade with terraces and restaurants – and not a car in sight. The sweep of coarse golden sand, fronting clear, moderately shelving water, sees families and firm-bodied clubbers working on their tans. The southern tip of Platja Gran, marked by the chic **Port Nàutic** and capped by the **Punta de Pinell** headland, gets slightly less crowded.

At the northern end of the Platja Gran, three incongruous nineteenth-century villas are a reminder of how the town has changed, while standing 100m further on is the huge standing stone known as **El Cavall Bernat**, backdrop to free summer jazz concerts. Its euphemistic name came into use in the sixteenth century to replace the ruder original Carall Bernat, thought to mean "revered phallus" (*carall* is Catalan for "phallus"). For details of the beaches north of town, see p.165.

The town centre

By day, Avinguda S'Agaró and Avinguda Cavall Bernat offer some of the region's best **shopping**, with exclusive designer clothes stores from Barcelona and Girona and some classy local establishments, including Valls, at Avgda S'Agaro 10, a rambling Aladdin's cave of a department store. Most are open all year and have extended summer hours (daily 10am–2pm & 5–10pm).

As evening suffuses into night, the same streets become the perfect arena for people-watching before dinner beckons, from one of the hordes of **pavement cafés** lining the main drag. Later into the night the population changes, as the stylish laid-back bars and thumping discos get going.

Every February, the shopping streets of central Platja d'Aro play host to one of the Costa Brava's best Carnival processions, with floats and extravagant fancy-dress parades accompanied by revelry all weekend long.

Ciutat de Palol

On the northern edge of town is **Ciutat de Palol**, one of the most important Roman villas in the region, although recent treatment of the site is a reminder of the unfortunate tourist-boom era and its contrast with the post-Franco desire to put things right. After decades of frenzied construction over the site, it was finally excavated in 1998, although by then much of it had been churned up or was completely inaccessible. What little remains is the work area of a large wine- and oil-producing villa, in use between the first century BC and the seventh century AD; the bases of oil jars can still be seen while the small circles of pottery visible are the tops of wine jars kept underground too delicate to be removed. Laid out as a public area and popular for an evening stroll, the site centres around a paved seating area bearing a large **modern mosaic** of a bunch of grapes, denoting the trade carried on in the villa, with the name Porcianus, who is thought to have been the owner.

EATING

In among the ubiquitous fast-food joints and nondescript eateries along the seafront and main street, Platja d'Aro has some good **restaurants**. Most are on Avinguda S'Agaró,

Avinguda Cavall Bernat and the little streets connecting these and the beach, while there are also some excellent places out of town and in neighbouring Castell d'Aro and Santa Cristina d'Aro.

Alhambra
c/Josep Bas 9.
Daily noon–11pm.
On the corner with Avgda Castell d'Aro, this small Moroccan restaurant makes very good authentic dishes and has a great choice for veggies. The mint tea and pastries are superb. Budget.

Aradi
Avgda Cavall Bernat 76.
One of the oldest restaurants in town, with a pleasant and surprisingly quiet terrace – rightly famous for the quality of its cooking. Specialities are rice dishes, *suquets* and grilled meats, or you could try one of their huge summer *mariscades* (seafood platters). Moderate.

Big Rock
Avgda Fanals s/n ☎ 972 818 012.
Closed Sun eve and Mon.
A superb Catalan restaurant in an old *masia* some 3km northwest of town – follow signs to Mas Nou – serving seafood and local grilled meats in sumptuous tranquillity. Their *suquet* is beaten only by the roast shoulder of lamb. It's advisable to reserve a table, as the place is very well known locally. Expensive.

Can Japet
Avgda Cavall Bernat 50.
This old tavern is rightly popular for its tasty home cooking, specializing in baked fish and lovely *suquet* and *sarsuela*. Inexpensive.

Can Poldo
Punta d'en Ramis 17.
Closed Nov–Feb.
This large, plush restaurant in *Hotel Costa Brava* has a lovely terrace overlooking Cala Rovira and very good rice and seafood dishes. Moderate.

Els Cinc Pebres
c/Església 64.

Daily 8pm–midnight.

One of the most alluring restaurants on the Costa Brava, this warm red- and cream-decorated family-run restaurant serves imaginative variations on traditional Catalan cooking, accompanied by an excellent wine list. Especially good are the generous platters of cheese and *embotits* and the spinach cannelloni. Inexpensive.

Palapa
Avgda S'Agaró 129.

Daily noon–midnight; closed Nov–March.

Spread over a large terrace, this fun establishment is divided into a pizzeria and a Mexican restaurant and serves delicious food and cocktails. Inexpensive.

La Pizza
Pl Europa 21.

Daily noon–midnight;
Nov–March closed Mon–Thurs.

This smart but reasonably priced Italian restaurant is in an arcade connecting the main drag with Plaça Europa. Its pizzas and sweet and savoury crêpes are the best in town, served in an unhurried atmosphere. Inexpensive.

Villa Elena
c/Onze de Setembre 3.

This busy and popular restaurant in an old mansion has a pleasant terrace. Specializing in Catalan and international cuisine, it has superb fish, pasta and rice, and the *patates d'Olot* (baked potatoes stuffed with meat) and cod carpaccio are excellent. Moderate.

DRINKING AND NIGHTLIFE

Despite the number of **bars**, Platja d'Aro is a long way from the organized drunkenness of Lloret de Mar. Platja offers chic, image-conscious enjoyment – truer to the Catalan style of going out. The best **terraces** (open all day from 10am to 2am) are on Avgda Sant Feliu, while bars of

PLATJA D'ARO AND AROUND

all shapes, sizes and inclinations are on and around the same street and Avgda Cavall Bernat. Most of the **clubs** are in the same area.

Ambar

c/Pineda de Mar 31.

A mainly local crowd frequents this chic bar near the seafront to compare suntans and shake bodies; the dancing is amidst a heaving throng to a strangely wide variety of tunes.

Assac Bar

c/Pineda de Mar 22.

Catering mainly for twenty- and thirty-somethings, this lively terrace bar in a large house is a popular starting point for the night's entertainment or as a late-night cool-down, and serves good *chupitos* to thumping rhythms.

Atico

Avgda Cavall Bernat 114.

This stylish club, located in a cellar despite its name, has a broad age appeal, reflected in the wildly eclectic tastes in music and the even more eclectic crowds milling around the door from 2am onwards.

Maddox

c/Sa Musclera 1.

By day a swimming pool with a terrace bar serving snacks, this beachside venue becomes a six-bar club at night, spread over two floors – one for a younger house crowd and the other for an older salsa crowd. Overheated dancers can enjoy a midnight swim in the pool.

Mas Marcó

Ctra Roca de Malvet km1, Sta Cristina d'Aro.

Signposted off a roundabout at the western entrance to Santa Cristina d'Aro, 5km west of Platja d'Aro, this wildly extravagant bar and club for gay men and lesbians (straight men and women welcome) in a rambling old building is great fun, and stages epic parties and drag nights.

900 House Bar

c/Església 54.

This stylish, minimalist bar is

the only all-out house bar in Platja d'Aro and appeals to a lively younger crowd as the last stop of the night.

LISTINGS

Bike rental You can rent bikes, scooters and tandems at Rent d'Aro, Avgda S'Agaró 103 ⊤ 972 828 599.

Car rental Arotur, Avgda Cavall Bernat 10 ⊤ 972 816 281; Bravatur, Avgda Costa Brava 1 ⊤ 972 817 860.

Health centre Eurocenter 55–61, Illa 4, on Avgda Castell d'Aro 500m west of the centre (24-hour line ⊤ 972 816 324).

Internet Montbar, Avgda S'Agaró 27 (daily 10am–10pm); Cybercafé Trebolmail, Avgda Cavall Bernat 92 (daily 10am–2am); Ciber d'Aro,

Round Store (daily 10am–10pm).

Pharmacies Sala, Avgda Costa Brava 2; Utzet, Avgda Cavall Bernat 95.

Police Beside the tourist office at c/Cinto Verdaguer 2 ⊤ 972 825 777.

Post office Avgda Castell d'Aro 11, near the main roundabout ⊤ 972 817 477.

Taxis Ranks outside *Can Japet* on Avgda Palamós (⊤ 972 817 019) and at the south end of town on Avgda Sant Feliu (⊤ 972 817 032). Call for a radio taxi on ⊤ 972 825 050.

NORTH OF PLATJA D'ARO

North of Platja d'Aro, the Camí de Ronda footpath dips and climbs for 4km, from the northern end of the Platja Gran along the water's edge as far as Sant Antoni de Calonge, offering paths down to some beautiful beaches. Some can also be reached by footpaths off the C253 road towards Palamós, which has roadside parking.

Cala Rovira

The attractive but busy **Cala Rovira** was originally the Roman port for the area: remains of the dock and a watchtower have been found on the Punta de Cala Rovira, which separates the beach from the next cove north. Cala Rovira is also known as **Cala dels Escalencs** after fishing families from L'Escala (see p.255), who – until the advent of tourism in the 1950s – used to spend their summers here camped on the beach, fishing the waters and selling their wares in Sant Feliu de Guíxols. A terrifically colourful and emotive **festa** to mark this history takes place on the first weekend after the Diada holiday (Sept 11), when dozens of traditional *Vela Llatina* boats make the journey from L'Escala and families camp on the beach in makeshift shelters for two days of traditional crafts, *havaneres* and *cremat*. The highlight of the weekend is the *suquet* lunch for all-comers on Saturday (you can buy a ticket entitling you to join in the feast from the tourist office for around €15), but the most spectacular and moving sight is on the Friday evening, watching the fleet of timeless boats round the headland and ghost ashore.

Cala Sa Cova and around

The tiny, sheltered **Cala Sa Cova**, 75m north of Cala Rovira, is accessed by a footpath running down from the road alongside the *Cala Sa Cova* campsite (see p.158) which stretches to the edge of the low cliff overlooking the beach. The beach is also known as Cala dels Nens (Children's Cove), owing to its gentle shelving and safe bathing up to a clearly defined line of underwater rocks, and its pine-clad prettiness helps you to overlook the number of people.

A clearly signposted path from the road takes you to the even smaller and more inviting **Cala del Pi**, 200m further north along the Camí de Ronda, whose underwater rocks and craggy point make it perfect for snorkelling. From here, a fairly long tunnel on the Camí de Ronda leads to the rocky stretch of **Ses Rodones de Terra**, where stone steps lead down through clumps of bamboo to a rugged mosaic of boulders and beach. This short section – popular with gay men – is mainly given over to nude bathing.

On to Platgeta de l'Ermita

A signposted stepped path alongside the *Hotel Cap Roig*, 2km along the road to Sant Antoni de Calonge, descends to the chic **Cala Belladona**, which gets less busy still than its neighbours. Here you'll find good snorkelling and swimming a long way out into the steeply shelving sea. The slightly finer sand of the beach houses a *xiringuito* and gives great views of Palamós over the bay. Between here and the very similar **Platja de Cap Roig**, 500m north, where you can rent kayaks for exploring the rocky inlets, is the minuscule **Platgeta de Sant Jordi**, a scaled-down version of its two neighbours.

The pine-topped Cap Roig (Red Cape) marks the northern boundary of Platja de Cap Roig, separating it from the eddying waters and washed-up driftwood of the **Platgeta de l'Ermita**, accessed by steps past the *xiringuito* and small boathouse and overlooked by the *Hotel San Jorge* (see p.157). Platgeta de l'Ermita is almost always empty and is more a place to explore the rockpools than to sunbathe or swim as there's little beach to speak of.

The Camí de Ronda continues a further 600m to Platja de Can Cristus (see p.173), although this requires a perilous, steep clamber through spiny bushes above the rocks.

CASTELL D'ARO

The charming narrow streets and ancient houses forming the medieval core of **CASTELL D'ARO**, 3km west of Platja d'Aro, perch hidden on a small hill above the main road. Most of the houses bear dates above the lintels along with the names of their original owners; the most attractive is the **rectory** next to the church, dating from 1569, which bears a pilgrim's shell engraved in the stone window surround.

During the last weekend of August, Castell d'Aro's church square and surrounding streets host a medieval market, with traditional crafts and food on sale to the accompaniment of troubadours and players.

Built in 1784, the solid Gothic-style **Església de Santa Maria** rises above a small square, with a facade as simple as its interior. Inside the main door, an octagonal font from 1670 harks back to an earlier building. Most of the chapels are plain plaster or stone, except for two on the right of the door, which have highly intricate murals of the Ascension.

Beside the church, the restored **Castell de Benedormiens** gives the appearance of having grown out of the rock. Originally built in the eleventh century, it was burnt in 1462 and then destroyed by an explosion in 1879, after which it was left to moulder until restoration last century. Little of the original structure remains, although excavations in the old moat are turning up some finds, including many relating to an iron-working industry in the area. Its three floors house changing free art exhibitions.

Practicalities

Places to **eat** in Castell d'Aro include the French-run *Bistro Art*, c/Carme (Mon–Thurs 4pm–midnight, Fri–Sun 1–4pm & 7.30pm–midnight), serving imaginative, moderately priced French cuisine in a lovely eighteenth-century building. About 500m east towards Platja d'Aro, the palatial *Cal Rei*, Barri de la Crota 3 (daily 1–4pm & 8–11pm), serves superb, but also moderately priced, Catalan food in its airy rooms and shaded patio.

Some 3km west of Castell d'Aro is the village of **Santa**

Cristina d'Aro, a very good place to **stay** with some excellent **restaurants** to boot. Providing both is the fabulous *Mas Tapiolas*, Veïnat de Solius (☎972 837 017, ℻972 837 134, ⓦwww.euro-mar.com; ⑧), a converted mansion in lush gardens which has nearly forty exquisite rooms and an expensive modern Catalan restaurant. Equally good is *Les Panolles*, Ctra Girona, on the western outskirts of the village, which has a lovely garden terrace and extremely good, moderately priced local cooking. *El Molí d'en Tarrés*, an old mill 1km along the road to Sant Feliu de Guíxols, serves filling regional and *mar i muntanya* cuisine at similarly moderate prices.

The attractive village of Romanyà de la Selva (see p.175) is accessible from Castell d'Aro on the minor GI661 road which passes through Santa Cristina d'Aro before winding up into the hills.

Sant Antoni de Calonge and around

SANT ANTONI DE CALONGE, 4km northeast of Platja d'Aro on the C255, is almost becoming an extension of its neighbour Palamós. It's not particularly picturesque, but has good-value accommodation and benefits from a lovely beach on its doorstep and even lovelier coves a short walk away. Palamós is within walking distance, and Platja d'Aro is a bus or taxi ride away.

The dusty approaches to Sant Antoni give it the air of being still under construction, and the stylish new

promenade, with angled street lamps decked in flags, further adds to the notion of a town only just beginning to establish itself. Framed by low- and medium-rise buildings, the promenade is cheerfully low-key and tranquil. The good **beach** can get a little crowded; its south end, known as **Torre Valentina** after a watchtower that still stands in the gardens of plush apartment blocks, is the preserve of sculpted sun-worshippers.

Boca Dolça, at *Hotel Reimar* (☎ 972 661 504) in the Torre Valentina area, offers diving courses in English. On the beach, Jet School (☎ 609 640 441) rents jet-skis, and Tsunami Center (☎ 972 825 792) rents windsurfs and kayaks.

PRACTICALITIES

With no discernible centre, Sant Antoni spreads from the Platja d'Aro–Palamós road eastwards to a parallel smaller road and then the beach. **Buses** stop on the main road at the entrance and exit to the town, 300m from the beach. There are a dozen or so **car parks** on and around the main road, and a metered zone one street back from the beach. **Boats** from Lloret and Palamós come in to the beach.

Also on the main road is the very good **tourist office**, Avgda Catalunya s/n (Easter–Sept daily 10am–2pm & 4–8pm; Oct–March Sat 10am–1.30pm & 4–6pm, Sun 10am–1pm; ☎ 972 661 714, ⓦ www.calonge-santantoni .com), with information about Sant Antoni de Calonge and Calonge. A noticeboard outside gives daily updates of accommodation availability. There's a summer branch office on the beach at Torre Valentina (July & Aug daily 10am–1.30pm & 4–7pm). The public library, c/Sant Antoni 56 (Mon, Tues, Thurs & Fri 4.30–8.30pm, Wed & Sun 10.30am–2pm), offers inexpensive **internet** access.

SANT ANTONI DE CALONGE AND AROUND

Accommodation

Sant Antoni is rarely noisy, so you're fairly safe looking for **hotels** on the seafront. Rental **apartments** abound, although you tend to pay more for sea views; Bigrup, Avgda Torre Valentina 24 (℡972 650 711, ℻972 652 619, @jariart@teleline.es) has a wide choice.

The best of the **campsites** on the main Palamós road is the well-equipped Internacional Calonge, Ctra St Feliu–Palamós km7.5 (℡972 651 233, ℻972 652 507, @www.intercalonge.com; ❶), a terraced campsite that is one of the few on the Costa Brava to stay open all year. At the southern entrance to town, the shaded, family-run Camping Costa Brava, Avgda Unió s/n (℡972 650 222; closed Nov–Easter; ❶), is much smaller and quieter.

Pensió Can Fabrellas
c/Vermell 25 ℡972 651 014.
Closed Oct–April.
An unprepossessing building on the road parallel to the seafront hides a very pleasant *pensió* with a decent restaurant and a quiet patio garden, run by an amicable family. Rooms are basic but comfortable and all have balconies. ❷

Hostal Guillermo
Pg Mundet 68 ℡972 650 564, ℻972 651 425,
@www.capitanes.com/guillermo.
Closed Oct–Jan.
This high-quality seafront *hostal* has very good, spacious rooms, some overlooking the beach. The room-price includes breakfast. ❺

Maria Teresa
Pg Mundet 3 ℡972 651 064, ℻972 652 110.
Closed Nov–March.
A pleasant, family-run seafront hotel. The large, en-suite, balconied rooms give onto the beach or the interior garden, while the restaurant serves good traditional food. ❸

Hostal Olga
Pg Mundet 48 ℡972 650 764,

SANT ANTONI DE CALONGE AND AROUND

Ⓣ 972 661 900.

Closed Oct–March.

Old-fashioned but comfortable seafront *hostal*, with prices – including breakfast – that differ greatly between rooms at the front or back of the building. ❸

Príncep Ben-Hur

c/Josep Mercader 2 Ⓣ 972 651 138, Ⓕ 972 652 577.

Closed Nov & Dec.

Small two-storey hotel on a quiet side street half a block in from the beach at Torre Valentina; despite dating from the 1960s, it has an old-world, oak-furniture charm. No sea views, but the rooms, all en suite, are airy and well furnished. ❹

Reimar

Pg Torre Valentina Ⓣ 972 652 211, Ⓕ 972 651 213, Ⓦ www.welcome.to/hotelreimar.

Closed Oct–April.

A plush three-storey hotel in the quiet Torre Valentina area with a rooftop sun terrace boasting a pool, jacuzzi and views of the bay. Also with its own diving school. ❻

Rosa dels Vents

Pg Mundet s/n Ⓣ 972 651 311, Ⓕ 972 650 697.

Closed Oct–April.

Comfortable hotel overlooking the beach near Torre Valentina; it has spacious bedrooms, most with balcony, and a relaxing bar and terrace. ❺

Eating and drinking

There are a few places to **eat** on the seafront. The cheapest option is *Versailles*, Pg Mar 80 (Easter–Sept daily noon–11pm), which offers a variety of filling set menus between €10.30 and €16. *Kubansky*, c/St Antoni 41 (Easter–Sept daily 1–4pm & 8–11.30pm), one street in from the beach, serves imaginative Catalan fare, and the extremely good *El Racó* (same hours), at the south end of the beach under the Torre Valentina tower, serves some of the best fresh fish in the area, at about €30 a head. The best place for a **drink** is the cheerful seafront *O'Higgins*, c/Josep

Mundet 81 (daily 10am–3am), which has a happy hour from 5pm to 7pm and also runs an English book-swap service.

SOUTH TO PLATJA DE CAN CRISTUS

The irregular **Camí de Ronda** footpath leads south from Sant Antoni past Torre Valentina to a string of delightful coves, most of which are reached by stone steps from the trail.

The first of four equally beautiful coves – all with iridescent turquoise waters ideal for swimming and snorkelling among the rocks – is **Cala Murtra**, protected by the Roca Grossa island (popular as a goal for swimmers). Beyond these, the path divides around expensive walled houses to join up on the picturesque little **Cap de Roques Planes** headland, where it's easy to find your own spot on the rocks or small patches of sand. On the south side of the point is the wonderful sandy beach of **Cala de Roques Planes**, which rarely gets crowded and is good for swimming despite rocks and seaweed underfoot. A footpath connects to the main Platja d'Aro road, as is also the case with the next cove, **Cala de la Roca del Paller**, a popular beach for snorkelling that gets slightly busier than its neighbour. Last of the small coves is the secluded and pretty **Cala dels Esculls**.

The two southernmost beaches – **Cala del Forn** and, on the other side of a rock with a small passageway of sand, the much larger **Platja de Can Cristus** – are both very pretty and offer good swimming, but since they are the nearest to a string of campsites on the main road and also have *xiringuitos*, they get correspondingly more busy.

An enjoyable way of exploring among the coves is by kayak, which you can rent at Platja de Can Cristus.

The Camí de Ronda continues south from here, ending up in Platja d'Aro, 4km from Sant Antoni, although note that the route between Platja de Can Cristus and Platgeta de l'Ermita (see p.167) is a particularly treacherous clamber through slippery rocks and thorns.

CALONGE

Some 3km inland from Sant Antoni, accessed from the roundabout to the south of town, lies the medieval parent town of **CALONGE**, handy for an enjoyable morning's stroll around the small centre and remnants of the castle.

Calonge's weekly market fills the narrow streets every Thursday morning.

A summer-only **tourist office** (July–Sept Mon–Sat 10am–2pm & 4–8pm, Sun 10am–2pm; ☎972 660 481) is open in the town hall on Plaça Major. The quiet town is dominated by a Gothic **castle**, currently being restored; at the time of writing the only part open to the public was the original parade ground, reached through a pair of imposing towers on Plaça Major. The courtyard boasts superb acoustics, and stages a fun jazz and classical **music festival** in July and August. The castle is rivalled in grandeur by the **Església de Sant Martí**, separated from it by the town hall. Originally dating from the tenth century, the current Baroque church was built in the eighteenth century. Its painted interior is simple but made interesting by the remains of the original construction visible along the left-hand wall.

ROMANYÀ DE LA SELVA AND AROUND

The little-used GIV6612 road heading west, inland from Calonge, rises steeply through a pine wood for 11km before coming to the charming medieval hilltop village of **ROMANYÀ DE LA SELVA**. Turn into the village through an arched gateway and take the narrow road to the left where you'll find an open parking area after 200m.

The settlement and its tiny church, the **Església de Sant Martí de Romanyà**, were first recorded in 1016, although the church itself is thought to date from the end of the tenth century. Dedicated to St Martí, the patron saint of soldiers, knights and tailors, the charmingly simple building has a pantiled roof and rickety porch held up by a single stone column. Largely pre-Romanesque, as can be seen from the horseshoe-shaped arches, it does also contain Romanesque elements, such as the simple stained-glass windows and square belfry. The small square in front of the church houses an altar with the statue of the Virgin and Child in a niche under a lean-to roof for open-air services.

A couple of very good **restaurants** make Romanyà de la Selva an ideal place for a quiet lunch. *Can Suquet*, a large stone house below the church square, has an excellent terrace serving drinks and very good, moderately priced Catalan meals, while the more expensive *Hostal-Restaurant Les Gavarres* serves superb *mar i muntanya* cuisine. The *Les Gavarres* is planning in 2002 to open a small number of guest rooms in a late nineteenth-century annexe built around a spacious walled courtyard.

La Cova d'en Daina

About 1km back along the road from Romanyà de la Selva towards Calonge, a barely visible sign to the left suddenly marks the sharp turn-off into a small unpaved parking area for the megalithic tomb of **LA COVA D'EN DAINA**. From the car park, a short, straight avenue of cork oaks and granite rocks leads to the perfect, albeit slightly restored, four-thousand-year-old **burial chamber** set in a small clearing, with the only sounds being birds and the soughing of the wind in the trees.

Thought to have been built between 2200 and 1700 BC, the site was first discovered in 1894, and excavated in the 1920s by local archeologist Lluís Esteva Cruañas, who unearthed human bones and teeth, flint arrowheads, knife and pottery fragments and necklace beads. Thanks partly to having been partially reconstructed in 1956, the **cromlech** and **tumulus** are still clearly defined, as are the access and burial chamber proper. The **entrance** to the tomb is oriented to the southeast, which allows sunlight to reach the interior on the summer and winter solstices, presumably in accordance with religious beliefs. The whole site exudes such calm that many people choose not to enter the tomb out of respect.

Palamós

Immediately northeast of Sant Antoni de Calonge, **PALAMÓS** is an invigorating town, imbued with the sense of being a thriving community which has got on with its life parallel to the tourist shenanigans going on around it. Alive and kicking with a distinct personality, it cheerfully conveys the feeling that it would have developed along the same path whether foreigners had chosen to visit or not.

The modern extension of the prosperous new town surrounds a lively and pretty **old quarter** on a headland overlooking the port and beach, while the neighbouring **marina** is a bustling leisure port by day and hotspot by night. To the east, the popular **La Fosca** beach heralds the stunning beauty of **S'Alguer**, framed by colourful nineteenth-century fishing huts, and the ecological success of **Platja de Castell**, saved from the clutches of property developers, and which is crowned by the atmospheric ruins of an **Iberian settlement**, separating it from a necklace of idyllic coves.

Some history

The **Iberian** village at Castell dates back to 2000 BC, while subsequent written record of Palamós is from 1277, when **King Pere el Gran** bought the Castell de Sant Esteve, known to have been built on the remains of a Roman villa. His interest in the area ensued from his rivalry with the Comptes d'Empordà, who had inveigled their loyal supporters into diverting the River Ter, thus silting up the king's harbour at Torroella de Montgrí (see p.240), forcing him to look elsewhere for a trading port. Two years later, he granted the town its charter, from when the **Tuesday market** – still held today – dates.

Part of Palamós's week-long Festa Major celebrations around June 24, dedicated to Sant Joan, are traditional *gegants* (see p.44) representing King Pere el Gran and Queen Constança de Sicilia dancing through the streets, plus *sardanes*, fireworks and live music on the promenade.

A strongly fortified town in its medieval heyday, with nine defence towers, Palamós still fell victim to the Turkish pirate **Barbarossa**, who ferociously sacked the town in 1543, an event depicted by Cervantes in *La Galatea*. Expansion came in the eighteenth century thanks to trade with the Americas and the nascent **cork** industry, which, along with the **fishing** industry, laid the basis of Palamós' nineteenth-century prosperity. The two still rank alongside **tourism** as the town's main sources of income.

ARRIVAL AND INFORMATION

Palamós lies on the C253 **road** from Sant Feliu de Guíxols and the C255 from Palafrugell. Parking is available along the seafront and in large **car parks** by the beach and the La Planassa quarter alongside the old town. A regular **bus** service connects with towns up and down the coast as well as Girona and Barcelona, while **boats** pull up on the beach from Roses in the north, Blanes in the south and several points between.

The well-stocked and helpful **tourist office** (Mon–Fri 9am–2pm & 5–8pm; ☎972 600 500, ⓦwww.palamos.org) is midway along the Platja Gran at Passeig del Mar 22, 350m north of the centre, and there's also a seasonal **information kiosk** (Easter–Oct daily 9am–9pm) near the corner of Passeig de Mar and Avgda Onze de Setembre.

ACCOMMODATION

Since many holiday-makers are second-home owners, there are very few **hotels** in Palamós, and holiday **apartments** aren't always easy to come by; best agencies are Roura Soler, Pg del Mar 27 (☎972 601 947) and Soley Gubert, Pg Mar 1 (☎972 314 252).

Most **campsites** are in La Fosca. The best is *King's* (☎972 317 511, ⓕ972 318 935, ⓦwww.campingkings.com; closed Oct–March), a luxurious site centred around a huge swimming pool 200m from the beach. *Vilarromà*, c/Mar s/n (☎ & ⓕ972 314 375; closed Oct–March), a fifteen-minute walk south of the centre, is a small, shaded site 300m from

PALAMÓS

1 & La Fosca & Platja de Castell

CAFÉS, BARS & RESTAURANTS

Bel Air	I
El Castellet	D
Les Escales del Casino	B
La Fàbrica de Gel	K
Flor de Sal	H
La Fusta	C
Green Life	L
Kingcat	E
Maria de Cadaqués	F
La Menta	G
La Plata	M
El Portal de Palamós	A
El Racó	J

N

0   200 m

Marina

Sa Punta Lighthouse

Port

CLUB NÀUTIC

LA PLANASSA

Platja Gran

ACCOMMODATION

Àncora	1
Maria	5
Marina	4
Nauta	2
Trias	3

the beach with a terrace bar, children's play area and log cabins, apartments and mobile homes for rent.

Àncora

c/Josep Pla, La Fosca ⓣ 972 314 858, ⓕ 972 602 470, ⓦ www.6tems.com/ancora. Outwardly quite ordinary, this quiet, shaded hotel 200m from the La Fosca beach has spacious, well-equipped rooms. ❺

Hostal Maria

c/Allada 18 ⓣ 972 314 621. This cheerful *hostal* in the heart of the old town is close to the shops and nightlife, but away from any noise. The restaurant serves an excellent *menú del dia* for €14 and the bedrooms – some en suite – are simple but perfectly adequate. ❷

Marina

Avgda Onze de Setembre 48 ⓣ 972 314 250, ⓕ 972 600 024, ⓦ www.gironaweb.com/marina. This friendly central hotel grouped around a tiny courtyard is excellent value

for money and is a two-minute walk from the beach as well as the shopping and nightlife areas. ❸

Hostal Nauta

Avgda Onze de Setembre 44 ⓣ 972 314 833, ⓕ 972 314 600. Unassuming but comfortable *hostal* 200m from the beach and even nearer the old town. ❹

Trias

Pg del Mar ⓣ 972 601 800, ⓕ 972 601 819, ⓦ www.hoteltrias.com. Closed Oct–March. Delightful hotel in a shaded part of the promenade offering genteel charm with service to match, plus an excellent fish restaurant, free parking for residents and a heated pool. All the large, solidly furnished rooms have balcony and air conditioning. ❼

THE TOWN

Running the length of the new town, the tranquil, pine-shaded **Passeig del Mar** is flanked by rows of residential apartment blocks on one side and the sweep of the golden **Platja Gran** – catering almost exclusively for local families and sun-worshippers – on the other, only really lively where it meets the edge of the old town.

Where the Platja Gran curves southwards, a high medieval stone wall on the opposite side of the Avgda Onze de Setembre marks the boundary of the old town; this was where the sea used to lap in the fifteenth century when it was originally built. Steps lead up from the road to the small **Plaça Murada**, and alleys leading southeast to the **Plaça Major** and the busy **Carrer Major**, at the core of the warren of pedestrianized streets making up Palamós's vibrant **old town**, packed with shops and restaurants.

Turning south, c/Major leads 100m to **La Planassa**, a short avenue outside the medieval harbour wall which is now the lively heart of the old town. Bounded at its end by a small square with a solitary pine, La Planassa is lined with

PALAMÓS ACTIVITIES

A number of operators along Platja Gran offer kayaks, windsurfing and jet bikes. You could rent a traditional boat from Llaüts i Velers, c/Indústria 21 (☎ 972 600 957, ⓦ www .llautsivelers.com) at around €110 for the day, a bike from Bugui-Bike, Pg de Mar 3 (☎ 972 316 363), or a quad bike from Motor Access, c/Albert Pey (☎ 972 312 109). The luxurious *Rafael* traditional sailing boat (☎ 629 046 595) plies routes around the Illes Formigues off the coast by Calella, as well as running "Mar de Nit" night tours along the coast to the accompaniment of cava.

PALAMÓS

an array of stylish, laid-back terrace bars and restaurants, where you're most unlikely to hear any language other than Catalan.

The port and Sa Punta

About 150m west of La Planassa is the busy fishing **port**, built in 1902 to supersede the medieval harbour, and the scene every afternoon of a boisterous fish auction. South of the entrance, an old warehouse is being converted to house the **Cau de la Pesca** museum, chronicling the history of fishing in the town, scheduled to open in 2002.

Outside the port, a road leads to **Sa Punta**, the town's most southerly point, where a wide paved footpath skirts the edge of the port to the Far de Palamós **lighthouse**. The building itself isn't open to the public, but the belvedere beyond it is the perfect spot to savour one of the loveliest sunsets in the Mediterranean.

One of the most spectacular events in Palamós' calendar is the "Christmas Race", an annual competition in the bay that features a host of sleek yachts.

EATING

You're spoilt for choice in **restaurants**, the best of which are located in La Planassa and the narrow old-town streets. Palamós is renowned for the quality of its cuisine, especially fresh fish and locally caught prawns.

Les Escales del Casino
Pl Murada 3.
Daily noon–1am.
This brightly lit bar with a huge mosaic and old photos of Palamós serves excellent Basque tapas and a selection of cava and wines. Budget.

Flor de Sal
c/Pagès Ortiz 53.
Wed–Sun 1–3.30pm &
8–11.30pm; Easter–Oct also
Mon & Tues 8–11.30pm.
Inviting restaurant spilling out
of an old house onto a small
pavement terrace. The
innovative cooking has a
French influence, with pride
of place going to the tuna *mil-
fulls* in balsamic vinegar and oil
and the appetizing "chocolate
passion". Moderate.

La Fusta
c/Mauri Vilar 11.
Easter–Oct daily 9am–1am;
Nov–March Mon–Fri 5pm–1am,
Sat & Sun 1–11pm.
A cheerfully decorated
interior, or bustling terrace in
a tiny old-town street,
provide the setting for lovely
Catalan meals. Especially
good are the platters of
cheeses, *embotits* and pâtés
with *pà amb tomàquet*,
followed by crêpes for
dessert. Budget.

Green Life
Pl St Pere 13.
Easter–Oct daily 7.30pm–
12.30am.

Cosy vegetarian restaurant in
an old house in La Planassa.
The pasta choices, including
asparagus panzarotti and
gnocchi al pesto, are
outstanding. Inexpensive.

Maria de Cadaquès
c/Tauler i Servià 6 ⊤ 972 314
009.
Closed Mon & Dec–Jan.
Founded in 1936 as a
fishermen's tavern, this is one
of the most famous, and
busiest, restaurants in
Catalonia. In its wood-beam
interior, hung with artworks,
it serves superb local fish and
seafood cooked simply but
succulently. Particularly
noteworthy are the *suquet* and
rice casserole, while you
should leave room for the
homemade cakes. Expensive.

La Menta
c/Tauler i Servià 1.
Closed Wed & Nov.
The warm rooms of this
friendly old-town restaurant
are cheerfully cluttered with
knick-knacks. Specializing in
traditional Catalan fare, it
serves lovely fish dishes,
especially the *cap roig*

PALAMÓS

(scorpion fish) with pistachio oil and the sautéed squid with vegetables julienne and soya beans. Expensive.

El Portal de Palamós

Pl dels Arbres 10.

Daily 8am–3am; closed Wed in winter.

In a *masia* dating from 1700 on the fringes of the old town, this enticing tavern has a pavement terrace in the summer. Concentrating on charcoal-grilled meat, it's famous locally for the succulent kebabs served at your table on a huge skewer. Live music and *havaneres* play every Friday. Inexpensive.

El Racó

Pl St Pere 1.

July & Aug daily 1pm–midnight; rest of year Mon–Fri 1–4pm & 7pm–midnight, Sat & Sun 1pm–midnight.

First of a chain which now spreads to Barcelona and Madrid, this stylish and friendly restaurant comprises the original old house with marble and wrought-iron tables, and an adjacent light-wood and chrome annexe. Serving an imaginative fusion of Italian and Catalan cuisine, it has a wide choice for all tastes, particularly vegetarians. Moderate.

DRINKING AND NIGHTLIFE

Palamós **nightlife** makes no concessions to foreign tastes, steadfastly maintaining the Catalan idea of a night out; as a result, the town is infinitely more fun and spontaneous than a lot of its better known neighbours. You won't find any discos or clubs, but instead an impressive array of stylish **bars** and **terraces**, where you just get up and dance when the urge takes you. Most people begin the evening in **La Planassa** or the **old town**, moving on, as the small hours roll around, to the string of lively joints facing the **marina**, about ten minutes' walk east.

Bel Air

c/Onze de Setembre s/n.
Favoured by a younger crowd, this lively, unassuming bar is reached by a flight of steps from La Planassa and has a spectacular view over the port and beach from an upper-floor picture window.

El Castellet

c/Onze de Setembre 81.
Signed photos of George Harrison and a small tribute to Brian Jones give some idea of the age and provenance of this, the oldest bar in Palamós, which used to attract a hippie crowd from all over Europe. Much less esoteric these days, it's still a curiosity for the wonderfully kitsch decor and for its location in what was once the sea wall on the edge of the old town.

La Fàbrica de Gel

Pl St Pere 6.
In the former ice factory that once served the fishing port, this stylish establishment successfully combines designer decor with the irresistible charm of an uneven rock floor and pitted old stone walls.

Kinggat

c/Notaries 32.
Atmospheric bar in an old fisherman's house between the church and La Planassa. Downstairs is dominated by the different types of music from salsa to techno filling the standing-only room, while upstairs is more for chatting leisurely under the wooden beams.

La Plata

Pl St Pere 11.
A superb bar in a ruined building at the end of La Planassa. The youthful downstairs, dominated by a soaring thirty-metre high back wall, is for dancing, while the subtly lit, roofless upstairs area is perfect for a mellow drink.

PALAMÓS

LISTINGS

Banks The main banks have ATMs in the old town and along Avgda Onze de Setembre.

Hospital Hospital Comarcal, c/Hospital 23 ⓣ 972 600 160.

Internet Internet Planet, opposite the tourist information kiosk at Pg de Mar 2.

Pharmacies Baviera, c/Major 1; Clarés, Avgda President Macià 62.

Police Pl del Forn s/n ⓣ 972 602 077.

Post office On the corner of Avgda Catalunya and Avgda Onze de Setembre.

Taxis There's a rank on the corner of c/López Puigcerver and Avgda Onze de Setembre ⓣ 972 315 025.

LA FOSCA AND BEYOND

Skirting Palamós's marina, the Carretera de la Fosca leads 2km east to the neighbouring beach of **La Fosca**, which is also accessible on foot via a stretch of the Camí de Ronda hugging the Cap Gros headland (takes 45min). The bay's lovely golden sand and gently shelving water have conspired to make it one of the most popular in the area with upmarket second-homers – but it still doesn't ever feel overwhelming. A ten-minute walk east follows the shore past the ruins of the Castell de Sant Esteve to the much lovelier **Cala S'Alguer**, an idyllic beach framed by hundred-year-old fishermen's huts, now converted into beach cabins, and which rarely gets crowded.

Platja de Castell

Neighbouring **Platja de Castell** became a local cause célèbre in the 1990s when it was saved from development by popular referendum and allowed to remain in its semi-virgin state. The clear waters of the sheltered half-moon cove and the deep expanse of glittering sand are no secret, so don't expect to have it to yourself, but it still doesn't get too full.

Platja de Castell is accessible by car, via a signposted turning off the C255 Palamós–Palafrugell road. You'll find plenty of free parking in an open field 200m from the beach.

Platja de Castell is separated from S'Alguer by a five-minute stretch of footpath running near the **Mas Juny** mansion, built by the artist Josep Maria Sert with the proceeds of a commission to paint the murals in New York's *Waldorf Astoria* hotel; Philip Leacock's *The Spanish Gardener* (1957), starring Dirk Bogarde (see p.357), was almost entirely filmed at the house.

Perched on the headland bounding Platja de Castell to the north, but visited by surprisingly few people, are the atmospheric ruins of the **Poblat Ibèric de Castell**, an Iberian settlement dating from the sixth century BC. Left to deteriorate until it was bought by the Catalan government, the site has been excavated in earnest only since 2000: ninety percent of it is still to be discovered. What can be seen at the moment is a series of terraces guarded by the remains of two **defence towers** and crowned by an **acropolis** where a temple would have stood. For the time being, it's a magical place in which to enjoy the shade of the evergreen oaks and pines and the views out to sea. Immediately east of the headland is the spectacular sight of the Chartreuse-green waters of the idyllic **Cala de Sa Cobertera** lapping against the natural arch of **Sa Foradada de Castell**.

On to Cala Estreta

From Platja de Castell, a dusty dirt track bumps its way eastwards, giving access to a string of much quieter coves off the track; you'll spot cars parked under trees to the

LA FOSCA AND BEYOND

right. There's also a beautiful path following the cliff east from the headland, but you'll need to be fit to cope with some of the inclines, and there are frustratingly few places at which to get down to the coves below.

The best – and sometimes the only – way to visit the secluded coves in this area is to rent a kayak at Platja de Castell and paddle there yourself.

The first, **Cala dels Canyers**, is a tiny pebble bay with a couple of old boathouses and rockpools just made for snorkelling. From here, the dirt track continues north to the Jardí Botànic Cap Roig (see p.195) and on to Calella de Palafrugell, while a footpath leads to some tumbledown steps descending to **Cala dels Corbs**, two tiny coves popular with nude bathers which rarely get crowded. On from here, the same path opens into **Cala Estreta**, a trio of pretty sandy coves with mixed clothed and nude bathing where you can normally find plenty of space for swimming in the steeply shelving water.

Palafrugell

The busy market town of **PALAFRUGELL**, 7km north of Palamós, has remained largely aloof from the tourism surrounding it. It is eminently low-key in ambience, despite being the parent town of three of the loveliest villages on the coast – Calella (see p.191), Llafranc (p.199) and Tamariu (p.203), each with a distinct character, embracing tourism without being swamped by it.

Sprawling modern development on the fringes of Palafrugell circles a bustling centre, which, in turn, harbours a compact and lovely **old quarter**, whose charming pedes-

FESTES DE PRIMAVERA

Palafrugell's independent spirit is exemplified by its Festes de Primavera (Spring Fair). This exuberant celebration, held on the last weekend in May, was invented in 1962 to get round Franco's prohibition of Carnival throughout Spain, and has survived him to become one of the liveliest events in the local calendar, featuring a procession, live music and *sardanes*.

trianized streets all lead to the central **Plaça Església**, where you'll find congenial terrace bars to help you relax after the rigours of shopping.

Palafrugell's old quarter overflows every Sunday morning with the Costa Brava's liveliest and most important market.

Much of the town's history is linked to cork production, chronicled in the small but arresting **Museu del Suro** (Cork Museum; June–Sept daily 10am–2pm & 4–9pm; rest of year Tues–Sat 5–8pm, Sun 10.30am–1.30pm; ⓦ www.museudelsuro.org; €3), currently at c/Tarongeta 31 but moving to new premises in 2002. Static displays and a fascinating short documentary film recorded locally in the 1920s relate how cork is formed, while nineteenth-century machines show how the raw material was worked. An eclectic exhibition of cork sculptures – from altarpieces to abstract art – leads into a shop. The museum runs guided tours in English (Tues 5pm).

PRACTICALITIES

Palafrugell lies off the C255 Palamós–Girona **road** and acts as a junction-point for the link roads to the seaside towns of Calella, Llafranc and Tamariu. A regular **bus** service connects the town with Palamós and Girona.

PALAFRUGELL

In summer, buses run on a circuit from Palafrugell to Calella and Llafranc roughly every 30min (July & Aug), dropping to every 45min (early June & late Sept, when there's also a lunchtime gap 12.30–3.30pm). Four buses a day serve Tamariu (late June to mid-Sept only). Pick up timetable information at tourist offices or the Sarfa bus company (see p.24).

The **tourist office** is in a small pedestrianized lane beside the church on Plaça Església (April–Sept Mon–Sat 10am–1pm & 5–8pm, Sun 10am–1pm; Oct–March Mon–Sat 10am–1pm & 4–7pm, Sun 10am–1pm; ☏972 611 820, ⓦwww.palafrugell.net). There's a smaller **information office** on the main road near the junction for Calella and Llafranc, at c/Carrilet 2 (same hours year-round, except July & Aug Mon–Sat 9am–9pm, Sun 10am–1pm; ☏972 300 228).

As most people prefer to stay in the nearby coastal villages, there are very few **hotels**. Top choices comprise the *Hostal Plaja*, c/St Sebastià 34 (☏ & ℻972 300 526; ❸; closed Oct–Dec), which has large, comfortable rooms amid old-world charm, and *Fonda L'Estrella*, c/Quatre Cases 13 (☏972 300 005; ❷), a *pensió* with small but cheerful rooms around a shaded courtyard.

The best **restaurants** are *La Xicra*, c/Sant Antoni 17 (closed Tues pm & Wed), which serves excellent Catalan fare and *mar i muntanya* cuisine, and *Xado*, Avgda Corts Catalanes 12 (closed Mon & Tues, and Wed pm), outside the centre near the main roundabout for Calella, which offers an imaginative and tasty blend of Arabic and Catalan cuisine. *La Sala Gran*, 1km southwest at c/Barceloneta 44 (closed Jan), serves up superb Catalan cooking in a lovely old mansion on the Palamós road.

PALAFRUGELL

LISTINGS

Banks The main banks have ATMs around Pl Església.

Car rental Masca Motor, c/Lluna 51 ☏ 972 301 530.

Clinic c/Angel Guimerà 6 ☏ 972 610 607. The Red Cross is at c/Ample 1 ☏ 972 301 909.

Internet Can Palé, c/Cavallers 16; Café Internet La Muralla, c/Valls s/n.

Pharmacy Suñer, Pl Església 9.

Post office c/Torres Jonama 16.

Taxis 24-hour radio taxis on ☏ 972 610 000 or ☏ 972 612 222.

Calella de Palafrugell

Understated development in a perfect setting has helped make **CALELLA DE PALAFRUGELL**, 4km southeast of Palafrugell, one of the most enjoyable towns on the Costa Brava: it has succumbed neither to the mass tourism of the south nor to the near-snobbish exclusivity of some of its smaller neighbours to the north. Its seafront is a necklace of tiny coves strung along a backdrop of whitewashed arches and turn-of-the-century houses, while the tiny centre focuses on the thoroughly charming quarter of the minuscule **Calau**, **Canadell** and **Port-Bo** beaches. Having grown along the shoreline rather than any appreciable distance inland, Calella provides its main attraction in a rugged coastline, which extends some 2km south to the secluded **El Golfet** beach, nestling in the lee of the craggy **Cap Roig** headland, itself home to the most beautiful **botanical gardens** in Catalonia.

CALELLA DE PALAFRUGELL

Don't confuse Calella de Palafrugell with another town
named Calella, further south towards Barcelona but often
hyped by tour operators as being on the Costa Brava. Its
dismal high-rises and English breakfasts bear no relation to
the quiet charm of Calella de Palafrugell.

ARRIVAL AND INFORMATION

Instead of following the four-kilometre stretch of main road
from Palafrugell to Calella, you might prefer to use the
more picturesque and less busy **old road**, starting from the
main roundabout in Palafrugell and signposted to Santa
Margarida. A more rugged alternative is to drive or **walk**
the seven-kilometre dirt track from Palamós's La Fosca
beach (see p.186); if you walk, the first half of the journey is
along the spectacular but demanding Camí de Ronda,
which links up with the dirt track partway along (takes
3hr). **Buses** on the circular route between Palafrugell,
Calella and Llafranc stop at the bottom of Carrer Chopitea,
50m from the centre and its beaches.

See p.190 for details of buses between
Palafrugell, Llafranc and Calella.

A small **tourist office**, c/Voltes 4 (July & Aug daily
10am–1pm & 5–9pm; April–June, Sept & Oct Mon–Sat
10am–1pm & 5–8pm, Sun 10am–1pm; ☎972 614 475,
ⓦwww.palafrugell.net), housed in an atmospheric old fishermen's hut, stocks maps and information for the whole
area. The main **banks** have ATMs on c/Chopitea, and
there's a **pharmacy**, Frigola, at c/Pirroig 23.

ACCOMMODATION

Calella's few **hotels** are expensive. Rooms – all with terrace or balcony – at the good-value clifftop *Sant Roc*, Pl Atlàntic 2 (☎972 614 250, ☞ 972 614 068, ⓦ www.santroc.com; ❻; closed Dec–Feb), 300m southwest of the centre, offer spectacular views, while those at the summer-only *La Torre*, Pg de la Torre 26–28 (☎972 614 603, ☞972 615 171, ⓦ www .hotel-latorre.com; ❻; closed Oct–May), set on the headland dividing Calella and Llafranc, are similarly large, bright and comfortably furnished. The excellent-value *Port-Bo*, c/August Pi i Sunyer 6 (☎972 614 962, ☞972 614 065, ⓦ www.hotelportbo.com; ❺; closed Jan & Feb), about 200m from the sea, is run by extremely friendly and helpful staff and has huge, airy rooms; the price includes a copious buffet breakfast.

Finally, there's the extraordinary *Batlle*, c/de les Voltes 2 (☎972 615 905, ☞972 615 409; ❼; closed Dec), ideally located by the tiny Port-Bo beach. Its spacious rooms are extravagantly designed according to a floor-by-floor theme – Traditional, Regional or Artistic – with the most sought-after being the Salvador Dalí room, where the bedstead is a pair of gigantic carmined lips.

It is possible to find reasonably priced **apartments**, even on the seafront, but they get snapped up quickly; Port-Calella, c/Calau 10 (☎972 615 454, ☞972 615 564) is one of the few agencies to offer apartments on a day-by-day basis, rather than Saturday to Saturday.

The **campsites** are a fair walk from the beaches. *La Siesta*, c/Chopitea 110–120 (☎972 615 116, ☞972 614 416, ⓦ www.campinglasiesta.com; closed Nov–March) is an enormous complex off the main Palafrugell–Calella road, with bars, restaurants and a swimming pool. The quieter *Moby Dick*, Avgda Costa Verda 16–28 (☎972 614 307, ☞972 614 940, ⓦ www.campingmobydick.com; closed

Oct–March), is halfway between the town centre and El Golfet, about 500m from the beach. It's laid out on shaded terraces, the higher ones with sea views, and has a good bar and shop plus cabins.

THE TOWN

Calella has largely been left to get on with life as a fishing village and base for weekenders and holiday-makers seeking peace and quiet with an edge of luxury. Perpendicular to the beach, **Carrer Chopitea** leads into the tiny, cobbled **Plaça Sant Pere** at the bottom, offering a lovely vision of the Mediterranean shimmering between whitewashed arches and brightly coloured fishing boats.

Heart of the town is the narrow, bustling **Carrer Voltes**, adjoining Plaça Sant Pere and linking two minuscule horseshoe coves. The first, **Port–Bo**, a blue-flag beach bedecked with fishing boats pulled up onto the coarse sand, is framed by a tiny square with terrace cafés. Neighbouring **Calau**, separated by a craggy rock, stands at the foot of whitewashed arches (home to the best terrace on which to sample an evening drink) and is protected by a flotilla of small pleasure boats moored in the crystalline waters.

Port-Bo beach manages to accommodate upwards of 40,000 spectators on the last weekend in June for the thronging *havaneres* festival (see p.45), when sea shanties are sung from boats in the bay to a torchlit crowd.

Straggling lanes lead 200m north past Port-Bo to the larger but equally stylish **Canadell** beach, also winner of a blue flag, and lined by a promenade of nineteenth-century town villas. At the north end of the cove, stone steps lead up to the Camí de Ronda footpath, which rounds the point by the *Hotel La Torre* and meanders 1km along an undulating pine-clad path hugging the rocky shore to Llafranc.

South of Calau and separated from it by a steep finger of rock pointing out to sea, sheltered **Port Pelegrí** is favoured by divers and boaters, but still makes for some great bathing. This is the last sandy cove before a stretch of indented coastline running 1km to El Golfet, most of which can be followed along the serpentine Camí de Ronda, which starts after the *Hotel Sant Roc* and swoops up and down along the water, revealing secluded rocks and handkerchiefs of sand on which to sunbathe. At the southern end, the sheltered **El Golfet** cove is half-hidden at the foot of a steep, winding flight of steps, its deep waters framed by pines clinging tenaciously to the cliff.

At Port Pelegrí, the friendly Club Vela Calella, c/Noi Gran 3 (☎ 972 614 619) offers week-long sailing courses to kids and adults, and Poseidon (☎ 972 615 345), on the beach, runs diving courses and excursions.

JARDÍ BOTÀNIC CAP ROIG

Daily 9am–8pm; winter closes 6pm. €1.80.

At the end of the road climbing above El Golfet is the enchanting **Jardí Botànic Cap Roig**, 2km south of Calella via Avgda Antoni Rovira – follow the signs to Cap Roig – and also accessible via the Camí de Ronda footpath heading south from El Golfet. The gardens, made up of themed areas set out on terraces around a modern castle, were begun in 1927 by Nicolai Woevodsky, an exiled colonel from the army of Nicholas II of Russia, and his aristocratic English wife, Dorothy Webster, to combine his interest in architecture with hers in archeology and gardening. You should allow three hours for the delightful walk through the site; a **free map** shows the way.

The small entrance courtyard opens into the sloping **Camí del Castell** path offering the first panorama of the crisp blue sea beyond an outburst of bougainvillea, yellow sage and oleander. At the foot of the path, mimosas and cork oaks part to reveal a square dominated by the **castle**, a solid, twin-turreted building with an elaborate fifteenth-century doorway rescued from a ruin.

The castle isn't open to the public, but the square in front of it is the location every summer for a prestigious open-air jazz festival (information and €6 tickets from the tourist office).

The path winds slowly down through cypress-lined terraces, perfumed arches and past lily-ponds to the **Jardí dels Enamorats** (Lovers' Garden), where a Judas tree and olives shelter a carpet of fuchsias and busy lizzies. Below this, the marigold- and primula-lined **Jardí de Primavera** (Spring Garden) suddenly emerges into a **cactus garden**, where the towering forms of the cacti watch over a small offshore archipelago, Les Illes Formigues (Ant Islands), where the Catalan admiral, Roger de Llúria, famously defeated French invaders in 1285. Below the cacti, the **Mirador de les Formigues** is a relaxing spot to take in the vista.

From here, the **Passeig dels Geranis** (Geranium Promenade) climbs up to two small squares, set one above the other behind the castle. The first one in particular, the **Mirador de la Lady** (Lady's Belvedere), gives outstanding views over the white arches and beaded coves of Calella in the distance. Following on round to the castle square, a detour leads to a grove devoted entirely to Mediterranean species.

EATING

Along with a couple of reasonable seafront **restaurants** serving fairly ordinary but good-value meals, Calella has some very good places to eat traditional Catalan fare, specializing in fish and seafood.

Calella's *Garoinada* festival – during which the town's restaurants serve up sea urchins caught by hand – runs throughout February.

La Bella Lola
Pl Sant Pere 4.
Daily noon–midnight;
Oct–Easter closed Mon–Thurs.
A lively restaurant and bar specializing in tasty *pà amb tomàquet* meals with hams, cheeses and salads. It's popular with the *havaneres* crowd: the occasional impromptu singalongs are fun. Inexpensive.

La Gavina
c/Gravina 7.
Daily 7.30pm–midnight;
Oct–Easter closed Mon–Thurs.
One of the Costa Brava's most enjoyable Catalan restaurants, equally pleasant in the summer on the shaded terrace as in the winter in front of the open fire. The friendly owners create some fine salads, as well as superb *pà amb tomàquet* meals, succulent freshly caught fish and grilled meats. Moderate.

Sant Roc
Pl Atlàntic 2.
Closed Dec–Feb.
Boasting a wonderful view of the town and coves from its spacious terrace, this hotel restaurant serves particularly good *mar i muntanya* dishes, notably steak with clams and parmesan sauce, plus a few veggie options. Expensive.

Tango
c/Voltes 8.
Oct–Easter closed Mon–Thurs & Fri lunch.
This small Catalan restaurant beside the tourist office attracts a stylish crowd and

CALELLA DE PALAFRUGELL

197

serves excellent fish, rice and vegetable dishes – and the best paella and *fideuà* in town. Moderate.

La Torre
Pg de la Torre 26–28.
Closed Oct–May.
Overlooking Platja Canadell, this lovely restaurant specializes in local fish and rice dishes; for veggies, the grilled vegetable platter is a must. Moderate.

El Tragamar
Pg del Canadell s/n.
Easter–Sept daily noon–midnight; Oct–Easter Sat & Sun 1–11pm.
Beautifully located on a stone walkway at beach level below the Canadell promenade, this smart establishment serves imaginative, modern Catalan cuisine, including exquisite fish and rice dishes. Moderate.

Les Voltes
c/Voltes 7.
Closed Nov, and Dec–March closed Wed.
A popular choice (though no phone bookings taken), with the most sought-after tables on the terrace under the arches. The speciality among the tasty local dishes is fresh fish, especially cod, and the homemade desserts are good. Moderate.

DRINKING AND NIGHTLIFE

Calella's version of having a **drink** is a pleasant, laid-back affair best done in the open air, gazing out to the boats and the small lighthouse on the Illes Formigues. The perfect place for people-watching is at one of the half-dozen or so terraces at Calau or Port-Bo, ideally *Gelpí*, c/Voltes 11 (daily 10am–3am), a popular, friendly establishment which serves the best *cremat* in Catalonia. Equally alluring, but without the backdrop of the sea, is the laid-back terrace at *Habana Café*, Plaça Sant Pere (daily noon–2am). The twenty-something crowd favours lively *Xabec*, c/Lladó 6 (daily

198

10am–3am), a café by day and a bustling music bar at night, or the varying musical choices at *Arena*, Ctra Vella de Calella 6 (daily 10pm–5am), a huge **club** on the old road into town.

Llafranc

Stately **LLAFRANC** sits in a half-moon bay 2km northeast of Calella, the domain of second-homers and tourists in the know seeking tranquillity and gastronomy in splendid surroundings. More genteel than its neighbour, it's a self-consciously opulent place, with more yachts and restaurants than shops or bars.

The focus of town is the stylish promenade of **Passeig Cipsela**, the setting for the evening walk to show off your

LLAFRANC ACTIVITIES

To explore the stunning coves and caves either side of Badia de Llafranc, you can rent kayaks and motorboats from Tourist Service, c/Cipsela 1 (⊤ 972 301 748), or take an excursion with Barracuda, based in the port (⊤ 607 871 213; 2hr; €12), which uses boats and inflatables to explore the most inaccessible caves between Palamós and Begur. Berganti, Avgda del Mar 1 (⊤ 972 301 748; daily 10am–7.30pm; 1hr; €12), runs excursions by glass-bottomed boat in the same area. The area north of Llafranc is popular with divers, due to the spectacular Els Ullastres underwater mountains and trench, but you should dive only when accompanied by a reputable instructor; in Llafranc, Snorkel, Avgda del Mar s/n (⊤ 972 302 716) and Triton, Pl dels Pins (⊤ 972 302 426), offer courses and excursions.

LLAFRANC

199

finery or the ideal place to while away an hour or two on a terrace before heading off to eat. Framed by the promenade, the fine golden sand of Llafranc's sheltered blue-flag **beach** takes up where the strollers leave off – although don't expect much room in the height of summer.

The southern end of the short seafront is marked by modern buildings and a narrow but quite busy road; proceeding northwards, beyond the halfway point of the popular meeting place of **Plaça Promontori**, the road is restricted for residents and you'll see grander early twentieth-century villas, some adorned with Modernist patterns and balconies. At the far northern end of the beach are the yachts and dinghies of the **Port Nàutic**.

From the port, near the telephone kiosk, steps lead up to the Passeig Carles Vilà for the calf-aching climb through winding residential streets to the **Far de Sant Sebastià** lighthouse, where you'll be treated to some breathtaking views, and the signposted GR92 footpath cuts inland through pine woods as far as the cliffedge near Tamariu.

The Far de Sant Sebastià lighthouse is also accessible by road, signposted from behind Plaça Promontori; the route links up with the road north to Tamariu.

PRACTICALITIES

Llafranc lies just off the roundabout at the end of the main **road** from Palafrugell, or can be reached via the GIV6591, winding through the woods south from Tamariu. A more picturesque alternative is to take the thirty-minute **walk** along the lovely Camí de Ronda from Calella. A summer **bus** service runs on a circular route between Palafrugell, Calella and Llafranc.

LLAFRANC

**See p.190 for details of buses between
Palafrugell, Calella and Llafranc.**

The **tourist office** occupies a small cabin near the start of the seafront, c/Roger de Llúria (July & Aug daily 10am–1pm & 5–9pm; April–June, Sept & Oct Mon–Sat 10am–1pm & 5–8pm, Sun 10am–1pm; ⊤972 614 475, ⓦwww.palafrugell.net).

Accommodation

Llafranc has some very good **hotels**, most of which have excellent restaurants and are situated on the promenade or overlooking the town. A wide range of **apartments** and **villas** is available, the best choice belonging to the friendly Llafranc Villas, c/Xaloc 5 (⊤972 305 412, ⓦwww.llafranch -villas.com).

Casamar
c/Nero 3 ⊤972 300 104, Ⓕ972 610 651.
Closed Nov–March.
Perched halfway up a flight of steps on the south side of the cove, this award-winning hotel has fabulous views over the beach and port from its terrace bar and range of bright, superb-value rooms. ❸

Celimar
c/Carudo 12–14 ⊤ & Ⓕ972 301 374.
Closed Sept–Dec.
Friendly establishment on a quiet street 50m from the sea. The rooms are smallish but modern and very comfortable, all en suite. ❸

El Far
Platja Llafranc ⊤972 301 639, Ⓕ972 304 328, Ⓔhotelfss@intercom.es.
Closed Jan.
This tranquil haven offers vast panoramas over the sea from its perch near the lighthouse on Llafranc's northern headland. The sumptuous rooms have air conditioning and spacious balconies. ❼

LLAFRANC

Llafranch

Pg Cipsela 16 ⊤ 972 300 208,
Ⓕ 972 305 259,
Ⓦ www.hllafranch.com.
At the heart of the town on
the beach, with a lovely
terrace bar and restaurant.
The tastefully modernized
rooms have separate sitting
areas and most have sea-
facing balconies. ⑥

Llevant

c/Francesc Blanes 5 ⊤ 972 300
366, Ⓕ 972 300 345,
Ⓔ hllevant@arrakis.es.

On a pedestrianized section
of the seafront, this hotel's
relaxing terrace bar and restaurant, just made for cocktails
at sundown, are as enticing as
its charming, pleasantly
understated rooms. ⑥

Terramar

Pg Cipsela 5 ⊤ 972 300 200,
Ⓕ 972 300 626.
Closed Nov–Feb.
A shaded family-run hotel on
the seafront, with tranquil,
air-conditioned rooms, most
with sea-view balconies. ⑥

Eating and drinking

Llafranc's **restaurants** are pricey but rewarding – particularly for lovers of fresh fish and seafood. Most of the best are
in the hotels along the seafront, where you can also soak up
the views over a **drink** on the terrace.

El Far

Platja Llafranc ⊤ 972 301 639.
Closed Jan.
High above the sea, the hotel
terrace is the setting for this
sumptuous restaurant famed
for its seafood and local
cuisine. Especially good is the
fideuà and rice with wild
mushrooms. Expensive.

Llevant

c/Francesc Blanes 5 ⊤ 972 300
366.
Well known locally for its
generous fish and seafood
dishes, this seafront hotel has
a busy terrace. Particularly
appetizing is the pickled
anchovy salad in cava sauce.
Moderate.

La Pasta
Pg Cipsela 1.
Daily 1–11pm; Nov–Easter
closed Mon–Thurs & Fri
lunchtime.
One of the most economical
options in town, this brightly
lit restaurant serves good pasta
and pizzas, as well as some
tasty *mar i muntanya* and
traditional dishes. Inexpensive.

Simpson's
Pg Cipsela 10.
Closed Nov–Jan.
Midway along the seafront,
the tastefully subdued decor

of this popular restaurant is
the ideal match for the subtly
flavoured salads and fish
dishes, while the desserts are
sheer heaven. Moderate.

La Txata
**c/Carudo 12–14. Nov–Easter
closed**
Mon–Thurs & Fri lunchtime.
One street in from the beach,
this arty Basque restaurant,
decorated with the owner's
sculptures, specializes in
delicious *nouvelle cuisine* based
on traditional Basque fish and
seafood dishes. Moderate.

Tamariu

The smallest and quietest of Palafrugell's satellite towns,
TAMARIU, 3km northeast, is rather modest in the way
that only the very wealthy can be. It's more a spot in which
to relax than to sightsee, and everything is focused on the
small seafront. The **promenade** – lined with tamarinds,
source of the town's name – has a subtle, unhurried charm,
populated by Catalan children scampering around the feet
of their well-to-do parents. Lining the short curving
seafront is a jumble of small shops, pavement restaurants and
houses, where elderly locals sit outside on wicker chairs
chatting. The coarse sand of the blue-flag **beach**, sheltered
by the high walls of the cove, is the domain of young
Catalan families but few foreigners.

TAMARIU

Walking north a short distance past the restaurants, a paved footpath ends at the tranquil, rocky **Cala d'Aigua Dolça**, popular with evening strollers and anglers. The coves beyond here are inaccessible by foot or car, but the area around **Foralló d'Aigua Xelida**, a rock standing off the neighbouring Punta d'Esguard point, is very good for **diving** as it's riddled with caves and features the submerged mountain of Llosa de Cala Nova. Less well known than other dive sites on the Costa Brava, the area is still relatively untouched.

Divers can explore the area around Foralló d'Aigua Xelida with the English-speaking outfit Stolli's, Pg del Mar 26 (☎ & ⓕ 972 620 245, ⓦ www.stollis-divebase.de; Easter–Oct).

South to Cala Pedrosa

Leading south from the end of the main beach, the rugged inlets carved out of the shoreline as far as Llafranc – including the pretty and secluded **Cala Pedrosa**, a bare kilometre south of Tamariu – are reached most easily by boat. Paco Boats (☎ 607 292 578) rents out small **motorboats** from the beach; these take about half an hour to reach Cala Pedrosa. Kayaking Costa Brava, also on Tamariu beach (☎ 972 773 806, ⓦ www.kayakingcb.com), rents **kayaks** and also organizes excellent **guided excursions** to Cala Pedrosa and other hidden coves and caves in the area; especially good is their moonlight trip to the coves north of Tamariu.

An alternative is to head there on **foot**. The Camí de Ronda footpath sets off from the bottom corner of the beach and skirts Tamariu's cove before climbing up to the treeline. The route from here hugs the cliff-edge to Cala Pedrosa; it's treacherous in parts and you should only attempt it if you're confident and reasonably agile. At

Pedrosa, it turns inland through less spectacular scenery as far as Llafranc's Far de Sant Sebastià (see p.200).

PRACTICALITIES

The winding GIV6542 **road** heads into Tamariu from Palafrugell, and the tortuous but more picturesque GIP6532 snakes its way south from Begur (see p.208) and Aiguablava over the villa-coated Aiguaxelida headland.

See p.190 for details of buses
between Palafrugell and Tamariu.

A small seasonal **tourist office**, next to the beach on Carrer Riera (June–Sept Mon–Sat 10am–1pm & 5–8pm, Sun 10am–1pm; ☎972 620 193, ⓦwww.palafrugell.net), stocks the same leaflets and maps as you'll find in Palafrugell, Calella and Llafranc.

Accommodation

Tamariu has some good **hotels**. Seafront *Tamariu*, Pg del Mar 2 (☎972 620 031, ⓕ972 620 500, ⓦwww.tamariu.com; closed Dec–Feb; ❺), was a fishermen's tavern in the 1920s. Today, still in the same family, it has an excellent seafood restaurant and seventeen large rooms, all beautifully furnished and some with sea views; pricier penthouses have large terraces. *Es Furió*, c/Foraió 5–7 (☎972 620 036, ⓕ972 306 667, ⓔacomas@intercom.es; closed Nov–Easter; ❺), on a quiet street 20m from the sea, also has a good restaurant and bright, en-suite rooms. The tranquil *Sol d'Or*, c/Riera 18 (☎972 620 172; closed Oct–Easter; ❸) is surrounded by trees at the top of low steps, its simple, en-suite rooms very comfortable and cool. Finally, *Pensió Tamariu Platja*, c/Foraió 20 (☎972 620 437; closed Oct–April; ❸),

TAMARIU

originally the annexe to the *Tamariu*, is now separately run by the same family to the same high standards. In a low building some 50m from the seafront, all the cheerful, airy rooms are en suite and come with large balconies.

Apartments are not always easy to come by and you should reserve well in advance; it's rare to find any near the beach. The best agency is Corredor-Mató, c/Riera 6 (☎972 620 016, ⓕ972 620 012, ⓦwww.corredormato.com).

There's one simple and well-shaded **campsite**, a good ten minutes' walk from the beach – *Camping Tamariu*, Paratge Costa Rica (☎972 620 422 ⓕ972 302 481, ⓔcampingtamariu@teleline.es; closed Oct–April).

Eating and drinking

Good places to **eat** need hunting down. Few of the waterfront restaurants are enticing and, as the terraces are set out on the small promenade, you can't help feeling on display while eating. *Es Furió*, c/Foraió 5–7 (moderate; closed Nov–Easter), serves an eclectic variety including pizzas, crêpes and salads, while some of the house specials, especially the orange salad with goat's cheese and the cod with roast garlic and *xamfaina* mousse, are superb. An alternative, hidden away at the start of the winding road to Aiguablava, is the cosy *El Mossec*, c/Pescadors 8 (inexpensive; closed Nov–Easter); eschew the small terrace in favour of the welcoming wood interior. Its imaginative menu includes a curious blend of rice and curry dishes cooked in a Catalan style and more traditional fare like roast lamb and the succulent *bacallà amb xamfaina* (cod with a ratatouille-like stew).

On the corner of the beach, *El Salí*, c/Riera s/n (inexpensive; closed Nov–Easter) offers fabulous views from its simple, raised terrace. The food is good, but nothing spectacular, concentrating on filling *pà amb tomàquet* meals and grilled fish. Its **bar** serves a heavenly range of cocktails and *chupitos*.

The Baix Empordà
– north

The **northern Baix Empordà** marks an abrupt change in scenery and style from the southern end of the region. By day, the rugged coves around the stylish hilltop town of **Begur** are a favourite haunt of well-to-do locals, who by night exchange looks in the chic bars and restaurants beneath the eleventh-century castle. North lies the long, sweeping beach of **Platja de Pals**, while inland the restored medieval town of **Pals** stands in contrast to delightful **Peratallada**, with its own brand of rural-chic and upmarket eateries. Nearby is the county town of **La Bisbal**, famed for its ceramics.

Map 2 at the back of the book covers the
whole Baix Empordà region.

As you venture further north towards the Alt Empordà, Salvador Dalí makes his presence felt in the sleepy inland hamlet of **Púbol**: the castle he bought and renovated for his Russian wife, Gala, now houses a museum. On the northern edge of the Baix Empordà and crowned by an unfinished

THE CAMÍ DE RONDA

The Camí de Ronda footpath (see p.49) in the northern part of the Baix Empordà comprises only disjointed fragments around Begur's beaches. From Fornells (see p.215), a short stretch runs to a neighbouring cove. Most recommendable is the longer section from Sa Tuna (p.215) to Aiguafreda (p.216) and on to the more strenuous kilometre-long cliff-edge route to Sa Riera (see p.216). From Sa Riera, a relaxing fifteen-minute section is the only way to get to the lovely coves north of the town.

medieval castle, the ancient town of **Torroella de Montgrí** channels traffic to its rumbustious child **L'Estartit**, an unashamed tourist centre that serves as a gateway to the offshore nature reserve of the **Illes Medes**.

Begur and around

Nestling in the shadow of a ruined castle on a headland, chic **BEGUR**, 6km northeast of Palafrugell, is the hub of an array of serpentine roads leading down to its tranquil and equally stylish **beaches**. Steeped in history, its narrow streets, with their exclusive shops and restaurants, all lead to the bustling **Plaça de la Vila** and the seventeenth-century **Església Parroquial de Sant Pere**. The medieval **Castell de Begur** overlooking the town gives superb views as far north as the Cap de Creus.

Begur has two patron saints – and so two Festes Majors: Sant Pere is around the last weekend in June, while the more sedate Santa Reparada is Sept 15–17.

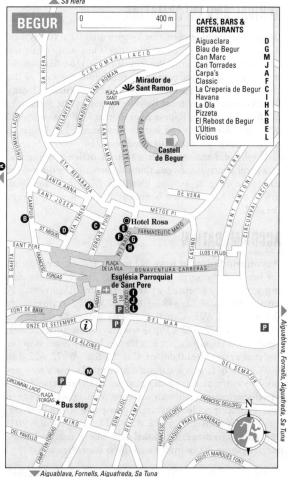

BEGUR

0   400 m

CAFÉS, BARS & RESTAURANTS

Aiguaclara	D
Blau de Begur	G
Can Marc	M
Can Torrades	J
Carpa's	A
Classic	F
La Creperia de Begur	C
Havana	I
La Ola	H
Pizzeta	K
El Rebost de Begur	B
L'Últim	E
Vicious	L

Sa Riera

Mirador de Sant Ramon

Castell de Begur

Hotel Rosa

Església Parroquial de Sant Pere

Bus stop

N

Aiguablava, Fornells, Aiguafreda, Sa Tuna

Aiguablava, Fornells, Aiguafreda, Sa Tuna

ARRIVAL AND INFORMATION

Begur is accessible via two well-signposted local **roads**; one turns off from the C255 at Torrent, 10km west, while the other leads directly from Palafrugell (see p.118), 6km southwest. **Parking** is not easy, and you should use one of the clearly marked car parks near the old town. **Buses** (1 daily from Girona, 4 daily from Barcelona) stop by the Sarfa ticket office, within the Ribera bookshop at Pl Forgas 6 (⊤972 622 446). A summer bus service runs from Plaça Forgas to the surrounding beaches, detailed on p.214.

The helpful and informative **tourist office** is at the rear of a small courtyard, Avgda Onze de Setembre 5 (June–Sept daily 9am–3pm & 4–9pm; Oct–May Mon–Fri 9am–2pm; ⊤972 624 520, ⊛www.begur.org); their website is very detailed.

ACCOMMODATION

Accommodation in town is limited, and most people go for hotels at the surrounding beaches. Two agencies offering a variety of rented **apartments** are Alquiventa, Pl Forgas (⊤972 622 348, ⊕972 623 277, ⓔalquiventa @cbi.es) and AVI, Urb Residencial Begur 33–34 (⊤972 622 505, ⊕972 622 016, ⊛www.avi-inmobiliaria.com). *Apartaments Aiguafreda*, set in a former luxury hotel atop the isolated craggy headland of Cap Sa Sal (⊤972 622 130 ⊕972 623 641, ⊛www.aiguafreda.com; ❸), has a seawater pool, waterfront restaurant, gardens and comfortable, serviced apartments – all with sea-view terraces – for between one and six people. The only **campsite** is the pleasant, shaded *El Maset*, (⊤972 623 023, ⊕972 623 901, ⓔelmaset@jazzfree.com; closed Oct–March), set on hillside terraces about 500m from Platja de Sa Riera beach.

Aiguablava

Platja de Fornells ⓣ 972 622 058, ⓕ 972 622 112, ⓦ www.aiguablava.com.
Closed Dec & Jan.

Plush hotel set in shaded gardens right on the water's edge, with a seawater pool and tennis courts. The sumptuous rooms all have terraces giving onto the garden or the sea. ❻

Parador d'Aiguablava

Platja d'Aiguablava ⓣ 972 622 162, ⓕ 972 622 166, ⓦ www.parador.es.

The Costa Brava's only *parador* – the highest class of Spanish hotel – this modern building on the rugged headland overlooking the beach boasts a gym with sauna, open-air pool and terraces high above the sea. The huge rooms, each with terrace, give onto the open sea or the coves of Aiguablava and Fornells. ❼

Pensió Sa Barraca

Ctra de Fornells s/n ⓣ 972 623 360.

Tiny, family-run *pensió* perched up a sharp incline halfway along the hilly road to Fornells, and offering superb views over the coves below, particularly from the breakfast terrace. The en-suite rooms are simply furnished but comfortable and quiet. ❸

Hostal Sa Rascassa

Cala d'Aiguafreda 3, Begur ⓣ 972 622 845.
Closed Nov–Easter.

The most tranquil of Begur's hotels, this beautiful old house a minute's walk from the protected inlet of Aiguafreda has five peaceful, stylishly decorated en-suite rooms and an excellent restaurant. ❺

Hotel Sa Riera

Platja Sa Riera ⓣ 972 623 000, ⓕ 972 623 460.
Closed Nov–Feb.

Friendly place set back from the beach, with a good pool and pleasant restaurant and sitting rooms. The simple but stylish air-conditioned rooms, all en suite, are large and shaded. ❺

Hotel Rosa

c/Pi i Ralló 11, Begur ⓣ 972 623

BEGUR AND AROUND

015, (F) 972 624 320,
(E) hotelrosa@hotmail.com.
Closed Dec–Feb.

Extremely friendly hotel in a lovely old building just off the main square that's far more comfortable than its rates suggest. The rooms, with air conditioning and hydromassage bathrooms, are excellent value, and internet access is available. ❹

Pensió Sant Cristobal
Platja Sa Riera (T) 972 622 228,
(F) 972 622 093.
Closed Oct–Easter.

To book at this no-frills *pensió* 50m from the beach, ask at the friendly *Restaurant* *Miramar* round the corner on the seafront. All rooms are cheerfully decorated and en suite, some with sea views. ❸

Hostal Sa Tuna
Platja de Sa Tuna (T) & (F) 972 622 198,
(W) www.hostalsatuna.com.
Closed Oct–March.

This welcoming *hostal* on a tiny beach is deservedly famous for its excellent seafood restaurant. Its five tranquil en-suite rooms were refurbished in 2001, and all but one has a seafront terrace. ❺

THE TOWN

Focal point of Begur is its paved **Plaça de la Vila**, site of the small **Església Parroquial de Sant Pere**, and focus for a web of stylish shopping and dining streets. Above the town, the **Castell de Begur** and the **Mirador de Sant Ramon** offer splendid views of the Baix Empordà coast-line.

Begur's alleys achieved fleeting Hollywood fame when Elizabeth Taylor filmed a few short scenes in the town for her 1959 film, *Suddenly Last Summer*.

Plaça de la Vila and around

Surrounded by a maze of charming pedestrianized streets, the heart of Begur is its **Plaça de la Vila**, which serves as venue for the Wednesday **market**, as well as *sardanes* most Saturdays in the summer, starting at 10.30pm. A smattering of terrace bars, which fill out during the early evening, occupy one side of the square, while a stone ledge known as Es Pedrís Llarg ("The Long Stone"), running the length of the adjacent church wall, has been used as a shaded meeting place and people-watching spot for as long as the church has been standing.

The simple lines of the seventeenth-century **Església Parroquial de Sant Pere**, renovated in 1996, belie its Gothic interior. Inside, a second nave parallel to the first was built in the eighteenth century in place of four original side chapels, in dedication to Begur's co-patron saint, Santa Reparada. In a side chapel to the right, a simple alabaster statue of the Madonna and Child, sculpted by Francesc Fajula in 1985 provides a pleasant contrast to the busy altarpiece, which depicts St Pere holding the keys to heaven.

Castell de Begur

The ruins of the **Castell de Begur**, in whose shadow Begur grew, stand 500m northeast of Plaça de l'Església. Built by Arnust de Begur in the eleventh century, the castle fell into the hands of Gilabert de Cruïlles in 1360, beginning an era of punitive feudal conditions for the townspeople which only ended when de Cruïlles' impoverished descendants sold the castle and the rights to the town in 1604. Devastated twice by the French and subsequently rebuilt, the castle was finally destroyed in 1810 by Spanish troops led by the English General Doyle, to stop further French occupation. The ruins that remain are scant testimony to such eventful history, but the gentle climb up to the low walls is worth it for the spectacular **views** as far north as Cap de Creus. Looking north, the Gavarres mountains come into alignment with the hilltop castle of Torroella de Montgrí (see p.240) and the small escarpment at L'Estartit (see p.244) to create the illusion of a figure lying on its back; some see a pregnant woman, others a sleeping bishop.

At the foot of the castle nestles the **Mirador de Sant Ramon**, where a tiny chapel stands on a low point offering equally inspiring views out to sea. First documented in 1605, it was razed to the ground during the Civil War and rebuilt as an exact replica in 1951.

BEGUR'S BEACHES

Begur's elegant and enticing **beaches**, all within a 3km radius of the town, could more accurately be described as beach villages: each has a distinct character and most have homes and a handful of restaurants, hotels and shops. This is the Costa Brava as it should be seen, crystalline turquoise waters lapping against bleached sand and reflecting pines clinging on to the gnarled cliffs.

From Easter to October, hourly buses – all of which display their destination – run from Plaça Forgas in Begur to the beaches: to Sa Riera (daily 10am–8pm on the hour; takes 15min), and to Fornells and Aiguablava (daily 10.30am–7.30pm on the half-hour; takes 15–20min).

All the beaches are accessible via well-signposted roads from Begur, and while some are connected with each other by road or the Camí de Ronda, you'll occasionally have to trek back up to Begur to cross between beaches.

Aiguablava

The beautiful cove of **Aiguablava**, 3km southeast of
Begur, shelters in the lee of the headland on which stands
the *Parador d'Aiguablava* (see p.211). Offering fabulous views
of neighbouring Fornells and the pine-covered hills, the
sandy blue-flag beach shelves quite steeply and is popular
with a chic local crowd. Overlooking the beach are a couple of *xiringuitos* and an excellent seafood restaurant (see
p.218). Parking costs €0.70/hr, free after 8pm.

Fornells and around

A turning to the east 1km north of Aiguablava leads to the
tiny and exclusive **Fornells**, dominated by fine villas and
the expensive *Hotel Aiguablava* (see p.211); more popular
with yachters than bathers, the beach is minuscule. If you're
looking for seclusion of a sort, a short section of the Camí
de Ronda runs north from Fornells (15min) as far as a long,
steep staircase winding down to the almost virgin **Platja
Fonda** at the foot of a steep cliff; the swimming here in the
deep water is wonderful.

Sa Tuna

One of the prettiest and most interesting beaches on the
Costa Brava, **Sa Tuna**, 500m northeast of Begur, nestles in
a small, steep-sided cove with a pebble beach and deep
waters ideal for strong swimmers. Popular with second-
homers and boating folk, the beach gets busy but rarely
overflows, while the car park hosts an all-day **market** every
Friday in July and August.

Sa Tuna's beauty is matched by the colourful tales surrounding it. A ruined watchtower on the northern headland
bears witness to the damage wrought by General Doyle and
his Spanish troops when they stormed the town in the war
against the French. In more peaceful times, returning
Indianos (see box on p.122) would land here on their home-

coming from the Americas; their distinctive mansions, amid the low pine-clad hills on the water's edge, have contributed to the genteel and uniquely characterful ambience of the town today. More reluctant visitors were the crew of a French steamship carrying a cargo of hats which ran aground on the rocks at the entrance to the cove; for years after, the townspeople did a roaring trade in headgear.

Aiguafreda and around

Some 500m northwest of Sa Tuna along the same road, the long channel of **Aiguafreda** has no beach to speak of and is more popular with boating people and divers. By walking to Aiguafreda on the Camí de Ronda from Sa Tuna, you'll pass the pretty and uncrowded **Cova des Capellans** (Chaplains' Cove), a secluded inlet where priests used to bathe.

Gym Sub, Ctra Aiguablava km3.6 (℡ 972 622 659, ⓦ www.gymsub.com), and Sa Rascassa, beside the small jetty in Aiguafreda (℡ 972 624 247), both offer diving courses, equipment rental and excursions; the latter also has kayaks for rent.

Sa Riera and around

The largest of Begur's beaches is **Sa Riera**, 2km north; it's nonetheless still a manageable size and retains its fishermen's quarter on the south side of the sandy, blue-flag beach. Backed by a short row of cafés and a couple of hotels, the beach is popular with local families but rarely gets packed. The beach is signposted off the Sa Tuna road, or you can follow a spectacular but arduous stretch of the Camí de Ronda from Aiguafreda (takes 1hr).

From the north end of the beach, steps take you on to a much gentler part of the Camí de Ronda, which is the only way to cover the 500m to the minuscule and almost empty beaches between Sa Riera and the **Platja de l'Illa Roja**, an idyllic nudist beach framed by steep cliffs. The red island which gives the beach its name is, in fact, joined to the mainland by a short spit of sand; at almost the same height as the cliff, the islet towers over the cove. To get to the beach, you'll need to walk another five minutes along to where steps lead down to the next cove, the longer **Cala Moreta** – with nude and clothed bathing plus a *xiringuito* – and double back along the shore.

EATING

Virtually all of the beach towns have terrace bars and **restaurants**, which are ideal for a snack or *plat combinat* at lunchtime, although you'll find that the less upmarket ones tend to close in the evening. Begur itself has a wide choice, mostly located around c/Pi i Tató and c/Pi i Ralló.

Aiguaclara

c/Sta Teresa 3, Begur ☎ 972 622 905.

Daily 8–11pm.

Set in a Indiano mansion, this is one of the priciest restaurants in town, known locally for its seafood. In summer, the walled garden provides an enchanting, torchlit setting for an unhurried dinner, while the high-ceilinged interior is nice and bright. Expensive.

Blau de Begur

c/Pi i Ralló 10, Begur.

Daily 8pm–midnight.

The best place in town for evening tapas, a tiny, modern bar in an old house that attracts a lively local crowd. Try everything, but make sure you don't miss the walnut bread with cheese or the *Xoricets al Txakolí* (Basque white wine). Budget.

Can Torrades

c/Pi i Tató 5, Begur.

Daily 8pm–midnight; closed all

BEGUR AND AROUND

Oct & Nov–April Mon–Thurs. For excellent traditional Catalan cooking, follow the bright young things past the art gallery anteroom into the warmly lit stone courtyard of this deceptively large old house off Plaça de la Vila. The grilled meats and fresh fish are superb, or try the *escalivada* or *manchego* cheese with *pà amb tomàquet*. Moderate.

Cap Sa Sal

Cala d'Aiguafreda ⓣ 972 623 254.

This luxurious place among the trees is set to become part of Girona's gourmet trail: its dynamic young chef specializes in marrying traditional ways of preparing local produce with an original, personal touch. Expensive.

Casa de la Playa

Platja d'Aiguablava.
Daily 8–11.30pm; closed Nov–March.

A sumptuous garden restaurant atop a staircase above the beach. With a quality to match its high prices, its outstanding dishes in a wide-ranging Catalan menu are the grilled fish, meats and sausages. Expensive.

La Creperia de Begur

c/St Josep 1, Begur.
Daily 7pm–2.30am; closed Oct–May.

Favoured by a younger crowd, this funky restaurant with a peaceful, verdant terrace is a good place for a meal of savoury Breton galettes, sweet crêpes and salads. There's live music of varying styles every Thursday in August. Budget.

La Ola

c/Pi i Ralló 4, Begur.
Daily 8pm–midnight; Oct–May closed Mon–Thurs; also closed Nov & Dec.

Also housing a lively bar, this unique French Catalan restaurant is reached through a modernistic blue-neon entrance which belies the warm traditional architecture of the interior. Specializing in imaginative meat, fish and salad dishes, the grilled *calamars* with pesto and romesco sauce are extremely tasty, and the mint courgette soup is a dream. Moderate.

Pizzeta

c/Ventura Sabater 2–4, Begur.

Daily 8pm–midnight; closed Jan & Feb.

An unprepossessing entrance leads into a surprisingly large, colonial-style garden. The pizzas are tasty and large, while the healthy portions of fresh pasta and salads are also good. Inexpensive.

El Rebost de Begur

c/Campuig 1, Begur.

Daily 8pm–midnight; Oct–May closed Mon–Thurs.

Cheerful restaurant in an old corner cottage about 100m from Plaça Església, which specializes in filling *pà amb tomàquet* meals – try the *fuet*, *llonganissa* or grilled cheese

ones – and large salads. Also generous servings of anchovy fillets and piping-hot stuffed aubergines. Inexpensive.

Sa Rascassa

Cala d'Aiguafreda 3.

Closed Nov–March.

This old stone house with a shaded garden 50m from the beach serves imaginative variations on traditional Catalan cooking and offers a good choice for veggies. Inexpensive.

Sa Tuna

Platja de Sa Tuna.

Closed Oct–March.

This lovely terrace restaurant on the beach is something of an institution and serves extremely good fish and seafood and solid Catalan fare, including some veggie dishes. Moderate.

DRINKING AND NIGHTLIFE

The beach towns wind down at night, so Begur is the place for an evening **drink**. Catering entirely for local tastes, the town's bars can either be laid-back affairs or lively hotspots. Most are great places to show off your tan, wealth, looks or all three, and many encourage impromptu dancing.

BEGUR AND AROUND

Can Marc

c/Creu 5.

Easter–Oct daily midnight–5am;
Nov–March Fri & Sat
11pm–5am.

Begur's only club, set in a
lovely old building with a
large garden overlooking the
town and castle. Catering for
all ages, the dance area plays a
mix of house and disco, while
the garden's three bars are
popular for chilling out. A
room off the garden starts
serving *torrades* from around
midnight.

Carpa's

Ctra d'Esclanya km1.

July & Aug daily midnight–5am;
April–June & Sept Fri & Sat
same hours. €6.

A complex of about a dozen
open-air nightspots set up
every summer by designer
bars in Girona, Barcelona and
Begur; look for white canvas
awnings and bright lights
amid the trees to the right,
just out of town on the
Palafrugell road. Drinks are
expensive, so look out for the
flyers in bars and restaurants
in Begur giving discounted
admission.

Classic

c/Pi i Ralló 3.

This curious nightspot –
which claims, without
apparent foundation, to be a
karaoke bar – spreads over the
first-floor rooms of an old
mansion, decorated in
Indiano style with cushioned
benches running around the
walls in the quieter areas.

Havana

c/Pi i Tató 7.

A stylish bar with a large
terrace at the rear looking up
to the floodlit castle, serving
the best caipirinhas and
mojitos in town. This is
where the smart crowd comes
after dining to dance to salsa
and merengue or just mellow
outside under the stars.

L'Últim

c/Pi i Ralló 13.

The last breathless stop in a
short street heaving with bars
and restaurants, this small
place still has room for three
areas. Behind the main bar is
a terrace with an enormous
Gothic font, while to the side
is a dark dance floor, playing
mainly house, with dimly

discernible erotic art on the walls.

Vicious
c/Pi i Tató 3.
The main reason for stopping off in this friendly bar is not the eclectic music or the laid-back atmosphere, but the sculptures created by the owner: he produces some amazing works of art, some of them highly erotic, from bits of recycled iron.

LISTINGS

Banks Most banks have branches with ATMs around Pl de la Vila; there's also one on Pl Forgas.
Health centre The nearest health centre is in Palafrugell; the hospital is in Palamós. There's a **Municipal Medical Dispensary** c/Pella i Forgas (☎ 972 622 025).
Internet La Creperia de Begur, c/St Josep 1 in Begur (see p.218).

Pharmacy Opposite the tourist office on Avgda Onze de Setembre.
Police In the town hall on Pl Església (☎ 972 624 020).
Post office c/Ventura Sabater 3.
Taxis The town's two taxis operate from c/Camí del Mar 1 (☎ 972 622 187) and Pl Forgas (☎ 630 980 895).

Pals and Platja de Pals

Well signposted from the Torroella de Montgrí–Palafrugell road, the old quarter of **PALS** sits atop a hill 6km north-west of Begur. The medieval town was destroyed and abandoned during the Civil War, and then painstakingly restored after 1948 by a local character, one Dr Pi i

Figueras, in a thirty-year labour of love. Winning numerous architectural awards and attracting wealthy second-home owners has had an unfortunate side effect, though: Pals suffers from swarms of visitors and has the feel of a showcase, although it has an interesting museum and craft shops. Northeast of town is the expansive sweep of the **Platja de Pals**.

THE TOWN

Pals is very compact, and you can take in everything of interest in a couple of hours; to see it at its best, arrive before lunch or in the late afternoon, both to catch the craft and pottery shops when they're open and also to avoid the deathly quiet of the middle of the day.

On the main street into the old town is the **Museu-Casa de Cultura Ca La Pruna**, c/La Mina (Mon–Sat 10am–2pm & 5–9pm, Sun 10am–2pm; €3), an alluring museum chronicling key aspects in Pals' history, most notably underwater archeology, wine and cava production, and a facsimile of an eighteenth-century pharmacy.

Hub of the town is the **Plaça Major**, 100m northeast of the museum, dotted with craft shops and a café. The atmospheric Carrer Major climbs off northeast, where pre-second century AD **Visigoth graves** were discovered during Pals' restoration; their shallow, boat-like shapes are clearly visible in alcoves to the right as you go up the street. Almost at the top of this rise is the **Església de St Pere**, built in the fifteenth century using stones from the ruined castle that once stood here. The site was first documented in 994, and the current building includes a tenth-century Romanesque layout, a fifteenth-century Gothic apse and nave, ornate seventeenth-century Baroque facade and eighteenth-century belfry. It's strangely austere inside, with an intricate vaulted ceiling framing a simple altar.

Above the church is the towering eleventh-century Romanesque **Torre de les Hores** clock tower. Some 50m north of here, a section of the twelfth-century **walls** is still standing, while at a small gap in them, the small **Mirador de Josep Pla** square gives great views towards the offshore marine reserve of Les Illes Medes (see p.252).

PLATJA DE PALS

The golden sands of the **Platja de Pals**, 6km northeast of the medieval town, sweep round their bay for 3.5km – although they're hidden by the last uninspiring stretch of road leading to the car park. Popular with a sporty set, it does get crowded, but if you're prepared to walk 100m or so in either direction you can usually find reasonably empty parts to bathe in and settle down for the day away from the hordes. Shelving fairly gently, the sea is very good for swimming, and there are stands along the length of the beach renting out windsurfing equipment or kayaks. The red and white masts that frame the beach are all that is left of Radio Liberty, a US station which broadcast propaganda to the Eastern bloc during the Cold War.

PRACTICALITIES

There's plenty of **parking** at the entrance to the medieval town and by Platja de Pals. **Buses** linking Pals with Girona and other nearby coastal towns stop on Carrer Enginyer Algarra, the main street running through the new town. In summer (July & Aug), four buses a day run between Pals and Platja de Pals (€1.50).

By the roundabout on the north side of town, the modern **tourist office**, c/Aniceta Figueres 6 (June–Sept Mon–Sat 9am–9pm, Sun 10am–2pm & 4–8pm; Oct–May Mon–Fri 9am–2pm, Sat & Sun 10am–2pm; ☎972 667

857), has good information about Pals and the region. There's a smaller **branch** in the town hall, Plaça Major 7 (Mon, Tues & Thurs–Sun 10am–2pm & 4–8pm, Wed & Sat 9am–9pm; ☎972 637 380).

Accommodation

The best **hotels** are in Platja de Pals or along the Carretera de Torroella. A short distance from the beach on one of Spain's most prestigious golf courses (see p.50) is the plush *La Costa*, Platja de Pals (☎972 667 740, ℻972 667 736, ⓦwww.lacostahotel.com; ❽; closed Dec & Jan), boasting a huge pool, good bars and some golfing holidays. The tranquil *Lindos Huespedes*, 1km north of Pals on the Torroella road (☎972 668 203; ❸), has rooms in a charmingly run-down old mansion beside a river, while the sprawling farmhouse *Mas Pericay*, Barri Camargues (☎972 636 871; ❷), offers large self-catering **apartments** around a pool in the peaceful Masos de Pals area 1km west of Platja de Pals. The **campsite** *Delfín Verde*, Mas Pinell (☎972 758 450, ℻972 760 070, ⓦwww.eldelfinverde.com; ❶), 2km north, is right on the beach and has a good pool and amenities.

Eating and drinking

Medieval Pals is short on **restaurants**, and the majority of those in the new town and Platja de Pals are generic *plat combinat* places. *Bona Vista*, c/Muralla 5 (closed Mon & Jan; moderate), a terrace restaurant in an old house in the town walls north of Plaça Major, serves excellent local rice dishes and desserts. Also in the old town, *El Pedró*, Placeta d'en Bou 29 (closed Thurs & Sun eve; also closed Jan; moderate), serves upbeat Catalan fare and some *mar i muntanya* dishes: plump for the apples stuffed with beef and pine nuts. There are a couple of terrace **bars** around Plaça Major and a few at Platja de Pals, but nightlife as such is non-existent.

Peratallada

The medieval walled town of **PERATALLADA**, 6km west of Pals, has managed to preserve its rustic feel while still injecting a vitality into its labyrinth of narrow streets and squares. Restaurants, hotels and craft shops coexist surprisingly harmoniously with their thirteenth-century Romanesque surroundings, while a relatively low degree of second-home ownership means Peratallada has less of a museum atmosphere than nearby Pals. It's a fine place for a pleasant stroll followed by a good meal, and serves equally well as a quiet, inland base from which to explore the whole Baix Empordà.

THE TOWN

Peratallada (which means "hewn stone") is separated from the outside world by a shallow **moat** carved out of the rock. In its medieval heyday, it was one of Catalonia's best protected towns, with a defensive system comprising three ranks of **walls**, parts of which can still be seen running parallel to the main road outside the moat.

Inside the moat, a short street leads to the low porticoes of the lively **Plaça de les Voltes**, with its terrace bars, craft shops. Adjacent is the larger **Plaça del Castell**, dominated by the **Castell de Peratallada**, the ancient palace of the Barons of Peratallada – now a hotel – where the atmospheric ruins of the Torre d'Homenatge dels Cavallers (Knights' Homage Tower), a five-storey tower with dungeons,

PERATALLADA

refectory and defences, is open to the public (€6). From July to September, both Plaça de les Voltes and Plaça del Castell host Saturday crafts and produce markets.

Outside the walls and across the main road to the northeast of the town is the thirteenth-century Romanesque **Església de Sant Esteve**, remarkable for its imposing facade with four bells. It's rarely open outside services, but it's worth getting in to see the unusual double nave connected by arches and the Gothic ossuary in the north nave, dated 1348, which contains the bones of Gilabert de Cruïlles, lord of Begur (see p.213).

The neighbouring village of **Palau-Sator**, 2km east, houses a medieval clock tower and walls, and where there are four equally good restaurants, while **St Julià de Boada**, 1km further east, boasts a beguiling tenth-century chapel.

PRACTICALITIES

The nearest **bus** stop to the town is on the Torroella de Montgrí road about 2km north of Pals; signposts point to Peratallada, which lies a further 5km west. There's a **car park** (€1.50 per day) outside the town. There's no tourist office, but most shops stock a free map.

Accommodation

Peratallada boasts a small number of exceptional **hotels**. The friendly *Hostal La Riera*, Pl de les Voltes 3 (☏972 634 142, ⨍ 972 635 040; ❹), occupies a seventeenth-century building under the arches at the entrance to the village, with huge rooms giving onto a private garden. Quiet and welcoming *Hostal Miralluna*, Pl de l'Oli 2 (☏ & ⨍972 634 304; ❻), in an eighteenth-century house set back from the street, stands shaded by its carefully tended private garden. All six rooms, including two suites, are individually designed. *El Pati*, c/Hospital 13 (☎972 634 069, ⓦwww.hotelelpati.net; ❻), is a tastefully decorated hotel in an eighteenth-century mansion near the church. All five rooms give onto the sunken garden, replete with hammocks and loungers, and breakfast (included in the price) is served beneath fig trees and bougainvillea. Finally, there's unadulterated luxury on offer at the tenth-century *Castell de Peratallada*, Pl del Castell 1 (☎972 634 021, ☏972 634 011, ⓦwww.castelldeperatallada.com; ❾), at the heart of the village. Its eight rooms, some with four-poster beds, are big enough to lose yourself in, and are beautifully decorated in keeping with the setting, while the restaurant is famous throughout Catalonia.

Can Massanes (☎972 634 235, ⓦwww.ruralplus.com /canmassanes; ❷), a lovely nineteenth-century **turisme rural** house with pool in the neighbouring hamlet of Fontclara, has self-catering apartments.

Eating and drinking

Peratallada – already well known for the outstanding restaurant at the *Castell de Peratallada* hotel – is rapidly gaining standing for the quality of its **restaurants**, while its terrace **bars** on Plaça de les Voltes stay open all day and into the small hours.

Bonay
Pl de les Voltes 13.
Closed Mon and Nov.
This cluttered restaurant, founded in 1936, specializes in Catalan cooking, with some *mar i muntanya* dishes, and is good for game in winter. Don't miss the mouthwatering dessert buffet. Moderate.

Candelària
c/Major 9.
July–Sept daily 8pm–midnight; Oct–June Fri–Sun 8pm–midnight, plus Sat 1–4pm; closed Feb.
A slightly surreal cavern with

PERATALLADA

dried corn and St John's Wort – Salvador Dalí's favourite flower – hanging from the ceiling and a hotch-potch of mirrors and paintings cluttering the walls. The food is eclectically inspired, especially the variety of duck dishes. Expensive.

El Castell de Peratallada
Pl del Castell 1 ☏ 972 634 021.
Set in the castle's oratory, this top-flight restaurant serves some of the best Empordà cuisine in the region and has a wine list to match. Expensive.

La Païssa d'en Cardina
c/Jaume II, 10.
Mon–Fri 7pm–12.30am, Sat & Sun 1–4pm & 8pm–12.30am; Nov–March closed Wed & Thurs.
Friendly, excellent-value pizzeria with a hugely stylish interior and terrace. There are 33 different pizzas,

complemented by an imaginative choice of fresh pasta, tasty salads and grilled vegetables. Moderate.

Papibou
c/Major 10.
Closed Wed.
Empordà cuisine only served in a subtly lit stone-vaulted interior or on the cosy terrace off the street. Highlights are duck and veal with aubergines, and platters of homemade cheeses and pâtés with *pà amb tomàquet*. Inexpensive.

El Pati
c/Hospital 13 ☏ 972 634 069.
Even more inviting than the eighteenth-century interior is the lush shaded garden for a meal of traditional Catalan fare under the stars. Specialities include local meat dishes and some veggie options. Expensive.

PERATALLADA

Ullastret

ULLASTRET, a peaceful walled town atop a low hill, lies 6km northwest of Peratallada. Although enjoyable in itself, it's known for the nearby **Poblat Ibéric d'Ullastret**, a ruined Iberian settlement. You'll really need your own transport to get to either, as the nearest bus stop is in La Bisbal, a good 7km south.

A burgeoning crafts centre, medieval Ullastret makes for a pleasant half-day's pottering among the maze of shops around the central **Plaça de l'Església**, venue for the town's lively Festa Major on the second weekend in August and site of the eleventh-century **Església de Sant Pere**, a charming Romanesque church adorned with an elaborate Baroque facade. Parts of the original Romanesque front were reused for the interior, such as the bases of the arches – one with the original eleventh-century carving of a lion, another with mermaids – which look slightly incongruous in their new setting.

POBLAT IBÉRIC D'ULLASTRET

Tues–Sun: Easter & June–Sept 10am–8pm; Oct–May 10am–6pm. €1.80.

Nestling amid olive groves and cypresses atop the Puig de Sant Andreu, which dominates the Empordà flood plain, the **Poblat Ibéric d'Ullastret** (signposted 3km east of the medieval town) is the most significant and extensive settlement in Catalonia of the Iberians, who are considered Spain's first historic culture: they had their own system of writing – as yet undeciphered – and money, as well as agriculture, metallurgy and pottery. The Ullastret settlement, located in what is thought to have been the heartland of the Indiketa tribe (see p.345), was populated between the sixth

ULLASTRET

229

and second century BC; there's still a great deal left to unearth, including a second site some 500m across the plain, which probably formed part of the same settlement.

There's a **car park** at the base of the hill, but you can also park near the main entrance; drive through the first gate past the ticket booth. Running north inside the entrance, the sixth-century BC **walls**, the oldest and one of the largest Iberian defences in Catalonia, house seven circular towers and, 50m from the gate, a newer **square tower**, where the remains of an earlier round structure can be seen at the base; traces of a stairway still cling to the sides. The most striking feature of the settlement is its modern layout: you can easily make out the **streets**, including a beautifully preserved cobbled roadway leading to a water cistern, flanked by the foundations of rectangular **houses**.

Outside the museum, at the top of the hill, you can discern the outlines of two **temples**; it's still not known which gods were worshipped here. Another curiosity is the ruin of a **medieval castle** wall and tower, built in the ninth century and abandoned three hundred years later, about which little is known.

The museum

The superbly laid-out site **museum** on the summit of the hill chronicles the history of the settlement, and uses finds to explain Iberian lifestyles. You can pick up a free returnable booklet at the entrance, which contains an English translation of the display panels. The most fascinating exhibits are some lead tablets marked with writing to record commerce, along with coins for trading with other tribes and – more gruesomely – the skulls of victims of ceremonial execution, pierced by spikes.

ULLASTRET

PRACTICALITIES

The atmospheric *Hostal El Fort*, c/del Presó 2 in Ullastret town (Ⓣ972 757 773; ❹), is a peaceful **place to stay**; rooms are large and cheerful, and there's a good **restaurant** which takes an imaginative slant on traditional Catalan cuisine. A short distance northeast of town, in the hamlet of Llabià, *Can Pau* (Ⓣ972 760 262; ❷) is a good **turisme rural** option, with rooms for rent in the stone family home.

La Bisbal and around

The medieval market town of **LA BISBAL**, the county seat of the Baix Empordà located midway between Girona and the coast, is famous for its distinctive **ceramics**, produced here since the seventeenth century; people come from all over the region to buy ceramic wares from a string of outlets in the town, and the industry is chronicled in the fascinating **Museu Terracota**. The old town retains the imposing and beautifully preserved **Castell Palau de La Bisbal**, with its chapel built intriguingly on the roof, and a seventeenth-century bridge spanning the River Daró.

Northwest of La Bisbal is the small town of **Púbol**, site of a castle once owned by **Salvador Dalí** that is now a major museum.

ARRIVAL AND INFORMATION

La Bisbal straddles the busy C255 **road** between Girona and Palamós, and has ample **parking**. Regular **buses** from Girona and around the region stop near the traffic lights on the central Avinguda de les Voltes.

The small but informative **tourist office** is inside the imposing Castell Palau de La Bisbal on Plaça Castell (Easter–Sept Tues–Sat 10.30am–1.30pm & 4.30–8.30pm, Sun 10.30am–1.30pm; Oct–March Mon–Fri 5–8pm, Sat 11am–2pm & 5–8pm, Sun 11am–2pm; ℡ 972 645 166, Ⓦ www.labisbal.org).

ACCOMMODATION

Accommodation in town is limited: *Pensió Adarnius*, Avgda de les Voltes 7 (℡ 972 640 957, Ⓕ 972 600 112; ❸), in the central arcaded avenue on the main road opposite the old town, is the best on offer; its en-suite rooms are small, and some can get noisy, but they're comfortable enough for a short stay. Dominating the bluff-top hamlet of Castell d'Empordà, 2km north, is an 800-year-old castle which once belonged to Pere Margarit, one of Columbus's captains. It's now a hotel, *Castell d'Empordà* (℡ 972 646 254, Ⓕ 972 645 550, Ⓦ www.castelldemporda.com; ❽), its sumptuous bare-stone rooms warmly decorated with tapestries and rugs.

Arcs de Monells, 3km northwest at c/Vilanova 1 in Monells (℡ 972 630 304, Ⓕ 972 630 365, Ⓦ www.hotelarcsmonells .com; ❽), is a lovely hotel in a fourteenth-century former hospital surrounded by lawns and boasting a superb restaurant and a three-tier swimming pool. Choose from huge, luxurious air-conditioned rooms (some with jacuzzis) within the cool stone walls of the original building, or modern ground-floor bedrooms on the edge of the lawns; prices are discounted off season. *Mas Torrent*, a secluded five-star hotel 9km east in Torrent (℡ 972 303 292, Ⓕ 972 303 293, Ⓦ www.mastorrent.com; ❾), is made up of suites grouped around lush gardens and a pool.

The best **turisme rural** is 3km west in Cruïlles, at *Mas Masaller*, Ctra La Bisbal km2.3 (℡ & Ⓕ 972 641 046,

ⓦ www.ruralplus.com/masaller), which has six spacious double rooms and offers B&B.

THE TOWN AND AROUND

Strung out along the main road running northwest to southeast, La Bisbal's **new town** is clearly divided into two by the River Daró, with the **old town** tucked away to the south, away from the main road and protected from passing traffic. The new town – dominated by ceramics and antiques – features the enjoyable **Museu Terracota**, while the old town boasts the splendid **Castell Palau de La Bisbal**. Nearby is the atmospheric old village of **Monells**.

The new town

Although connected by a modern road bridge, the two sides of the new town have very distinct personas. To the northwest, **Carrer Aigüeta** holds all the **ceramics shops**, most of which offer similar stock. You'll find innovative creations at El Rissec, which produces and sells good quality tableware and ornaments; Ceramiques Martí, set in an Indiano house, has more functional wares; and Rogenca d'Ullastret and Vila Clarà both offer progressive variations on traditional designs and methods. Characteristic colours are blues, greens and mustards, and look out for plates depicting the winds as points on a compass, tiles portraying traditional trades and the *auca*, a framed tile representation of crafts such as winemaking or baking.

Southeast of the bridge, the arcaded **Carrer de les Voltes** is home to a couple of terrace bars, before becoming Carrer Sis d'Octubre, where a variety of **antiques shops** sell all manner of objects from the sublime to the bizarre.

LA BISBAL AND AROUND

Museu Terracota

c/Sis d'Octubre 99. May–Sept Mon–Sat 10am–1pm & 5–9pm, Sun 10am–1pm. €3.

Housed in a former factory, which was founded in 1922, the **Museu Terracota** offers an alluring insight into La Bisbal's ceramic industry, its exhibits spanning pottery and tile-making from early manual methods to the machinery of the 1930s; you'll find artistic pieces lying alongside domestic and industrial wares.

After a room charting early processes of working clay before machinery stepped in, the cavernous main room, once the factory floor, concentrates on the industry on which the town's wealth was created. Moulds for shaping tiles stand alongside the unbearably complicated machinery used in creating them. La Bisbal pottery was widely used by Modernist architects, and a display of prototypes for the pillars built by Rafael Masó (see p.80) in S'Agaró and design elements for the seafront houses in Llafranc (see p.199) show how traditional materials were adapted to create the distinctive Modernist style. Huge brick kilns and glass floor inserts showing the colourfully tiled underground *nevera* (fridge), where clay was stored to keep it malleable, serve as a reminder that this was once a busy working factory.

The old town

Opposite the arches on Carrer de les Voltes, a number of side-streets lead into the **old town**, host to a Friday **market** since 1322 and once home to a significant Jewish quarter, the sole remnant of which is the rather drab Carrer del Call, where you can still see the grooves for the enclosures either end that sealed the ghetto at night. On the northwestern edge of the old town, the seventeenth-century Renaissance **Pont Vell**, now a footbridge, stands on the site of an earlier Romanesque bridge washed away by the once-raging torrent – hard to imagine on the evidence of the meagre trickle of the river today. The bridge was originally planned with a single arch, but the bishop of the time feared it would be swept downstream a second time and insisted on an imposing two-arched design.

Castell Palau de La Bisbal

Pl Castell. Easter–Oct Tues–Sat 10.30am–1.30pm & 4.30–8.30pm, Sun 10.30am–1.30pm; Nov–March Mon–Fri 5–8pm, Sat 11am–2pm & 5–8pm, Sun 11am–2pm. €1.80.

Highlight of the old town is the imposing eleventh-century **Castell Palau de La Bisbal** on Plaça Castell, west of the Pont Vell. The fortified palace of the bishops of Girona, it's remarkable for the fortified chapel built on the roof and the heavy defences, including a large **machicolation** over the main door. A fourteenth-century extension to the palace added outer walls and a **parade ground**, two sides of which, complete with embrasures, still stand, marking the present Plaça Castell.

Inside, to the left of the entrance, the **stables** and stone troughs are in excellent condition. Opposite the front door, excavations in 1993 turned up discoveries such as the original **well**, covered over in the fifteenth century and still containing water, while a section of wall and two silos provide evidence of a building predating the palace by up to two hundred years. To the right of this room are two perfectly preserved eighteenth-century **wine presses** connected to a stone collection pool. The remains of a small dungeon are visible off this chamber.

Steps lead up to the crenellated roof, which offers terrific views over the countryside. In one corner, the **chapel** is very simple, with a rounded stone apse, and has a trapdoor which once communicated directly with the bishop's quarters below.

Monells

The compact, fortified village of **Monells**, 3km northwest of La Bisbal, is a warren of untouched tiny squares and streets grouped around the impressive porticoed **Plaça de Jaume I**. Under the arches opposite the town hall is a reminder of the village's medieval splendour – an 1818 reproduction of the Mitgera de Monells, a standard grain measure which Jaume I decreed in 1234 was to be used for markets throughout the see of Girona.

EATING AND DRINKING

The **cafés** under the arcades on c/de les Voltes or along c/Aigüeta are good for snacks or a daytime drink, while most **restaurants** are in the old town or surrounding villages. For an evening **drink**, the liveliest places are on Pg Marimon Asprer northeast of the modern bridge, some of which have summer-only terraces on the riverbank.

Arcs de Monells

c/Vilanova 1, Monells. ☎ 972 630 304.

Overlooking the hotel gardens, this modern restaurant is fast becoming famous for its extremely good Catalan *nouvelle cuisine*. Expensive.

La Cantonada

c/Bisbe 6.
Closed Tues.
Small, stylish restaurant between the Palau Castell and the river that serves modern variations on Empordà cooking. Especially delicious are the aubergine *mil fulls* with mascarpone and tomato, and the pork chops in grape juice and honey. Inexpensive.

El Taller del Museu Abras

Ctra Girona km22, Corçà.
Much of the appeal of eating in this restaurant, 2km north of La Bisbal, lies in the surreal setting of figurative sculptor

Joan Abras's studio in an old flour mill. The traditional Catalan cuisine is very good, specializing in grilled meats and *pà amb tomàquet* meals. Moderate.

Mas Pastor

Ctra Girona km20, Corçà.

Closed Wed and Feb.

Run by a larger-than-life owner, this restaurant in an old *masía* 4km north of La Bisbal is very popular with locals, thanks to its generous servings of traditional Catalan cooking. Especially good are the baked fish, shoulder of lamb and *mel i mató*. Moderate.

Monells

c/Vilanova 11, Monells.

Closed Tues and July.

Occupying an atmospheric old house and specializing in cod – especially baked in honey – and hearty Catalan meat dishes. Inexpensive.

LISTINGS

Banks Main banks with ATMs are on c/de les Voltes.

Health centre On c/Marqués de Cruïlles, parallel to c/Aigüeta.

Pharmacy Piera de Ciurana, c/de les Voltes 1.

Police Next to the Palau Castell de La Bisbal on c/Peixateries ℡ 972 640 292.

Post office Corner of Avgda Prat de la Riba and c/Hospital, on the southern edge of the old town.

Taxis By the bridge at Pl Francesc Macià ℡ 972 643 050.

PÚBOL

The sole reason for visiting **PÚBOL**, 8km northwest of La Bisbal, is a compelling one, since this is where Salvador Dalí bought and renovated a derelict castle for his Russian wife Gala, and where he lived and worked for a couple of years after her death in 1982. The **Castell Gala-Dalí** is now a

LA BISBAL AND AROUND

museum giving an engaging insight into the couple's bizarre life together.

Castell Gala-Dalí

Tues–Sun: July–Sept 10.30am–7.30pm; March–June & Oct 10.30am–5.30pm. €4.20. ⓦ www.dali-estate.org.

Dalí bought this dilapidated fourteenth-century castle – designed on three storeys around a courtyard – in the 1960s to fulfil a promise he'd made to Gala decades earlier; he conceived it as his wife's refuge, a place where she could get away from him and which he claimed he would never visit without her permission. As he set about restoring it, Dalí preserved all the cracks, most notably a huge one running down the main facade; although it was very much Gala's domain, he couldn't resist stamping his own sense of mischief on the decor. The Costa Brava's other Dalí museums are in Figueres (see p.297) and Portlligat (see p.314).

The first floor

The first room up the steps from the courtyard is the **Sala dels Escuts** (Room of the Escutcheons), dominated by an elaborate false door in front of you. A throne in the far corner with a landscape painted on the backrest was originally for Gala, but was used by Dalí himself, after her death, to receive visitors. Gala had insisted on the radiators being covered up, so Dalí painstakingly created an alcove in the adjacent **Saló del Piano** (Piano Room), only to paint it to look like a radiator. In this same room hangs the magnificent painting *Camí a Púbol*, featuring a narrow trail leading to the castle of Púbol and tall poplar trees (the name of the village is derived from the Catalan word for poplar). In the foreground is Gala, her back turned, wearing the sailor's uniform in which Dalí often depicted her.

Next door is the **Blue Room**. Originally Gala's bedroom,

Dalí took to sleeping here after her death, and it was here that he was badly burned in an accidental fire in 1984 and forced to move to Figueres, where he lived until his death in 1989. Adjacent is the old kitchen, which the artist converted into a private **bathroom**, hiding the lavatory under the curving sweep of the fireplace. As Dalí's cryptic tribute to Vermeer and Velázquez, the tiles either side of the hearth are from the Netherlands and Seville.

In the other direction from the Blue Room are the **Lost Library**, containing a chess set designed by Dalí and dedicated to Marcel Duchamp, and the strangely austere **Red Room**, used as a guest room.

The second floor

From the Red Room, stairs lead up to the exhibition of **Gala's dresses**, featuring creations by Givenchy, Christian Dior, Pierre Cardin and Elizabeth Arden and background music from *Tristan and Isolde*, her favourite piece. The displays take on a rather macabre note when you come across a lifesize, posed model of Gala wearing the same leopard-skin print jacket and purple trousers as she did for Dalí's *Batalla als Núvols* painting. The final room upstairs is the elegant and sad **Dining Room**, where the easel on which Dalí's last works were painted stands against a wall.

The crypt, garage and gardens

Sadder still is the sight of two tombs side by side in the **crypt**. Gala is buried in one, but the other, where Dalí insisted he wanted to be interred, lies empty: the executors of his estate instead laid the artist to rest in a mausoleum in Figueres. After Gala died in Portlligat, her body was brought to Púbol in the Cadillac now displayed in the **garage** above the crypt, the same car which took Dalí away from Púbol for the last time to Figueres in 1984.

In the grounds, the **garden walk** loops past busts of

Richard Wagner around a pool as well as giant sculptures of elephants teetering on storks' legs; the crows that stand on the elephants' backs also appear on the crest of the castle's original owners.

Practicalities

Púbol is signposted off the C255 Girona road 5km north-west of La Bisbal, about 3km along the minor GI643. **Trains** on the Girona–Portbou line stop at Flaça, 4km northwest of Púbol, from where you can get a taxi (€6). **Buses** stop a short walk away on the main C255 at the GI643 junction.

The village of Foixà, 4km northeast, has a good, moderately priced Catalan **restaurant**, *Can Quel*, c/La Vila 3 (closed Mon and Sept). You can rent decent, quiet rooms at good **turisme rural** houses in La Pera, 1km northwest of Púbol: in the centre of the village is *Can Massa*, c/Vell (℡972 488 326; ❸), the smaller of the two, while *Mas Duran* (℡972 488 338; ❸) is more isolated, set in its own grounds.

Torroella de Montgrí

The Massis de Montgrí ridge runs in a straight line towards the sea, linking **TORROELLA DE MONTGRÍ**, 6km north of Pals, with its coastal offspring of L'Estartit (see p.244). Torroella is a compact and sedate medieval town which retains a fiercely Catalan feel; the best time to visit is during the summer music festival, which lends a vibrant air to the otherwise peaceable streets.

Torroella's glory days began when King Jaume I declared

The river Onyar in Girona

Cadaqués

Santa Pau

Cala Sa Bona, Tossa de Mar

SALVADOR DALI

Donació del Centre d'Art Perrot-Moore
al Poble de Cadaqués

Dalí statue, Cadaqués

NEIL SETCHFIELD

Café table, Figueres

MICHAEL JENNER

Tossa de Mar

FESTIVAL INTERNACIONAL DE MÚSIQUES

Every year, from the last weekend in July to the last weekend in August, Torroella de Montgrí stages the renowned Festival Internacional de Músiques, featuring Baroque, chamber, orchestral and world music performed in several venues around town. Tickets (€12–30) are available from mid-June onwards from the festival office (☎ 972 760 605, ⓦ www.ddgi.es/tdm/fimtdm). At the same time, there's a lively free festival of classical, jazz and traditional Catalan music staged in various town squares.

it a royal port in 1273, making it one of the most important in medieval Catalonia, following the Lords of Torroella's participation in his conquest of the Balearics. The king's long-standing rivalry with the neighbouring Counts of Empúries came to a head when the counts diverted the River Ter, destroying the port's livelihood. Since then, the town's economy has relied on agriculture, primarily the growing of rice.

THE TOWN

Torroella de Montgrí's grid-plan streets – a beautifully preserved example of thirteenth-century town planning – radiate from the porticoed **Plaça de la Vila**, which was designed as a meeting-point on the model of the Greek agora and Roman forum and boasts the fifteenth-century Ajuntament and a huge sundial dating from 1725. It is now the site of the town's bustling Monday **market**.

North of the square, the narrow Carrer Església leads 50m to the **Museu de Pintura Palau Solterra**, c/Església 10 (June–Sept Mon & Wed–Sat 5–10pm; Oct–May Sat 11am–2pm & 4.30–10.30pm, Sun 10.30am–2.30pm; €4.20), a sumptuous medieval mansion displaying temporary

TORROELLA DE MONTGRÍ

A WALK TO THE CASTELL DEL MONTGRÍ

Dominating the town and the surrounding area from its vantage point on the summit of the Massís de Montgrí, the thirteenth-century Castell del Montgrí was built by King Jaume II during his struggles with the Counts of Empúries. It was only ever partially completed, and all that stands today are the walls and towers. The steep but relatively easy kilometre-long walk from Torroella de Montgrí to the castle is best tackled early or late in the day, to avoid the midday sun and the haze which can obscure the summit views.

Set off along c/Fàtima north of the roundabout on Plaça Lledoner, following signs to the castle, and then watch out for the red and white GR92 footpath markings painted on rocks. Follow this steadily climbing footpath for half-an-hour to three tiny, derelict chapels either side of the track, originally used for worship of Santa Caterina and later occupied by shepherds. Shortly after, the path divides at a stone cross; follow the right fork. The castle is straight on, but it's worth taking a short, scrambling detour signposted to the right for El Cau del Duc (The Eagle's Lair), one of a series of fifty-odd caverns hereabouts; archeological finds have shown that this strategic site – named after the eagle owls which used to nest on the massif – was occupied by humans 300,000 years ago. Backtracking to the original path, there's just another 50m to go before you come out onto a plateau, where the castle's massive walls rear up in front of you.

The interior of the castle was laid out around a square inner courtyard, and, although the structure was never built, keystones and arch bases set into the walls give an idea of how the finished castle would have looked. Inside, steps lead up to the walls, from where you'll be rewarded with a breathtaking panorama of the coastline from Begur in the south to Cap de Creus in the northeast, and the Pyrenees to the northwest.

exhibitions of contemporary Catalan paintings that is also a venue for the music festival. At the end of the street, a passage at the north end of the broad Passeig de l'Església (which itself holds world **crafts market** on the second weekend in Aug) leads into a small square giving access to the imposing Gothic **Església de St Genís**. Started during the prosperous years of the fourteenth century, it was intended as a cathedral – which explains its size and outward splendour – although the town's decline in fortune is marked by the unfinished eighteenth-century belfry. The interior is contrastingly simple, the only highlight being the medieval font. North of the church, the fourteenth-century **Portal de Santa Caterina** is the only remaining part of the town wall.

Heading south towards Palafrugell, you cross a **road bridge** built in the summer of 1942 by the slave labour of 300 Republican prisoners of war, and subsequently known as "The Bridge Over the River Ter". A road off to the left (east) after this leads 6km to the sweeping **Platja de la Gola**, a less-crowded extension of L'Estartit's sandy beach.

PRACTICALITIES

A natural crossroads, Torroella de Montgrí links the network of local roads connecting the Baix Empordà and the Alt Empordà, and channels traffic along the single road heading out to L'Estartit. There's a free **car park** on the road to L'Estartit, next to a very helpful seasonal **tourist information** stand (June–Sept Mon 10am–2pm, Tues–Sat 10am–1pm & 5–8pm).

Fifteen **buses** a day (hourly 7am–10pm) link Torroella with L'Estartit, and Torroella has good regular links up and down the coast from its bus stop on Plaça Lledoner. There's a **taxi** rank at the corner of Passeig de Catalunya and Plaça Ledoner (☎972 757 964).

TORROELLA DE MONTGRÍ

For **accommodation**, the charming *Fonda Mitjà*, north of Plaça de la Vila at c/Església 14 (⊤ 972 758 003; ❷), offers good-value en-suite rooms. Beside the church, the fabulous ninth-century *Palau Lo Mirador*, Passeig de l'Església 1 (⊤ 972 758 063, ⨍ 972 758 246, ⊛ www .palaumirador.com; ❾), once the royal palace of Jaume I, provides king-sized luxury rooms and a refreshing swimming pool set in lush grounds. The fortified eighteenth-century farmhouse of *Mas d'en Bou*, 4km east of Torroella (⊤ 972 752 177, ⊛ www.ruralplus.com/masdenbou; ❷), has three large self-catering **apartments**.

The moated medieval town of Verges, 7km west of Torroella, hosts the macabre Ball dels Morts (Dance of the Dead; see p.46) every Easter.

L'Estartit and Les Illes Medes

At the end of the road from Torroella de Montgrí, **L'ESTARTIT**, 6km east, grew in the nineteenth century as Torroella's port, exporting rice and wine, but the balance between the towns changed with the advent of tourism. These days, L'Estartit has a deserved reputation for being a classic pack-'em-in tourist spot. Parts of it are an unsightly sprawl of high-rises – with places serving all-day English breakfasts depressingly apparent – but the area around the **port**, favoured by the locals, has retained much of its original identity.

The **Les Illes Medes** marine wildlife reserve 1km offshore plays host to an extraordinary variety of species of flora and fauna. Now strictly protected, the islands have turned L'Estartit into a magnet for divers and watersports enthusiasts in general.

ARRIVAL AND INFORMATION

Buses run to L'Estartit from Barcelona (4 per day) and Girona (another 4 per day); from other places, you'll have to change at Torroella, from where there are regular services (see p.243). All arrive at the bus stop on the Passeig Marítim, near the helpful **tourist office**, Pg Marítim 33 (Easter–Sept Mon–Sat 9am–2pm & 4–9pm, Sun 9am–2pm; Oct–March Mon–Sat 9am–1pm & 3–6pm, Sun 10am–2pm; ☎972 751 910, ⓦwww.ddgi.es/tdm). There's plenty of **parking** on the beach (free) or by the port (€1.50/hr).

ACCOMMODATION

Most of L'Estartit's **hotels** deal with package-tour operators and are not always as comfortable as they might be, despite their star rating. Unless you take a package, you'll often get better value for money at a two-star hotel or *hostal*. Good **campsites** abound, while self-catering **apartments** are mainly at the Griells end of town, some distance from the centre; Ceigrup, Avgda Grècia 20 (☎972 751 744, ⓕ972 751 957, ⓦwww.torrent-api.com), has a wide selection.

HOTELS

Bell Aire
c/Església 39 ☎ 972 751 302,
ⓕ 972 751 958,
ⓦ www.hotelbellaire.com.
Closed Oct–March.

This reasonable-value hotel is 100m from the beach and has decent-sized en-suite rooms overlooking its own garden. ❺

L'ESTARTIT AND LES ILLES MEDES

Hostal Egara

c/Església 38 ⓣ & ⓕ 972 751 120, ⓔ hs_egara@hotmail.com. Closed Nov–April.
One of the quieter options, a friendly, central *hostal* set back from the road behind a shaded garden. Rooms are simple but comfortable, all with their own bathroom and balcony. ❸

Les Illes

c/Illes 55 ⓣ 972 751 239, ⓕ 972 750 086,
ⓦ www.hotellesilles.com. Closed Feb.
Top choice for serious divers, opposite the port, offering a wide range of reasonable packages that include diving lessons or excursions; half or full board is compulsory. Rooms are a little dark, but are all en suite with a balcony. ❺

Miramar

Avgda Roma 13–21 ⓣ 972 750 628, ⓕ 972 750 500,
ⓦ www.hotelmiramar.net. Closed Nov–April.
Pleasant, old-fashioned seafront hotel set in dense gardens; the owners work with agencies, so you might get a better deal through a tour operator. The airy rooms are all en suite with a balcony giving onto the gardens. Half board only in August. ❻

Santa Anna

c/del Port 46 ⓣ 972 751 326, ⓕ 972 750 842,
ⓦ www.hotelsantaanna.com.
Smart hotel near the port with comfortable en-suite rooms, some with balcony. Organizes golfing, diving and cycling holidays. Prices include breakfast. ❺

Univers

c/Victor Concas 7 ⓣ 972 750 570, ⓕ 972 750 687,
ⓦ www.hotelunivers.com. Closed Nov–March.
Pleasant two-star hotel about 100m from the beach near the town centre: revellers in the street below can make it noisy at night. All the rooms are airy and pleasant, each with bathroom and balcony. ❹

Pensió Vila

c/Santa Anna 41 ⓣ 972 751 113.

Closed Nov–March.
Cheerful *pensió* in the centre (and so noisy at night), catering mainly for a younger crowd. The rooms are very simple but good value for money. A filling *menú del dia* for €5.50 is also available. ②

CAMPSITES

Castell Montgrí

Ctra de Torroella km4.7 ⓣ 972 751 630, ⓕ 972 759 906, ⓦ www.campingparks.com.
Lovely site arranged in terraces on a hill 500m outside town. Amenities are excellent and the large, shaded pitches are fairly secluded. Spacious mobile homes also available.

Les Medes

Paratge Camp de l'Arbre ⓣ 972 751 805, ⓕ 972 750 413, ⓦ www.campinglesmedes.com.
Closed Nov.
Best site around, with a quality award to show for it; 2km from L'Estartit and about 800m from the beach. Built around a landscaped pool with plenty of shade, amenities are exemplary, as are the plush chalets.

Rifort

Ctra de Torroella ⓣ 972 750 406, ⓕ 972 751 722, ⓔ campingrifort @mx3.redestb.es.
Closed Oct–March.
Most central choice, beside the roundabout at the entrance to town, and well shaded with a pool and decent apartments for rent.

THE TOWN

L'Estartit gives the impression of being divided into two unequal parts. There's no reason to linger in the first, larger, section, which includes the entrance to the town from Torroella and the residential district of **Griells** to the south. In contrast, the **port** area is attractive and characterful, home to some good bars and restaurants, and is also a thriving

L'ESTARTIT AND LES ILLES MEDES

BOAT TRIPS FROM L'ESTARTIT

Lined up along L'Estartit's port at c/Gambina are the kiosks of about a dozen companies offering boat trips to the Illes Medes and various other spots. Most of what's on offer is self-explanatory, although there are a few trips that stand out. Nautilus has good trimarans with underwater viewing hulls for trips to the islands (€12), while the snazzy *Subcat* submergible catamaran (book on ☎ 972 752 505; €18) goes 15–30m under the waves around the islands and along the coast. Marina Princess (☎ 972 750 643, ⊕ www.marinaprincess.com) runs trips to Palamós in the south and Cadaqués in the north (€22), while La Sirena (☎ 972 752 233) offers shorter trips to L'Escala and Roses, as well as moonlight cruises (€18).

fishing concern and leisure marina based around diving and visits to the Illes Medes. Framed by the pine-covered Roca Maura escarpment, where the Gavarres range drops into the sea, the port hasn't been blighted by high-rise development, thanks largely to the fact that the land is too unstable to support new buildings.

An efficient mini-train runs between Griells and the port (daily 9.30am–midnight, every 30min; €1.50 one-way, €2.70 return). Buy tickets from the tourist office.

A road past the quayside, the Passeig Molinet, leads out to the windswept **Cap de Barra** headland, a favourite venue for early evening strolls, which affords excellent views of the islands and the choppy waters and gull-strewn cliffs of the Molinet cove. The rest of this headland is only really accessible by sea, and it's worth taking one of the **boat trips** that hug the coastline here to see the natural arch of Roca Foradada or to **snorkel** or **dive** in the species-rich waters of the Golfet del Falaguer.

From the port, L'Estartit's **beach** stretches some 5km south, boasting fine golden sand all the way along, with very gently shelving water. It gets pretty crowded in August, although you can find less populated parts if you're prepared to walk away from town. Several beach operators run water-skiing, jet-bikes and the like. The Aero Club, Ctra de Torroella (☎972 752 058, ⓦwww.ultraligeros.com), has accompanied microlight flights, and Club Hípic Estartit, c/del Riu 43 (☎972 751 472), offers horse riding on the beach.

Framing the port, the **town centre** is surprisingly small, centring on the Plaça de l'Església, a short section of the pleasant Passeig Marítim and the fairly ordinary shopping street of c/Sta Anna. On one side of its square, the **Església de Santa Anna**, built in 1920 and open during the day, is beautiful in its simplicity: its whitewashed walls and sturdy belfry are set off by a single palm beside the door and the backdrop of the escarpment. Inside, two non-figurative stained-glass windows illuminate both ends of the transept. Crowned by a wrought-iron representation of the town's seafaring history, the marble altar and pink marble altarpiece with a wood and glass insert are supremely elegant.

EATING

L'Estartit holds a broad choice of **places to eat**, ranging from the burger bars around the Avgda de Grècia and in Griells to fresh fish and seafood restaurants and some excellent tapas bars in the port.

Els Arquets
Pg Marítim 21.
Daily 1pm–midnight; closed Nov–Easter.
Best pizzas and pasta in town, as borne out by the queues. There's a pleasant terrace downstairs, and a more private upstairs balcony with great views of the port. Moderate.

La Gaviota
Pg Marítim 92.
Closed mid-Nov to mid-Dec.

One of the town's most traditional restaurants, famous throughout Catalonia for its seafood – including some *mar i muntanya* dishes – and good wine list. Anchovies, or turbot with truffles, are worth trying, as is the strawberry cheesecake. Expensive.

Gourmet
c/de les Illes 21.
Closed Feb.

Modern Catalan restaurant that is very popular with the locals and serves upbeat versions of traditional fare, the best dishes being rice casserole, roast lamb and the selection of seafood tapas. Inexpensive.

N'Gruna
Pg Marítim 20.
Daily 9am–3am; Nov–March closed Mon–Fri.

Friendly terrace bar serving an excellent range of tapas and one of the best breakfasts in town. Try the banana and strawberry *granissat* for a cooling drink during the day. At night it doubles up as a bar, with a good line in cocktails. Inexpensive.

Noray
Pg Marítim 13.

Small, imaginative restaurant serving tapas at lunchtime and an eclectic choice of meals at night. Fondues are the speciality (chicken and beef as well as cheese), and the deep-fried Camembert is good, too. Inexpensive.

Robert
Pg Marítim 59.
Nov–March closed Mon–Fri.

Occupying a Modernist house dating from 1917, with a beautiful shaded garden on the seafront, this imaginative Catalan restaurant is excellent value for money, offering a range of *menús del dia* from €12 to €21. The wine list is superb and the fish and seafood grills are huge. Good choice for vegetarians. Moderate.

DRINKING AND NIGHTLIFE

L'Estartit has two distinct **nightlife** areas. The block around Plaça del Timó by c/Coral, c/Eivissa and Passatge Vela houses a raucous collection of dismal British-style pubs, while the port offers a more Catalan feel with stylish music **bars** and mellow terraces.

Absolut Vodka
c/Eivissa 57.
Closed Nov–March.
The best of the bars around Pl Timó, playing some excellent Spanish Caribbean sounds, mainly salsa, cumbia, merengue and rumba, and offering free salsa lessons every night. The mojitos and caipirinhas are great.

Can Bernat
c/del Port 2.
Daily 10am–2am.
Traditional fishermen's tavern founded in 1926, serving *torrades* during the day; at night, the terrace is a great place to kick back with cocktails or a *cremat*.

Líquid
Pg Marítim 25.
Nov–March closed Mon–Fri.
Trendy but laid-back bar with an excellent terrace for watching the world go by. After midnight, as the crowds build up, the pre-club drinking moves inside.

Mariscal
c/Barcelona 51.
Dust off your air guitars for the best craic in town. Ageing and not-so-ageing rockers, both local and tourist, flock to this hugely enjoyable bar playing sixties, seventies and eighties rock. Two or three live bands play live each week for an enthusiastic audience – watch for posters around town or in the tourist office.

Maxim's
c/Primavera s/n. €6.
A five-minute walk from the centre, along the road leading to the rock overlooking the town, this huge club – spread over four floors and playing mainly house – caters for a

L'ESTARTIT AND LES ILLES MEDES

young crowd. The large garden is a welcome respite from the packed dance floors.

Podium
c/Áncora s/n.
This small disco-bar in the Pl

Timó area plays dance and house to a young, primarily tourist, crowd. The action gets underway by 9pm, very early by Catalan standards.

LISTINGS

Banks The main banks have ATMs around Pl Església, Pl Dr Fleming and Pg Marítim.
Car rental Olimpia, Avgda Grècia 29 (☎ 972 750 389, ⓦ www.olimpiarent.com).
Health centre At c/Església 100 (☎ 972 750 063). A Red Cross station for emergencies is on the beach towards the port end of town (☎ 972 752 222).
Internet Ciberindian, c/Sta Anna 30 (April–Sept daily 10am–11pm).
Pharmacy Surribas, c/Sta Anna 62, near the port; Alaball, Avgda de Grècia 27, near the roundabout at the entrance to the town.
Police Ctra de Torroella 104 ☎ 092.
Post office c/Roca Maura 29, near Pl Església.
Taxis By Cafeteria Alba on Pl Església (☎ 972 751 422).

LES ILLES MEDES

Comprising seven islets and a scattering of reefs, the **Les Illes Medes** archipelago is the most important marine reserve in the western Mediterranean, home to over 1300 animal and plant species. During the early days of tourism, lack of controls on diving and fishing led to large tracts of **coral reef** being destroyed, but subsequent laws passed by the Catalan government seriously restrict all activity around the islands, and this has gone a long way towards redressing the ecological balance.

All **boating, diving** and **snorkelling** in the area is strictly regulated. Only 450 divers are allowed to dive here each day, and then only while accompanied by a certified instructor or divemaster. Consequently, for novices and experts alike, it's essential to use only a recognized PADI or CSL diving centre. Best of the bunch are Medes Poseidon, Pg Marítim 63 (☎972 752 477, ⓦwww.medasposeidon.com); Medaqua, Pg Marítim 13 (☎972 752 043, ⓦwww.medaqua.com), which also offers a variety of activities including sailing, parasailing and bird-watching; and El Rei del Mar, Avgda Grècia 5 (☎972 751 392).

The largest island, **Meda Gran**, can be visited on boat trips (not March–June), but you must stick to the signposted paths, which lead to the belvedere at the topmost part of the rock. Nesting **birds** here include cormorants and shags, while you can also spot kestrels, hoopoes and linnets. The most usual species of **fish** range from amberjack and barracuda to conger eels and groupers; even more exotic are the marbled electric ray and angler fish, found over 20m down.

L'ESTARTIT AND LES ILLES MEDES

The Alt Empordà — south

Comprising the wide, curving Golf de Roses and the lush Empordà plain, the long beaches and flat marshland of the **southern Alt Empordà** lie between the rocky coves and hills of the coast on either side. Fine sand beaches line the entire semicircle of the bay and the flat hinterland features lush fields and orchards.

Map 3 at the back of the book covers
the whole Alt Empordà region.

The deep coves south of the smart fishing port **L'Escala** flatten out to much straighter sandy beaches north of town. There are superb Classical ruins at **Empúries**, 2km north, while neighbouring **Sant Martí d'Empúries** is the oldest inhabited village in Catalonia. As the terrain becomes flatter, it opens out onto the marshlands of the **Parc Natural dels Aigüamolls de l'Empordà**, a haven for bird-watchers and walkers that also boasts a splendid beach. The park's main town, **Sant Pere Pescador**, lies 3km inland, a fact which saved it from the depredations of the tourist boom.

THE CAMÍ DE RONDA

Walking in most of the southern Alt Empordà involves skirting the Golf de Roses on the beach or the road. At the very northern end, beyond Roses, the Camí de Ronda (see p.49) takes over, following the gruelling GR92 as it snakes along the shoreline – from the port in Roses (p.283) through the outlying beaches, bypassing Cap de Norfeu, as far as the cove at Jóncols (p.289). From here, the path cuts inland across a barren, sun-baked landscape towards Cadaqués (p.307).

North of the park sits the fascinating Gothic town of **Castelló d'Empúries**, dominated by its would-be cathedral and cobbled alleys. The nearby modern development of **Empuriabrava** went up in the 1960s around a giant marina and 30km of canals, instantly turning it into a favourite with yachties. Finally, crowning its bay, the 3000-year-old town of **Roses** has thrown itself body and soul into tourism.

L'Escala and around

The lovely seaside town of **L'ESCALA** stands at the southern end of the Golf de Roses, catering primarily for local tourists. Development has been low-key, helped greatly by the **old port** and town having been saved from the tourist boom by construction of the outlying resort of **Riells**. L'Escala is elevated to greatness thanks to the stunning Greek and Roman ruins at **Empúries**, 2km north along the coast – one of the most important archeological sites in Spain. Beside the ruins is the medieval hamlet of **Sant Martí d'Empúries**, its postcard prettiness drawing in the crowds.

L'Escala's history owes much to the Greeks and Romans

▲ Riells & Cala Montgó

L'ESCALA AND AROUND

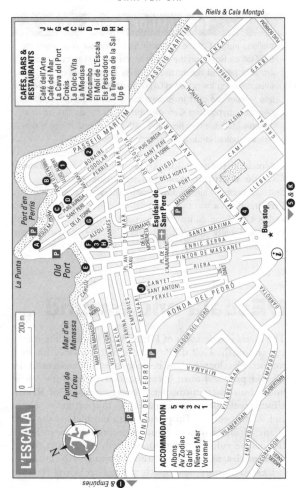

L'ESCALA

| 0 | 200 m |

CAFÉS, BARS & RESTAURANTS

Café dell'Arte	J
Café del Mar	F
La Cava del Port	G
Crokis	A
La Dolce Vita	C
La Medusa	E
Mocambo	D
El Molí de l'Escala	I
Els Pescadors	B
La Taverna de la Sal	H
Up 6	K

ACCOMMODATION

Albons	5
Av Zodiac	4
Garbí	3
Nieves Mar	2
Voramar	1

Bus stop

Església de Sant Pere

▲ & Empúries

who colonized the area; techniques of **anchovy** fishing and salting, first used by the Greeks, are still followed today. The town grew as the fishermen's quarter of Sant Martí d'Empúries – the earliest houses still standing were built in the 1640s. A flourishing twentieth-century cultural scene was curtailed after the Spanish Civil War, and Riells was steadily developed for tourism from the 1960s, happily leaving the old town largely untouched.

July and August's Festival Internacional de Mùsica L'Escala–Empúries features classical and contemporary music staged most nights at 10pm in the Empúries ruins and the church in Sant Martí d'Empúries. The tourist office has information and tickets (€3–12).

ARRIVAL AND INFORMATION

Exiting the A7 at junction 5 leads you to the GI623, on which L'Escala is 16km due east. Several **buses** arrive daily from Girona, Barcelona and on the Figueres–Sant Feliu de Guíxols route. All stop at the top of Avgda Ave Maria near the Plaça de les Escoles, about 500m west of the Pg Marítim and 500m south of the old port.

The **tourist office**, Pl de les Escoles 1 (daily 9am–9.30pm; ☏972 770 603, ⓦ www.lescala.org), stocks plenty of material, as do two more **information points** (both Easter–Sept daily 9am–9.30pm) – at the northwestern entrance to town by the roundabout on Ctra Viladamat, and at the western end of the beach at Riells.

ACCOMMODATION

The best **hotels** and **hostals** are around the old port, though – with no midrange options – the choice is between modern three-star seafront places, which are expensive in season, or very variable one-star establishments. Fonti Nugué, Port d'en Perris 6 (☎972 770 168, ☏972 773 888, ✉fontinugue@grn.es), is one of the few agencies to offer **villas and apartments** both in Riells and around the old port. *Avenida Zodiac*, Avgda Ave Maria 37–39, Apartado 281 (☎972 770 110; closed Nov–March; ❸), is a well-equipped apartment complex with pool very near the beach.

Two good **campsites** at Cala Montgó are *Neus* (☎972 772 751; closed Oct–May; open at Easter), a quiet, family-run site about five minutes' walk from the beach, and bigger *Cala Montgó* (☎972 770 866, ⊛www.betsa.es), with a good range of facilities near the beach.

Alberg d'Empúries

c/Les Coves 41, Empúries
☎972 771 200, ☏972 771 572,
⊛www.gencat.es/catalunyajove.
Closed Jan & Feb.
Under extensive renovation at the time of writing, this friendly hostel stands in a mansion near the Empúries ruins and offers a tranquil base for exploring the area or simply basting on one of the nearby beaches. The large, airy dorms sleep between four and twenty. ❶

Albons

Ctra La Bisbal–Figueres km18, Albons ☎972 788 500, ☏972 788 658,
⊛www.hotelalbons.com.
On a bluff 6km southwest of L'Escala stands this convivial four-star hotel. Modern in design, the low buildings are grouped around the sunny lawns and swimming pool. All rooms are huge, some with four-poster beds, and have air conditioning and stunning countryside views. ❻

Garbí

c/Sta Màxima 7 ☎ & ☏972 770 165.
Closed Feb.
Located in a small street near the old port, this tastefully renovated old merchant's house offers good value. The loquacious owners are very helpful and cheery, while the

simple but comfortable en-suite rooms, some facing the sea, are bright and cool. ❸

Nieves Mar

Pg Marítim 8 ⓣ 972 770 300,
ⓕ 972 773 605,
ⓦ www.nievesmar.com.
Closed Nov–Feb.

Between the old port and Riells, this modern hotel, famous for its excellent restaurant, has large gardens, tennis courts and a swimming pool. All of the large, brightly decorated bedrooms have sitting areas and balconies with sea views. ❻

Riomar

Platja del Riuet, Sant Martí d'Empúries ⓣ & ⓕ 972 770 362.
Closed Oct–April.

On the beach at nearby Sant Martí d'Empúries (see p.271), this quiet hotel has comfortable rooms, tennis courts and a pool. ❺

Voramar

Pg Lluís Albert 2 ⓣ 972 770 108, ⓕ 972 770 377.
Closed Jan–March.

On the seafront next to the old port, this otherwise ordinary modern hotel has a terrific saltwater swimming pool and bar above the sea crashing over the rocks. The rooms are simply decorated and most have balconies offering great sea views. ❹

THE TOWN AND AROUND

The core of the town is the **old port**, with the mainly pedestrianized **Barri Vell** running inland from it; both areas have preserved a great deal of their charm. West and north of the centre, a shaded **Camí de les Dunes** footpath leads along the shoreline past a string of small coves as far as the Greek and Roman ruins at **Empúries** and the neighbouring hamlet of **Sant Martí d'Empúries**. East of the old port, the seafront meanders past the small **La Punta** headland and the tiny **Port d'en Perris** beach before turning south along the Passeig Marítim to the modern tourist development of **Riells**. Rows of villas and apartments stretch back from the beach here to the lovely, if busy, horseshoe bay of **Montgó**, popular with divers.

The Barri Vell and old port

Heart of old L'Escala is its charming, historic **port**, previously the main fishing harbour until the new one south of Riells was built in the 1960s. Fishing boats still pull up onto the small **beach**, which shelves gradually, while the original quayside runs along one side past medieval mooring posts to towering stone mounds built in the eighteenth century – the round-topped ones for salting anchovies, the square-topped ones for mooring.

On the north side of the harbour, at c/Joan Massanet 2, a cannonball – fired in May 1809 – is embedded in the wall of a house that subsequently belonged to Surrealist artist Joan Massanet.

All the buildings lining the port were once related to the fishing industry. Many of today's bars and shops were fishermen's taverns, while a lot of whitewashed fishermen's cottages, built around patios for storing nets and tools, are still homes. On the corner of the seafront and the busy shopping street of c/Alfolí, the imposing **Casa de la Punxa** was built in 1919 as an ice factory, while further along the same street stands the towering seventeenth-century **Alfolí** or salt warehouse. The small street to the right from here houses **Can Maranges**, the fortified family seat of the local Maranges family, a dynasty of famous local politicians, soldiers and writers. Nearby **Plaça Pequín** is where a bomb fell in 1939 killing fifteen townspeople.

The **Església de Sant Pere** (daily 9am–1pm & 6–9pm), on c/Santa Màxima opposite the town hall, was built in

1700 in Gothic style with a Renaissance facade. Most interesting feature is the small chapel to the right of the altar, the Capella Santíssim, where a large model of a fishing boat bears Christ on the cross as the mast and features the names of the fishermen disciples carved around the gunwales in acknowledgment of the town's reliance on fishing.

L'Escala's lively market is held in the streets of the Barri Vell every Sunday morning.

Along the Camí de les Dunes

Heading west from the old port, the paved **Camí de les Dunes** footpath leads along the shoreline past **Mar d'en Manassa**, a beach with a row of working fishermen's huts, and **La Creu**, equally so-so for swimming. Over the road from the Camí, and reached by steps in the wall, the **El Pedró tower** (no public access) was originally built in 1543 as a defence against pirates and as part of a chain of warning beacons. Rebuilt in the eighteenth century by the Maranges family, whose shield is above the door, it has also been used to house the poor.

Back on the Camí, before it turns to the right away from the road, a huge statue of a hand commemorates the arrival here in 1992 of the **Olympic Torch** from Greece. This section of the footpath leads past a string of outstanding sandy **beaches**, which stretch along the shoreline below the ruins at Empúries and Sant Martí d'Empúries, both of which can be reached easily from the two-kilometre long track. The most interesting beach is **Moll Grec**, by Empúries, where part of the remains of the original Greek dock stands proud above the dunes.

L'ESCALA AND AROUND

La Punta and Port d'en Perris

Back in town, above the quayside, separate statues to fishermen and their wives dominate the low **La Punta** headland. Treacherous in stormy weather, the small harbour entrance has witnessed countless shipwrecks over the years. The high seafront leads east past restaurants and bars to **Port d'en Perris**, a pleasant beach for swimming, which was once a secondary port and housed the **anchovy** warehouses. There's still a number of family fishmongers dotted about, where you can buy the local delicacy.

South to Riells and Montgó

Past the Port d'en Perris beach, the seventeenth-century **Casa Gran**, which was fortified in 1711 by the Bourbon dynasty in the War of Succession, marks the start of the **Passeig Marítim**, a kilometre-long seafront promenade, lined with crafts stands in the summer, that is a local favourite for the evening stroll. It leads eventually to **Riells**,

RIELLS' LITTLE PRINCE

The French author and World War II pilot Antoine de Saint-Exupéry was shot down over the Golf de Roses, and in commemoration the Riells seafront has been charmingly themed on his most famous story, *The Little Prince*. A haunting statue of the little prince sits on a seafront wall at the start of the promenade, and the references pile up from hereon, including a slithering chain symbolizing the snake, palms planted to re-create constellations, a small stone amphitheatre with a statue of the fox, bronze asteroids set into the ground and, at the far end of the promenade, a baobab tree and rose next to tiny volcanoes emerging from the pavement.

a resort suburb 1km south of the centre, developed in the 1960s to cater for the influx of tourists. Its sweeping, sheltered **beach**, with fine golden sand, can get extremely crowded.

Various operators on Riells beach offer windsurf, ski-bus, water-skiing and kayaking, the best being Funtastic (☏ 972 774 184, Ⓦ www.funtastic-emporda.com). Boat tours run by Mare Nostrum, c/Maranges 3 (☏ 972 773 797), head from the new port, beyond Riells, north to Cap de Creus and south to Palamós. Also in the new port, Jets Marivent, c/Romeu de Corbera (☏ 972 775 379), rents jet skis.

Rows of villas lead on from here to **Cala Montgó**, a lovely deep and sheltered bay with fine sand, but which gets very busy in August. Tiny inlets, handkerchiefs of beaches and sunken wrecks make it popular with divers and kayakers, equipped by Montgó Sub, Avgda Montgó 297 (☏ 972 771 307) and Kayaking Costa Brava (☏ 972 775 394, Ⓦ www.kayakingcb.com). It's worth the half-hour walk up to the top of **Punta Montgó** for the superb views.

EATING

The best places to **eat** are in the old port area. Fish and seafood – especially anchovies – are a dominant feature, while there are also some excellent tapas places. For fast food, head to Riells, where you'll find plenty of outlets for snacks and pizzas.

La Cava del Port
c/del Port 33.
Daily 7.30am–midnight.
In a small street set back from the old port, this lively bar in

an old cottage serves a huge range of tapas washed down with cava. Worth trying are the *flautes* (tiny, thin sandwiches) and the platters of cheeses, pâtés and local anchovies. Budget.

La Dolce Vita
Port d'en Perris 1.
Daily noon–midnight.
One of the most popular places in town, serving great fresh pasta, pizzas and local meat dishes in a brightly lit upper-floor dining room giving splendid sea views. Inexpensive.

La Medusa
Platja de les Barques.
Easter–Oct daily 11am–3am.
In a corner of the beach in the old port, this amiable restaurant has a wide and imaginative choice, especially for vegetarians, with superb salads and sweet and savoury crêpes. Once the kitchen closes at midnight, it mutates into a bar with a great waterfront terrace. Budget.

El Molí de L'Escala
Camp dels Pilans ⊤ 972 774 727, ⓦ www.el-moli.com.
Nov–March closed Wed.
Near the roundabout at the western entrance to L'Escala, this sumptuous Catalan restaurant occupies a rambling sixteenth-century watermill in lush gardens. The top-range fish and seafood are superb, while there's also a reasonable selection for vegetarians and a list of over 150 wines. Expensive.

Els Pescadors
Port d'en Perris 5 ⊤ 972 770 728.
Closed Nov.
This traditional restaurant is renowned for the quality of its excellent seafood, almost matched by the range of imaginative vegetable and meat dishes. Carrot *gazpacho* with avocado and duck magret in port are especially good. Expensive.

La Taverna de la Sal
c/Sta Máxima 7.
Mon, Tues & Thurs–Sun 1pm–1am.
Bustling restaurant in the same building as *Hotel Garbí*, with a welcoming pavement terrace where a great selection of tapas and *pà amb tomàquet* meals is served alongside an extensive meat, fish and salad menu. Budget.

DRINKING AND NIGHTLIFE

A string of identikit **bars** lines the seafront in Riells, but most locals in the know head for the old port, where places range from stylish bars to down-to-earth taverns in old fishermen's cottages.

A couple of bars between La Punta and Port d'en Perris, *Bar La Cala* and *Bar La Punta*, have terraces below the sea wall, where you can enjoy tapas and a late drink with the water lapping at your feet and the lights of Roses glittering in the distance.

Café dell'Arte
c/Calvari 1.
Daily 5pm–1am.
In a small square between the town hall and the old port, this small, friendly bar, cluttered with antiques, is a great place for a laid-back drink. Also serves fondues and tapas.

Café del Mar
c/Alfolí 1.
Daily 10am–1am.
Originally the town's social centre for the fishing fleet, this high-ceilinged, old-fashioned bar in the old port is now a stylish place to sit and watch the world go by.

Crokis
Pl de la Punta.
Daily 9.30pm–2.30am.
Trendiest spot in town, occupying a terrific position atop La Punta. Downstairs is noisy with a small dance area playing anything from house to salsa, while the upstairs bar, with a pantile-roofed terrace, is perfect for relishing the sea views.

Mocambo
Port d'en Perris 3.
Daily noon–2.30am.
In the western corner of Port d'en Perris, this small, modern bar in an old fisherman's cottage serves an enticing range of cocktails to

L'ESCALA AND AROUND

accompany a selection of salads and sandwiches.

Up 6

Ctra Torroella.
Daily 10pm–6am; €6.
Some 2km southwest of the centre, this is one of the most popular clubs in the region, with two distinct areas and a chill-out bar. One part plays house and features visiting DJs from Ibiza, while the other has a buzzing salsa dance floor. Admission includes one drink.

LISTINGS

Bike rental Cycle Point, c/Mallols 46 ⓣ 630 246 194.
Car rental Tot-Rent Aventura, Avgda Montgó 10 (ⓣ 972 772 753, ⓦ www.totrentaventura .com) offers cars, quad bikes, scooters and jetskis.
Health centre At c/Gràcia 12, near the western end of the old port ⓣ 608 094 333.
Internet Les Gavines, Pg del Mar 15 (daily 11am–11pm); Si

no fos, Pg del Mar 17 (daily 8pm–3am).
Pharmacies Alarcón, c/Port 50; Planas, Avgda Riells 18.
Police In the town hall at c/Pintor Joan Massanet 34 ⓣ 972 774 818.
Post office Plaça de les Escoles 2.
Taxi Stand at Plaça de les Escoles ⓣ 972 770 940.

EMPÚRIES

Daily: Easter & June–Sept 10am–8pm; rest of year 10am–6pm. €2.50.
Located 2km north of L'Escala by the Camí de les Dunes footpath (or a five-minute drive along a small signposted road immediately after the Olympic Torch statue), the ruins of **EMPÚRIES** comprise one of Spain's most important and engaging archeological sites. More has been excavated of the **Greek city**, immediately west of the beach, where foundations and streets give a good idea of layout. A short

L'ESCALA AND AROUND

stroll west, past the **museum**, lies the **Roman city**, much less of which has been unearthed, although intact mosaics and columns mark individual buildings clearly. You can cover everything in half a day, and still have time for a dip at one of the beautiful beaches below the site. **Parking** is free with your admission ticket. An **audioguide** costs an extra €3.60.

If you're a reasonable swimmer, check out the guided snorkelling tour from the CASC hut on the beach outside the car park entrance (July & Aug daily 10am–7pm; €3.15 with a site admission ticket, otherwise €3.60; mask and snorkel included), which takes you some 50m out to sea to view the now-submerged Greek port.

In the early sixth century BC, the **Greeks** founded the Palaiopolis on what was then a small island – the site of Sant Martí d'Empúries (see p.271), now joined to the mainland. Shortly afterwards, they founded a new city, or Neapolis, nearby, known as **Emporion** – literally "Trading Post" – which grew thanks to flourishing trade with tribes around the Iberian peninsula, and, in turn, exerted a significant influence on these tribes.

In 218 BC, at the outbreak of the Second Punic War, a **Roman** army commanded by Scipio landed at Emporion to block the Carthaginians, and effectively began the romanization of Iberia. In 195 BC, Marcus Portius Cato established an army camp at Empúries, nucleus of the city that was founded anew in around 100 BC. Under Emperor Augustus, the Greek and Roman settlements were united under the name **Municipium Emporiae**. However, whereas Roman settlements such as Barcino (Barcelona) and Gerunda (Girona) flourished, Emporiae declined and was abandoned in the third century AD.

L'ESCALA AND AROUND

The Greek city (Ciutat Grega)

Even before you enter the site, the **car park** offers an interesting glimpse into the excavations. A dig here ruled out the claim of Classical sources that the Greek city had been built over an Iberian settlement; instead, it turned up fourth- and third-century BC burial tombs, covered by a large second-century BC building of unknown use, in turn covered by a first-century BC **metallurgy complex (0)**. The most exciting find was a small vase containing 88 Roman denarii and one Iberian coin, now in the museum.

Our account follows the numbering used on the free site plan, which is given to you on arrival. (Note that points within the Greek city have round numbers, points within the Roman city have square numbers.) Don't be confused by the information boards around the site, which follow a different numbering system.

The impressive **gateway (1)**, cut into the southern defensive walls, leads directly into a religious quarter. Inside the entrance to the right is the **Serapeion (3)**, a sanctuary dedicated to the Egyptian deities Isis and Zeus Serapis. Opposite it, left of the entrance, is the more interesting **Asklepeion (2)**, sanctuary to the Greek god of medicine. The path leads past open-based amphoras, which acted as water filters for purifying the sick. In the middle stood a small temple, where a model of the near-intact statue to Aesculapius stands; the original is in the museum.

Ahead on the main path from the entrance, six different-sized tanks mark the site of a **salting factory (6)**, precursor to the fish-salting industry that subsequently made the area's fortune. On from here past family residences is a large **public cistern (8)**, which would have been lined with crushed pottery mixed with lime, sand and water to stop the water from seeping away. This originally stood in the centre of a *macellum*, or small market, whose sloping roof channelled rainwater into the cistern for use by the small businesses in the building. At the end of this street stood the **agora (9)** – the public square and hub of the city – and **stoa**, a porticoed building housing shops and businesses. Little but the ground plan remains. The drainage system behind the *agora* is still visible, while a little west, just before the museum, a **mosaic (12)** bearing the inscription "how sweet it is to be reclined" suggests that the room was used as a banqueting hall.

The museum

Admission free with site ticket. Audiovisual exhibition runs every 30min (€1.50 extra).

All finds from the site, including funeral urns, coins and jewellery and the statue of Aesculapius, are housed in the small but beautifully presented **museum**, which stands above the Greek city. Video screens inside the door show constantly changing close-ups and aerial shots of the two cities, while display cases and panels in several languages provide a good chronology of the settlements and aspects of everyday life, such as worship, work, and play. Next to the museum, an award-winning twenty-minute **audiovisual exhibition** offers a neat potted history of the development and decline of the cities.

The Roman city (Ciutat Romana)

Behind the museum, a path leads out of the Greek walls west across a lawn to the **Roman city**, larger and potentially much more splendid than its Greek counterpart. To date, only ten percent of it has been excavated, and you'll see the extent of what's left to be done by the steel fence

L'ESCALA AND AROUND

defining future digs; it's been divided into seventy blocks, or *insulae*, scheduled for excavation up to 2008.

To the right of the path, **Domus 1** (**1**) is one of the largest houses, remarkable for its symmetrical mosaics. The upper level, distributed around an atrium, was the living area and is where the finer mosaics are to be found, while the lower area, which you come to first, would have been for domestic and service use.

Opposite a similarly large house nearby (**2**) and behind a fence, **Insula 30** (**3**) is where, at the time of writing, excavations have revealed the **public baths**, complete with hypocaust. Also uncovered is a black and white mosaic, unfortunately sliced in two by an anti-aircraft trench dug during the Spanish Civil War.

Past an incongruous vine grower's shed from 1913, the straight road leads to the **forum** (**4**), the political, religious and financial heart of the city. The north side of the square was dominated by temples, most notably the **Capitoline temple** (**7**) probably devoted to the Capitoline Triad – Jupiter, Juno and Minerva – of which only the outline and some stones remain. Directly opposite, on the south wall, and best viewed from here, a reconstruction of the high porticoes gives some idea of what the forum would have looked like in its heyday. On the east wall were the **basilica** and **curia** (**5**), which included the law courts and legal offices.

South of the forum, the **cardo maximus** (**9**), or main north–south street, runs past a row of small shops, while to the left (east), the **tabernae** (**10**) is the only complete block of dwellings to be excavated to date. Their location near the city centre suggests that they were combined shops and dwellings.

The **city walls** at the southern end of the *cardo maximus* are well preserved, despite parts having been hollowed out in modern times for use as vine growers' huts. The low

main gate (**12**) was originally protected by an inner bastion, and has a deeply rutted threshold, showing the passage of traffic. Outside the wall and to the left, a carved phallic symbol in the wall at head height invoked the protection and prosperity of the city.

To the right (west) of the gate is the base of the **amphitheatre** (**13**), probably constructed on an earlier wooden structure. Built in the first century AD, when the city had begun its decline, it lacks the usual underground chambers, indicating a considerable shortage of funds. East of this, on the path back to the car park, is the **palaestra** (**14**), a porticoed sports field, of which very little remains.

SANT MARTÍ D'EMPÚRIES

Five minutes' walk along the Camí de les Dunes north of Empúries, or a 2km signposted drive from L'Escala, is **SANT MARTÍ D'EMPÚRIES**, site of the original Greek settlement of Palaiopolis, founded in the sixth century BC. Regarded as the **oldest town in Catalonia**, Sant Martí d'Empúries has been occupied without interruption since the Bronze Age and was the first capital of the region at the time of Charlemagne, a position it held until the eleventh century. Its medieval **walls** mark the original Greek enclosure, while its rather austere sixteenth-century **church** stands on the site of a tenth-century pre-Romanesque temple. Attacked numerous times between the thirteenth and the seventeenth centuries by the French, it always survived, while its separate fishing quarter subsequently grew to become the town of L'Escala.

Possessing a fascinating history and promising much from the outside, the hamlet is ultimately something of a disappointment, as its undeniable prettiness attracts hordes of visitors to the tiny, café-lined **main square**, and its buildings give the feel of having been renovated just a tad too zealously. Despite that, it remains a pleasant place for a short stroll through the narrow streets or an evening drink, with superb beaches and fine views of the bay.

Parc Natural dels Aigüamolls de l'Empordà

Halfway around the Golf de Roses is the **Parc Natural dels Aigüamolls de l'Empordà** (Empordà Wetlands Park), an important reserve created by the Catalan government in 1983 as a refuge for wildlife and nesting and migrant birds. The park comprises two areas either side of the modern development of Empuriabrava (see p.280), and is what remains of the **marshland** which once covered most of the coastal plain but which has been destroyed over the years by farming and tourism.

Now, almost a hundred species of **birds** nest in the park, and a further two hundred have been observed. The most common are moorhens, coots and mallards, and the reserve is also active in reintroducing endangered species, such as the garganey, a rare breed of duck only found here on the Iberian peninsula, and the purple gallinule, which had previously not nested in Catalonia for over fifty years. **Mammals** include water voles and otters as well as weasels, polecats, badgers and red foxes, which help control the numbers of rats and rabbits, while bats control **mosquitoes**, which breed in the marshland pools.

The largest numbers of birds are to be seen during the two migration periods (March–May & Aug–Oct), when herons, flamingoes and the occasional crane also pass through.

ARRIVAL AND INFORMATION

Entrance to the park (unlimited access; free) is at the excellent **information centre**, signposted from the Castelló d'Empúries road 4km north of Sant Pere Pescador at El Cortalet (daily: April–Sept 9.30am–2pm & 4.30–7pm; Oct–March 9.30am–2pm & 3.30–6pm; ⊤972 454 222, ⓦ www.aiguamolls.org). There's a free car park at El Cortalet; the nearest **bus stop** is in Sant Pere Pescador. **Walking routes** through the park are outlined on a free map available from the centre, while, throughout the year, free **guided tours** in English for groups or specialist ornithologists can be arranged in advance.

To get the most out of the park's wildlife-spotting opportunities, you can rent a pair of binoculars at the information centre for €1.80 for the day.

THE PARK

There are two principal **routes** through the park, both of which set off from the information centre.

The **La Massona** route (2hr round trip) takes in the most interesting areas, following a shaded track to the beach and back. Dotted along the way are a series of **hides**; in the summer, huge numbers of birds are attracted to the watering holes in front of nos. 5 and 7, which tend not to dry up. Between these are four towering silos used to dry rice

PARC NATURAL DELS AIGUAMOLLS DE L'EMPORDÀ

grown in the paddy-fields nearby – an industry discontinued after 1969, although reintroduced since; one of the silos has been turned into an **observatory**. You'll need a good head for heights but the views are stunning and, provided you have binoculars, you'll be treated to a good range of bird species. Below the observatory, opposite a toilet block, **wild horses** graze in a field with egrets strutting proprietorially alongside.

The last part of the La Massona track, from a gate leading into a dusty road alongside a campsite, has little to offer, making the observatory a good point to turn back if you don't mind missing out on the beach.

The other track, **Can Comas**, is a looping route for hardcore walkers that takes about five hours on foot (or 1hr 30min on a bike), best attempted in the early morning before the summer heat hits. The first part is exposed, with few species of bird apparent unless you know what to look for, although it eventually doubles back along the beach to follow the La Massona route back to the information centre.

SANT PERE PESCADOR

SANT PERE PESCADOR, 12km northwest of L'Escala on the banks of the pretty River Fluvià, is regarded as the gateway to the Parc Natural dels Aigüamolls. Built 3km inland to escape the attentions of pirates, it was passed by during the tourist boom and – with its newfound protected status – remains a cheerfully aloof town populated by fruit-growers and the occasional tourist.

The centre is tiny, with narrow pedestrianized streets grouped around the quiet **Plaça Major**, dominated by an ornate Gothic-style fountain and the simple seventeenth-century Baroque church. The town's real draw, though, is its outstanding **beach**. At the end of a signposted 3km road past fruit orchards, the spectacularly long **Platja de Sant Pere Pescador**, with its beautiful golden sand, stretches off into the distance to the north and south. There's plenty of parking space amid the dunes, and, although it gets busy, the beach is so expansive that a short walk away from the cars and campsites will find you a relatively isolated spot.

There are several windsurf rental operators on the Platja de Sant Pere Pescador, or you could have a go at flysurf – dangling on a surfboard from a parachute; get information from Wind Station, next to *Camping Aquarius* (☎ 972 193 190, Ⓦ www.ventilador.com).

Practicalities

Several **buses** a day on the Figueres–Sant Feliu de Guíxols and Cadaqués–Girona–Lloret de Mar routes stop on c/Delicies at the northern entrance to town. The **tourist office**, c/Verge Portalet 10 (June–Sept Mon–Fri 10am–1.30pm & 4–6pm, Sat 10am–noon; ☎ 972 520 050, Ⓦ www.ddgi.es/santpere) stocks a selection of maps and information about the town and park.

Hotels and turisme rural

The outstanding **hotel** *Can Ceret*, c/Mar 1 (☎ & ⓕ 972 550 433; ❺) – originally a farmhouse, built in 1723 – occupies a cool stone building with large gardens. All its beautifully decorated rooms have sumptuous bathrooms and air conditioning. *El Molí*, Ctra de la Platja 36 (☎ & ⓕ 972 520 069, Ⓦ www.hotelelmoli.com; ❸; closed Oct–March), between the town and the beach, is a quiet place around gardens and a swimming pool. Its large rooms – some en suite – are simple but comfortable.

The village of Torroella de Fluvià, 4km southwest, has a couple of **turisme rural** houses, both with spacious double rooms for rent in the family home. *Can Forés*, Ctra St Pere Pescador 11 (☎972 520 545; ❷), offers B&B, while the larger *El Sugué*, Ctra St Pere Pescador 1 (☎972 550 067; ❷), can do B&B or half or full board.

Campsites

Most visitors stay in one of the numerous **campsites**. The small *Aquarius* (☎972 520 003, ℻972 550 216, ⓦwww.aquarius.es; closed Feb–Easter) gives onto the beach at one of the most popular windsurfing sections, with mediocre shade but good modern facilities. *La Ballena Alegre 2* (☎600 400 200, ℻972 520 332, ⓦwww.ballena -alegre.es; closed Oct–April) lies immediately east of town, popular with windsurfers but not for those who prefer small and simple. *Nautic Almatà*, Ctra Castelló-St Pere Pescador km11 (☎972 454 477, ℻972 452 330, ⓦwww .campingparks.com) is a large site 6km northeast of town, mostly shaded, with a landscaped pool, shops and restaurants. Finally, *El Rio* (☎972 520 216, ℻972 549 022, ℮el-rio@apdo.com; closed Oct–April) is a well-shaded site set back on a bend in the river, still with excellent amenities and a good pool.

Mosquitoes can be a problem at St Pere Pescador.

Eating and drinking

For a **meal**, *Can Ceret*, c/Mar 1, serves delicious Catalan food in an eighteenth-century farmhouse and garden. There are several more economical options on Plaça Major which also serve drinks. In keeping with the town's rustic feel, **bars** tend to double up as day and night venues, the best being *Placeta de la Muralla*, c/del Mar 15 (daily

10am–2am) and *Ruki*, c/Delicies 7 (same hours), the latter also offering **internet** access.

Castelló d'Empúries

The delightful inland town of **CASTELLÓ D'EMPÚRIES**, 8km north of Sant Pere Pescador, is characterized by fine Gothic buildings and cobbled alleys. Home of the Counts of Empúries from the eleventh century, when the town reached its height of splendour and from when many of its buildings date, the small old quarter retains a wholly untouched charm.

Every year around Sept 11, Castelló d'Empúries stages the Festival dels Trobadors, featuring a medieval market, live music and dancing in the streets.

THE TOWN

Heart of the town is the porticoed **Plaça dels Homes**, from which narrow streets emanate invoking the old trades in their names, such as c/Sabateries, "Cobblers Street" (look out too for c/Bordell, "Brothel Street"), while parts of the medieval **wall** and towers are still intact.

Castelló's medieval prison (daily 9.30am–1pm & 4–8pm; €1.80) is on a closed courtyard off c/Presó, worth a look for the graffiti that prisoners scratched on the walls of its tiny cells, counting off the days or recording prayers.

Referred to as the Cathedral of the Empordà, the giant

Església de Santa Maria was intended in the thirteenth century by the Counts of Empúries to be the centre of an episcopal see, but opposition from Girona, who didn't relish a rival bishopric so close, meant that this never came about and Castelló d'Empúries was left with a huge church out of all proportion to the town. The **facade** features a high belfry to the left (let down by an unfinished twin on the right) and an elaborate **doorway**, which features statues of the apostles in niches. Of these, the most curious is Judas Thaddeus, on the far left, which is a hundred-year-old copy, as the original was defaced by the medieval townspeople hurling rocks at it in the mistaken belief that it was Judas Iscariot.

Inside, the unique eleventh-century **font** resembles two huge kettle drums, one for children and one for adults. The rear of the nave reveals the ornate but ungilded fifteenth-century alabaster **altarpiece**, towering more than six metres over the altar. Behind this, the **museum** (€1.80), where you will be given a returnable leaflet describing the exhibits, includes the original defaced statue of Judas Thaddeus. On a small terrace in the museum offering views over to Roses, a Hebrew gravestone found in the church is evidence of a medieval Jewish community in the town.

Butterfly Park

Ctra de Castelló a Empuriabrava. Daily 10am–9pm. €5.25.

Castelló's enchanting **Butterfly Park**, at the east end of town on the Empuriabrava road, is one of the largest in Europe, beautifully laid out under an arched roof to resemble a tropical rainforest.

Your entry ticket allows you to come and go during the day, which is useful as the humidity inside can get oppressive.

There's no set route, but you can explore the maze of paths weaving between trees and ponds, spotting the butterflies described in the free booklet; some are curious and flutter up to inspect you. Pictorial signs point out caterpillars, eggs and chrysalises clinging to leaves, and you'll occasionally spot small birds, which eat the insects that would otherwise kill the butterflies. The most impressive specimens to watch out for are the Blue-banded Swallowtail and perfectly camouflaged Indian Leaf. The giant atlas moths and owl butterflies spend the day resting by the water; between 8 and 9pm, staff shutter the windows to allow them to fly – a spectacular sight as they swoop through tunnels of palm leaves.

PRACTICALITIES

Over thirty **buses** a day stop in Castelló, by the *Hotel Emporium* on the main road a short walk southeast of the centre. A small **tourist office**, Pl dels Homes 1 (Easter–Sept Mon–Sat 9am–1pm & 4.30–8pm, Sun 10am–1pm; ⓣ 972 250 426, ⓦ www.castellodempuries.net), has information on both Castelló and Empuriabrava.

The best place to **stay** is the atmospheric *Hotel Canet*, Pl Joc de la Pilota 2 (ⓣ 972 250 340, ⓕ 972 250 607, ⓦ www.hotelcanet.com), which has large en-suite rooms and a pool. *Camping Mas Nou*, Ctra Roses km38 (ⓣ 972 454 175, ⓕ 972 454 358, ⓔ masnou@intercom.es), has well-shaded sites and spacious wooden cabins. For a **meal**, *Hotel Canet* serves tasty Catalan food on its shaded terrace, while *Portal de la Gallarda*, c/Pere Estany 12 (Nov–March closed Mon–Fri), nestles in the shadow of the town walls behind the church.

CASTELLÓ D'EMPÚRIES

Empuriabrava

The dedicated tourist haven of **EMPURIABRAVA** was built in the 1960s to re-create a little Venice of canals, low houses and apartment blocks by the sea. Row upon row of whitewashed buildings snake back from the lovely sandy beach following the 30km of interlinking canals, where boats of all shapes, sizes and bank balances are moored. It's the ideal base for lazy holidays pottering about the canals or taking advantage of the excellent sports facilities, but with little else to recommend it.

ARRIVAL AND INFORMATION

Empuriabrava is well served by **buses** from Barcelona, Girona and Figueres, which stop either on the main C260

EMPURIABRAVA ACTIVITIES

Prime attraction is the network of canals, which you can explore in an electric boat from Eco Boats, c/Poblat Típic (☎ 972 454 946; €30/hr) or a motorboat from Rent, Avgda Carles I (☎ 972 454 162). Several operators offer organized trips on larger boats. Cormora, Club Nàutic 10 (☎ 972 452 845, Ⓦ www.cormora.com) offers diving courses, while Empuria Sailing, Club Nàutic (☎ 651 657 968, Ⓦ www.empuri-asailing.com) gives short sailing courses at €30/day.

Empuriabrava has its own aerodrome, and so has become a favourite with skydivers: the Centre de Paracaigudisme Costa Brava, Aeròdrom d'Empuriabrava (☎ 972 450 111, Ⓦ www.skyrats.com) offers tandem jumps for beginners (plus jumps for more experienced folk) for €20 and upwards, plus courses for €1300.

Roses road at the entrance to town or by the beach. The canals extend 1500m from the main road to the beach; most action is around the beach and port areas. The **tourist office**, near the beach at Centre Cívic (June–Aug daily 9am–9pm; ℡972 450 802, ⓌWWW.empuriabrava.com) has a good selection of free maps and information on both Empuriabrava and Castelló d'Empúries. There's also an **information point** (same times; ℡972 450 088) in the police station at the entrance to town. The bar *Barazza* (see below) on the main drag has **internet** access.

ACCOMMODATION

The majority of visitors to Empuriabrava rent one of the many **apartments**. Apart-Rent, Avgda Carles Fages de Climent (℡972 450 262, ℻972 450 522, ⓌWWW.intercom .es/apartrent) has one of the best selections, while *Comte d'Empuries*, Avgda Pompeu Fabra (℡972 450 796, ℻972 451 175, ℮comte@empuriagrup.com; ❸) is a hacienda-style complex one street back from the sea offering self-catering or half or full-board for a week minimum (Sat to Sat) in comfortable apartments sleeping between two and eight.

As for **hotels**, the new *Castell Blanc*, Sector Aeroclub 56 (℡ & ℻972 456 145, ⓌWWW.hotelcastellblanc.com; ❻; closed Jan & Feb), is in an unprepossessing part of town near the aerodrome but has a sunny pool and large, bright rooms. *Port Salins*, Avgda Castelló 21 (℡972 454 907, ℻972 456 047, ℮trinfinco@intercom.es; ❽) backs onto a marina where the big boats hang out, with plush balconied rooms and a stylish dining room and terrace. At the northern end of the beach near the Club Nàutic, *Briaxis*, Port Principal 25A–30C (℡972 451 545, ℻972 451 889, ⓌWWW.briaxis.com; ❾) is much more luxurious than it seems from the outside and boasts spacious rooms with

EMPURIABRAVA

waterside balconies and a terrific pool on the edge of the canal.

Internacional Amberes (℡972 450 507, ℻972 671 286, ⓦwww.inter-amberes.com; closed Oct–April) is a shaded **campsite** on the north side of town, five minutes from the beach. *La Laguna*, Can Turies (℡972 450 553, ℻972 450 799, ⓦwww.campinglaguna.com) is a leafy site on the beach south of town next to the Parc Natural dels Aigüamolls.

EATING

Dozens of **cafés** for snacks and sandwiches line the streets; stylish *Café Blume*, c/Sant Mori 12 (daily 8am–midnight) serves the best breakfasts in town and has a selection of fabulously sinful homemade cakes and pastries.

The area on and around Avinguda Carles Fages de Climent, parallel to the beach and one street in, has some decent **restaurants** offering a variety of culinary styles. *Bodegón*, just off the main drag at Avgda Joan Carles I, 12–24 (closed Nov & Dec; moderate), serves very good fish and seafood, plus lovely homemade desserts. At *El Celler de Can Serra*, c/Sant Mori 17 (closed Jan & Feb; inexpensive), a mock-rustic interior with a pleasant pavement terrace is the setting for some very good traditional cooking, while *I Sapori d'Italia*, c/Sant Mori 8 (Easter–Sept daily 5pm–1am; inexpensive), serves excellent pastas and has a good selection of Italian and Spanish wines. *Taberna del Mar*, Avgda Carles Fages de Climent 1 (closed Nov; moderate) is a lively fish and seafood restaurant near the beach that also offers a wide selection of tapas.

DRINKING AND NIGHTLIFE

Some **clubs** are on the main road at the entrance to town, but the best atmosphere is on and around Avgda Carles

Fages de Climent, where a string of **bars** thump out live and recorded music of all types. Between the avenue and the beach, the side streets offer more relaxing terrace bars, some with live music. *Barazza*, Avgda Carles Fages de Climent 18 (Mon–Sat 9am–2am, Sun noon–2am) is a relaxing terrace bar next to a canal, playing laid-back live music to the accompaniment of a great selection of cocktails and fresh juices. The mellow terrace at *Caipirinha's*, c/Moxó 2 (daily 9pm–3am), heralds a spacious interior with large dance area featuring a noisy selection of salsa and Spanish Caribbean music. *Passarel.la*, Pg Marítim (June–Sept daily 11pm–5am; €10), is a happening beach club, with several bars grouped around a large dance floor and pool playing mainly house and dance, often by visiting DJs from Ibiza. Admission buys your first drink; a flyer from the tourist office gets you €2.50 off.

Roses and around

The palm-shaded town of **ROSES** occupies a grand position at the head of its broad, sandy bay, tucked under the protective wing of the rugged Cap de Creus headland. Founded in the eighth century BC by Greek colonists, who named it Rhodes after their home, it was subsequently developed by the Romans, who established the fishing industry which is still very active today. After Roses had been sacked in 1543 by the Turkish pirate Barbarossa, Carlos I of Spain ordered the building of the Ciutadella, which was later dismantled by French troops.

However, there's very little left which hints at the town's splendid past. Instead, Roses has thrown itself into making the most of its 4km of sandy **beach**. It's packed in the summer, and is much more pleasant outside July and August, when the restaurants and beach can be enjoyed to their fullest. West of town, **Platja Salatar** and **Santa Margarida** offer more of the same with rows of apartments and hotels, while the pine-clad coves of **Canyelles Petites** and **Almadrava** to the east are much prettier, but get very crowded. A bumpy track leads further east to the more spectacular **Montjoi** and **Jóncols** coves.

> Operators all along Roses beach offer windsurfing, paragliding and ski-bus, while divers should head to Poseidon, Pg Marítim (☎ 972 255 772).

ARRIVAL AND INFORMATION

Roses is a hub for many of the routes around the northern Alt Empordà. **Buses** pull in at the seafront stop on the corner of Avgda Rhode and Plaça Catalunya. The **tourist office**, 50m northwest at Avgda Rhode 101 (daily: June–Sept 9am–9pm; Oct–May 9am–1pm & 4–8pm; ☎ 972 257 331, ⓦ www.rosesnet.com), has good local maps and can help with accommodation.

ACCOMMODATION

Many of the fifty-plus **hotels** in the area are booked solid well before high season; you should always reserve ahead. Best-value choices are *La Cala*, c/Sant Sebastià 61 (☎ 972 256 171, ⓕ 972 151 020; closed Nov & Dec; ❸), with a good terrace but slightly poky en-suite rooms with air conditioning; and the sumptuous *Almadraba Park*, Platja Almadrava (☎ 972 256 550, ⓕ 972 256 750; closed Nov–March; ❼), set on a low crag overlooking a busy cove east of town, with a lovely garden. Family-run *Marítim*,

Platja Salatar (Ⓣ & Ⓕ972 256 390; closed Oct–May; ❻), on the seafront towards Santa Margarida, has a lovely pool and spacious balconied rooms, while plush *Monterrey*, Urb Santa Margarida (Ⓣ972 257 650, Ⓕ972 253 869, Ⓦwww.monterrey.es; closed Dec–Feb; ❻) is in a seafront development south of Roses, also with a great pool and gym.

There are hundreds of **apartments**, primarily in Santa Margarida and Salatar; the agency with the widest choice is *Bigrup*, Avgda Rhode 159 (Ⓣ & Ⓕ972 152 400, Ⓔbigrupprose @mail.cinet.es). In the hills 5km northwest of Roses, the village of Palau-Saverdera has a lovely **turisme rural** fortified farmhouse, *Mas de la Torre* (Ⓣ972 255 453; ❹), which offers seven double rooms for rent individually. The best of the **campsites** is the small, shaded *Salatà*, c/Bergantí 1–15 (Ⓣ972 256 086, Ⓕ972 150 233, Ⓦwww.campingsalata .com), 130m from Santa Margarida beach.

THE TOWN

What little remains of Roses' past is best found in the ruins of the **Ciutadella**, by the beach south of the main promenade. The first sight you get of the vast pentagonal defensive citadel is its imposing Renaissance gate, reached over a short wooden bridge from the side facing the sea. Beyond this grand entrance, all that's left of the broad interior is a curious mishmash of the fortress's origins dotted about the grounds, including the layout of the original Greek streets on which it was built and the remains of a seventeenth-century monastery built within the walls. Of the defensive structure, large sections of the wall and the moat are left, but little else.

Beyond here, the town centres on the peaceful, café-lined Avinguda de Rhode and Plaça Catalunya, parallel to the promenade. The jumble of busy streets running back

ROSES AND AROUND

from them are awash with generic tourist shops and restaurants.

Above the port, a tortuous footpath leads up a small hill to the extensively ruined **Castell de la Trinitat**, built in 1544 in the shape of a five-pointed star for defence. After an arduous climb, you're rewarded by the remains of a medieval artillery fortress, comprising three levels of cannons and mortars, and stunning views.

Boat rides leave from Roses port north to Cadaqués and Cap de Creus and south as far as Palamós, organized by Creuers i Catamarans, c/Dr Ferran 68 (Ⓣ 972 152 196; daily 9.30am–5.30pm; €4.80–8.50). Mini-train trips to Cap de Creus and Cadaqués (1–3hr) are run by Roses Expres, c/Pescadors 19 (Ⓣ 972 256 625, Ⓦ www.trenrosesexpres.com).

EATING

Roses boasts an improbable range of **restaurants**, from the very bad to a handful of top-rated establishments, including one of the most prestigious in the country. Top local delicacy is seafood, particularly a variety of huge prawns.

La Avenida

c/Jaume I, 28.

Small, friendly restaurant near the fishing port specializing in fresh cod. Also with a good range of tapas. Budget.

El Bullí

Cala Montjoi.

Closed Oct–March.

Occupying beach-view gardens 5km east of town, this is one of the most famous restaurants in Spain, whose chef has earned three Michelin stars for his superb original take on traditional Catalan cuisine. The *menú del dia* alone costs a stiff €90. Expensive.

Flor de Lis
c/Cosconilles 47.

Easter–Sept daily 7–11pm.

A enticing town-centre restaurant in a beautiful stone cottage that has earned a Michelin star for its French *nouvelle cuisine*. It's worth trying the *menú degustació*, which includes a sample of everything. Expensive.

Mar y Sol
Pl Catalunya 20.

Tasteful seafront restaurant offering excellent fish and seafood, including regional rice dishes and local prawns and anchovies. Moderate.

Il Retrovo della Dolce Vita
Pl Catalunya 18.

Closed Jan.

With a busy seafront terrace, this friendly place serves some of Roses' best Italian food, specializing in fresh pasta. Inexpensive.

DRINKING AND NIGHTLIFE

There are dozens of pavement cafés and **bars** strung along Plaça Catalunya and the streets behind. Roses has an odd variety of **nightlife**, ranging from 1960s-era discos to an array of stylish bars in the streets back from the seafront and by the beach in Santa Margarida, which is one of the main late-night spots.

Caribeño
Riera Ginjolers.

Daily 8pm–5am; Sept–May closed Mon–Thurs.

Set back from the beach, this enjoyable bar has a large dance floor and plays a fun selection of salsa, merengue and Spanish Caribbean sounds for a lively crowd of mainly Catalan tourists and second-homers.

Chic
Ctra Figueres.

Daily 10pm–5am; Sept–May closed Mon–Thurs.

A huge and wonderfully kitsch disco at the entrance to town from Figueres, with an eclectic crowd and famous annual summer party.

Picasso

c/d'en Mairó 36.

Daily 10.30pm–5am; Sept–May closed Mon–Thurs.

Stylish town-centre club playing mainly trip-hop, drum 'n' bass, hip-hop and techno to an appreciative audience.

Si Us Plau

Pg Marítim 1.

June–Aug daily 10am–5am; Sept–May Fri–Sun 8pm–5am.

A café by day, this pleasant bar comes to life in the evenings, drawing in the pre-clubbing crowd and last-drink revellers. A varied programme of live music plays every summer weeknight.

Zodiac's

Avgda Gola Estany 10–20.

Daily 10pm–5am; Sept–May closed Mon–Thurs.

Chic nightspot with a large dance floor and a mellow bar one street back from the beach in Santa Margarida. Music ranges from salsa to Spanish pop, but the main reason for coming is to be noticed.

EAST OF ROSES

Following road signs **east of Roses** for Cala Montjoi and Cala Jóncols leads you along a road – extremely bumpy in parts, after the asphalt runs out at Montjoi – that snakes up through the hills to some of the northern Costa Brava's loveliest **coves**. Many are set below the road, meaning you'll have to park and then clamber down to the beach, a fact which has helped keep them relatively unspoilt. The coves can also be reached by the tricky, coast-hugging **Camí de Ronda**: allow 4hr to reach the main draw, the region's finest **diving centre** at Jóncols.

About 1km east of town is the peaceful Creu d'en Cobertella, the oldest dolmen in Catalonia, dating from 3000 BC and topped by a huge four-ton granite slab.

Cala Murtra is a lovely horseshoe cove popular with snorkellers and yachties, while alongside it is the even more idyllic, pine-clad **Cala Rostella**, with turquoise waters, a pebble beach and steeply shelving waters excellent for swimming. Both are popular with naturists. Picturesque **Cala Montjoi** – location of the famous *El Bullí* restaurant (see p.286) – is dominated by a Spanish holiday camp, but is a good place to rent a kayak. Beyond, the desolate **Cap de Norfeu** headland is a deceptively long walk from the road, but offers spectacular views from a ruined tower on the summit, and has the pebbly **Cala Canadell** down below.

Cala Jóncols

At the end of the road, a bumpy kilometre beyond Norfeu, is the wonderful **Cala Jóncols**, whose sheltered waters are perfect for swimming and diving. Nestling in its own gardens behind the beach is the lovely **hotel** *Cala Jóncols* (☎972 253 970; ❹; closed Nov–Easter), which has a terrific seafood **restaurant** and offers residents a boat-taxi service to Roses. The biggest attraction, though, is the award-winning Cala Jóncols Diving Centre (☎972 253 970, ⓌWww.pro-dive.de), undoubtedly the best **diving centre** on the coast, owned by Volkmar Göldner, a passionate ecologist. Offering courses for beginners to instructors, the centre also runs the best diving trips to Cap de Creus and the Illes Medes.

ROSES AND AROUND

Figueres

T he capital of the Alt Empordà, **FIGUERES**, 37km north of Girona and 25km south of the border, is forever destined to be associated with **Salvador Dalí**, who was born here and whose extravagant **Teatre-Museu Dalí** attracts more visitors than any other in Spain, apart from Madrid's Prado. Dalí's outrageous legacy rather puts the rest of this county town in the shade, but a stroll around town reveals a pleasant and prosperous old centre with some excellent museums, shops and restaurants. Figueres saw constant battling between the French and the Spanish, a fact made evident in the huge **Castell de Sant Ferran** perched over the town and in the curious feel of the place today, which draws on elements of both cultures: typical features of Catalan towns, such as a Rambla and central square, combine with a French flavour in the shops and cafés, while the local culinary tradition has long been a blend of the two.

It wasn't until the eighteenth century that Figueres grew in importance, prompted by the construction of the Castell de Sant Ferran (to fend off the French) and a burgeoning **wine** industry. Occupied by **Napoleon**'s troops in the early nineteenth century, it was eventually recovered by the Catalans and saw a period of steady growth until the end of the century when phylloxera wiped out the vineyards.

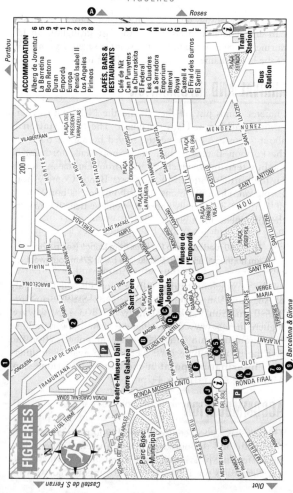

FIGUERES

FIGUERES

ACCOMMODATION
Alberg de Joventut   6
La Barretina   5
Bon Retorn   9
Duran   4
Empordà   1
Europa   7
Pensió Isabel II   2
Los Angeles   3
Pirineos   8

**CAFÉS, BARS &
RESTAURANTS**
Café de Nit   J
Can Punyetes   K
La Churraskita   B
El Federal   I
Les Quadres   A
La Serradora   H
Emporium   E
Interval   C
Royal   G
Castell 4   D
El Firal dels Burros   L
El Setril   F

FIGUERES

291

Figueres was always renowned in Catalonia for its **republican** and federalist ideals; it was the last stronghold to fall during the civil war, and was the seat for seven days in 1939 of the last parliament of the Spanish Republic.

ARRIVAL AND INFORMATION

Figueres stands just off the A7 and the N-II, with underground **parking** at Plaça Catalunya. The **train station** is about 750m east of the centre, served by regular trains on the Portbou–Barcelona line. It's a short walk northeast of the **bus terminus**, which has buses from Girona and towns on the northern stretch of the Costa Brava. Coming from Perpignan, changing trains at Portbou (not its border twin of Cerbère) is generally more convenient than waiting for the infrequent direct buses.

The C260 road runs into Figueres from Llançà (see p.328), 19km northeast, and from Besalú (see p.93), 27km southwest.

The very helpful **tourist office** is on Plaça del Sol (July & Aug daily 9am–9pm; rest of year Mon–Sat 9.30am–1pm & 4–7pm, Sun 9.30am–1pm; ☎972 503 155, ⓦwww.figueres.net, ⓦwww.ddgi.es/figueres), the opposite side of town from the train station, between the police station and a string of night-time bars. There's also a small summer-only **information point** at the train station (June–Sept Mon–Sat 9.30am–1pm & 4–7pm).

ACCOMMODATION

Figueres has a good choice of **hotels** and **pensions** both in the centre and the outskirts, plus a **hostel**. Further afield, there are some pleasant **turisme rural** houses, which make excellent bases for exploring the Alt Empordà coast, while

FIGUERES

campers have the simple but welcoming *Pous*, N-II km763 (☏ 972 675 496), some 3km north of the centre.

HOTELS

Pensió La Barretina

c/Lasauca 13 ☏ 972 676 412.
Small *pensió* about 250m
southwest of the Teatre-
Museu Dalí, offering good-
value, air-conditioned,
en-suite rooms. ❷

Bon Retorn

N-II km759 ☏ 972 504 623,
🅕 972 673 979.
This roadside hotel 3km
south of town appears quite
ordinary but has a congenial,
modern interior and a large
pool, making it a good out-
of-town base if you've got
your own transport. The
bright, comfortable bedrooms
have air conditioning and
satellite TV. ❹

Duran

c/Lasauca 5 ☏ 972 501 250,
🅕 972 502 609,
🅦 www.hotelduran.com.
This lovely old-world hotel,
founded as a carter's tavern in
1855, lies just off the Rambla
about 200m from the Teatre-

Museu Dalí, and is famous
for its very good restaurant.
The air-conditioned rooms
are on the dark side but very
comfortably furnished. ❺

Empordà

N-II km s/n ☏ 972 500 562,
🅕 972 509 358, 🅦 www
.hotelemporda.com.
An extremely comfortable
hotel grouped around a
pleasant, shaded courtyard
about five minutes' walk
north of the centre. All the
spacious, modernized rooms
have large terraces. ❼

Europa

Ronda Firal 18 ☏ 972 500 744,
🅕 972 671 117.
Only 50m from the tourist
office, this two-star hotel is
very good value and has
spacious, air-conditioned
rooms. ❷

Pensió Isabel II

c/Isabel II, 16 ☏ 972 504 735.
Cheerful *pensió* with a

pleasant terrace in a quiet backstreet one minute's walk from the Teatre-Museu Dalí. The rooms are small and simply furnished, but they have air conditioning and are adequate for a short stay. ❶

Los Angeles
c/Barceloneta 10 ⓣ972 510 661, ⓕ972 510 700, ⓔhangeles@olemail.com.
Friendly family-run hotel tucked away in a quiet street behind the Teatre-Museu Dalí, a short walk from shops and restaurants. The en-suite rooms are simply but pleasantly decorated, and are quiet despite the central location. ❷

Pirineos
Ronda Barcelona 1 ⓣ972 500 312, ⓕ972 500 766.
Modern, air-conditioned hotel opposite the tourist office with large, well-equipped rooms with en-suite bathrooms and satellite TV. ❹

HOSTEL

Alberg de Joventut
c/Anicet Pagès 2 ⓣ972 501 213. Closed Sept.
Modern hostel behind the tourist office, with good facilities including laundry and TV lounge, and comfortable dorms sleeping four, eight and fourteen people. ❶

TURISME RURAL

Ca La Maria del Marquès
c/Marinada 5, Fortià ⓣ & ⓕ972 534 300.
In the centre of a hamlet 9km west of Figueres, this three-bedroom stone house with a shaded garden and good kitchen and living room is rented out to groups of up to seven people. ❸

Can Navata
Siurana d'Empordà ⓣ972 525 174, ⓦwww.vsm.es/navata.
Beautifully located,

FIGUERES

atmospheric stone farmhouse with a communal sitting and dining area on the edge of a hamlet 6km southeast of Figueres. Very friendly, English-speaking owners offer B&B or self-catering; the six bedrooms are all large and comfortably furnished and have their own bathrooms. ❷

Manso Sant Nicolau

Ordis ⓣ & ⓕ 972 525 462.
A rambling nineteenth-century house 7km southwest of Figueres, with self-catering apartments for two to five people grouped around a

pool and tennis court. Horse riding is also available. ❸

Mas Molí

Siurana d'Empordà ⓣ & ⓕ 972 525 139,
ⓦ www.turismerural.com/elmoli.
Ten minutes' drive southeast of Figueres, this palatial, award-winning rural house is surrounded by huge gardens and has a small children's play area. Each of the rooms is large and cheerfully furnished with en-suite bathrooms, and the owners offer B&B or half board. ❸

THE TOWN

All signs in Figueres lead to the stunning **Teatre-Museu Dalí**. It stands on the northern limit of a small town centre embracing two more museums that are always fated to play second fiddle – the art-heavy **Museu de l'Empordà** and the **Museu de Joguets** toy museum. The jumble of the old town's shopping streets is framed by the focal **Rambla**. Overlooking the town on a low hill to the northwest is the **Castell de Sant Ferran**, billed as the largest fortress in Europe.

The Rambla and the old town

The short, plane-tree-lined **Rambla** defines the southern edge of the old town, but diverts from the Catalan norm:

it's less a pedestrian thoroughfare and meeting-point than simply a large traffic island, surrounded by shops and glass-fronted terrace cafés reminiscent of those in southern French towns, although it does host Figueres's regular Thursday market as well as other fairs and events throughout the year. Between the Rambla and the Museu-Teatre Dalí, some 100m north, the pedestrianized warren of the **old town** is brimming with a hotchpotch of designer shoe-shops and fashion boutiques intermingled with Dalí memorabilia and traditional food and houseware shops. Pavement cafés line the central **Plaça de l'Ajuntament**.

Museu de Joguets

c/St Pere 1. July–Sept Mon–Sat 10am–1pm & 4–7pm, Sun 11am–1.30pm & 5–7pm; rest of year closed Sun eve & Mon; also closed Feb. €4.50.

Occupying the old Hotel Paris, a mansion dating from 1767, the **Museu de Joguets** is a delightful cavern containing over four thousand antique toys, including some that once belonged to famous names such as Dalí, Federico García Lorca and Joan Miró. While the majority of exhibits are Catalan or Spanish – Meccano aside – may not evoke many memories for visitors, they nonetheless amount to a diverting array of kaleidoscopes, teddy bears and steam engines.

Museu de l'Empordà

Rambla 2. Tues–Sat 11am–7pm, Sun 10am–2pm. €2.50.

Some 50m further east along the Rambla, the unassuming **Museu de l'Empordà** holds local archeological finds and an outstanding art collection, bolstered by donations from famous Figuerencs and the vaults of Madrid's Prado. After a floor combining Iberian and Greek finds with Baroque art, the second level houses an impressive display of nineteenth- and twentieth-century Catalan artists, where the sombre figures of Vayreda and the Olot School stand in stark contrast to the vibrancy of Sorolla's expansive Mediterranean scenes. Equally engaging is the third floor's exhibition of abstract and figurative depictions of the region's landscape, including some by the ubiquitous Dalí. On the same floor is a small but eye-opening array of contemporary art by Spain's big guns, featuring Joan Miró's broad brushstrokes, the louring swirls of Antoni Tàpies and the attractive textured abstract portraits and depictions of nature by Modest Cuixart.

Teatre-Museu Dalí

Plaça Gala-Salvador Dalí 5. Daily: July–Sept 9am–7.45pm; rest of year 10.30am–5.45pm. Ⓦ www.dali-estate.org. €7.50.

A short stroll north of the Rambla sits the wildly extravagant **Teatre-Museu Dalí**. The building – not strictly a museum – went up in 1974 on the site of a ruined theatre where Dalí had staged his first exhibition in 1918 at the age of fourteen. The concept Dalí put forward was that this wasn't a chronological exhibition of his work to be seen on a specific route or a guided tour, but a monument to the senses, which should be savoured by every visitor individually. Consequently, it's far better to roam the galleries and rooms the way Dalí intended rather than try to stick to any trail. Neither should you expect to find his most famous paintings here, as they are dispersed far and wide – which is not to say that you won't nonetheless get an irresistible taste of his bizarre vision and genius from the works that are on display.

The region's other Dalí museums are in Púbol
(see p.238) and Portlligat (see p.314).

The exterior and courtyard

The surreal experience starts with the **exterior** of the building, which is topped by a giant metal and glass dome

FIGUERES

and crowned with huge eggs and figures. Hundreds of imitation bread rolls adorn the walls.

The moment you set foot in the door, you enter a fantasy world of one man's fevered imagination, ghosts and paranoia. The first sight to greet you is an open **courtyard**, where a buxom bronze statue of the biblical Queen of Persia rises above the bonnet of the *Rainy Taxi*, a Cadillac in which the rain falls inside onto two figures shrouded in ivy and snails. Towering above this, a totem pole of tyres is crowned by Gala's rowing boat, from which hang pendulous drops of water, made using condoms as a mould, while the whole centrepiece is dwarfed by rows of faceless art-deco mannequins threatening to leap from niches in the three-storey circular walls.

The dome and crypt

Beyond the courtyard, the former stage area under the **dome** houses an eerie skeletal *cobla*, or *sardana* orchestra, as well as one of Dalí's many trompe l'oeil paintings, which at first glance resembles a pixillated jumble with a portrait of Gala; viewing it through the inverted telescope placed in front reveals the face of Abraham Lincoln. Up a short flight of stairs from the stage, the **Mae West Hall** houses one of Dalí's beloved bits of mischief, where a pink sofa in the shape of lips and some carefully arranged drapes come together to form a giant portrait of Mae West.

Below the stage, stairs lead to a **crypt** where a simple marble stone marks the artist's tomb; sadly his body rests here and not in Púbol with Gala as he had wished. In the last years of his life, an increasingly depressed Dalí lived in the Torre Galatea alongside the museum, and stories of his being manipulated and even made to sign blank canvases are rife.

The Palau del Vent and upper floors

Among all the playfulness and love of illusion on display,

FIGUERES

there are some superb paintings where Dalí's consummate practical skill comes shining through. The **Palau del Vent** on the first floor, representing his idea of an artist's home – studio, living room and bedroom – is dominated by the ceiling painting of the huge feet of Gala and Dalí ascending to heaven, while beautiful pictures, such as the lithograph of Picasso in emperor's laurels or Dalí's haunting self-portrait in oils, go almost unnoticed. Other rooms on this floor house a series of variations inspired by Millet's *Angelus* and some enigmatic portraits of Gala, particularly *Gala Nude from Behind* and the lovely *Galatea of the Spheres*.

On higher floors you'll also find the work of other artists, most stunning being the paintings of Antoni Pitxot in the **Rue Trajan** section, in which moss-covered stones create figures such as the Muses in the *Allegory of Memory*. On the top floor, the **Room of Masterpieces** includes Dalí's works interspersed with paintings by the likes of El Greco and Marcel Duchamp in deliberate non-chronological or themed order.

Dalí-Joies

Next door to the Teatre-Museu Dalí, a permanent exhibition, dubbed **Dalí-Joies** (same hours; €4.50), displays the artist's weird and wonderful collection of jewels, although pride of place goes to Dalí's astonishing *Apotheosis of the Dollar* painting.

Castell de Sant Ferran

Daily: July–Sept 10.30am–8pm; rest of year 10.30am–2pm. €4.50. At the end of the Pujada del Castell, which climbs gently some 800m northwest from the Teatre-Museu Dalí, the **Castell de Sant Ferran** was considered in its day to be one of the most impressive fortresses in Europe and is still the most extensive. You can choose to roam among the buildings and battlements at your own pace, but in many ways it's more rewarding to shell out for an **audioguide** (€1.80) and follow the marked itinerary.

The best tours of the Castell de Sant Ferran take in a jeep ride around the walls followed by a dinghy trip through the cavernous underground water deposits (takes 3hr; €6); get tickets and information at the entrance.

The castle was built in 1753 to defend against the depradations of the **French**, but an unpromising start saw it fall twice to the French in the early nineteenth century without a single shot being fired. This was also where the leader of Girona's defence against Napoleon's troops, General **Alvarez de Castro**, died in imprisonment – an event which has imbued the castle with a popular mystique. In the Spanish Civil War, it was used as a **barracks** for the International Brigades and was the last home of the Spanish Republic before its leaders fled into exile in 1939. Most recently used as a **prison** for Colonel Tejero, who staged an attempted coup in 1981, it was opened to the public in 1997.

An imposing gateway leads through the defensive outer **walls**, over 3km in circumference, and the wide earth-filled moat to the inner walls, which conceal a vast **parade ground**. On the eastern side, the old **stables** comprise a huge double-galleried nave, which had room for a cavalry regiment of five hundred in its day, while beyond this, the **living quarters** are spread over nine two-storey stone buildings, where you'll also find the **caged chair** in which Alvarez de Castro is reputed to have died. Some of the inner buildings weren't ever finished, as is evident in the skeleton of the **church**. The real wonder lies beneath the parade ground, where cathedral-like **deposits** store water eight metres below the surface in a sabotage-proof marvel of hydraulic engineering designed to last out a year-long siege.

EATING

Figueres has a plethora of unimaginative **cafés** and **restaurants** on and around the Rambla and in the jumble of streets between there and the Teatre-Museu Dalí; it takes a little looking to unearth some better choices.

CAFÉS

Emporium
Rambla 10.
Daily 9am–10pm.
The friendliest café on the Rambla, with a relaxing terrace. Good snacks served throughout the day.

Interval
Pl Ajuntament 8.
Daily 8am–10pm.
This bustling terrace café in a busy square 100m southeast of the Teatre-Museu Dalí is a favourite meeting place for locals and tourists alike.

Royal
Rambla 28.
Daily 8am–10pm.
Resembling a quaint bygone railway bar, this old-fashioned establishment features wicker chairs and marble tables amid colourfully tiled walls.

RESTAURANTS

Can Punyetes
Ronda Firal 25.
Bustling restaurant 300m west of the Teatre-Museu Dalí, serving excellent Catalan food, specializing in *pà amb tomàquet* meals and chunky grilled meats amid a lively, rustic decor. Budget.

Castell 4
Pujada del Castell 4.
Fifty metres north of the Rambla, this Castilian restaurant serves lashings of chunky roast meat dishes and stews, and has a good selection of tapas.
Inexpensive.

FIGUERES

301

La Churraskita

c/Magre 5.

Closed Mon.

Busy Italian–Argentinian restaurant on a narrow backstreet, specializing in huge steaks and extremely good pizzas and fresh pasta. Inexpensive.

Duran

c/Lasauca 5.

Pleasantly cluttered old-world dining hall in a hotel off the Rambla, with well-cooked traditional Catalan fare. The menu includes a wide selection of meat and fish: the duck with pears and cod with *xamfaina* are very tasty, while the *crema catalana* ice cream with armagnac is glorious. Moderate.

Empordà

N-II km s/n.

The big, brightly lit restaurant in this pleasant hotel northwest of the centre is famous throughout Catalonia for its superb local food. Especially good are the *mar i muntanya* dishes and the fish and seafood. Expensive.

El Firal dels Burros

Ronda Firal 15.

Daily 9am–3pm & 5pm–1am.

This bodega 50m south of the tourist office serves a good *menú del dia* at €7.25 and appetizing platters of cheeses and pâtés. They also sell wines, cheese and *embotits* to take away. Budget.

Les Quadres

c/Baix 2, El Far d'Empordà.

This fabulous restaurant with stone vaulted ceilings and a lovely shaded terrace occupies a rambling 500-year-old tied cottage in a hamlet 1km southeast of Figueres. The house speciality is duck, cooked in a variety of ways, while you can also get salads, fish and *pà amb tomàquet* meals. Moderate.

El Setrill

Tortellà 10.

The pub-like frontage of this restaurant on a small street between the tourist office and the Rambla hides a lively eatery serving large portions of food from Catalan fare to pizzas, plus a reasonable *menú del dia* at €6.

FIGUERES

DRINKING AND NIGHTLIFE

For a daytime **drink**, there are plenty of bars on the northern side of the Rambla and on and around Plaça de l'Ajuntament. Traditionally, though, Figueres' **nightlife** has been comatose, most people departing to the brighter lights of L'Escala or Roses, although several new **bars** on Plaça del Sol are tempting some to stay. Lively *El Federal* is a great favourite, featuring surreal art, the re-creation of a living room clinging upside down to the ceiling and a fabulous interior garden for a long drink amid cooling greenery and subtle lighting. *Café de Nit* is for stylish thirty-somethings, its large dance floor covering music from 1980s pop to salsa, while thumping *La Serradora* (cover charge €4.80 includes first drink), occupying an old sawmill, is much younger, playing house with a mixture of Latin pop.

LISTINGS

Car rental Alfarent, Pl Estació 9 ⓣ 972 510 846.

Hospital 500m west of the Dalí Museum on Ronda Dr Aroles ⓣ 972 677 452.

Internet Bar Arcadia, c/St Antoni 7.

Pharmacy Cullell, Pl de l'Ajuntament 14.

Police Opposite the tourist office at Ronda Firal 4 ⓣ 972 510 111.

Post office 800m south of the Rambla at c/Sta Llogaia 60.

Taxis Stands on the north side of the Rambla ⓣ 972 500 008, and at the train station ⓣ 972 505 043.

AROUND FIGUERES

The most attractive of Figueres' outlying villages are **Vilabertran**, with its beautiful eleventh-century monastery, and the more cosmopolitan **Peralada**, boasting a Renaissance castle-casino and vineyards.

Vilabertran

Dominating the village of **VILABERTRAN**, 2km north-east of Figueres, is the **Canònica de Santa Maria de Vilabertran** (Tues–Sat 10am–1.30pm & 3–6.30pm, Sun 10am–1.30pm; Oct–May closes 1hr earlier & closed Sun; €2.40, free on Tues). Originally Augustinian, the monastery centres around its beautiful Romanesque church, setting for the marriage on Christmas Day in 1322 of the Catalan queen, Elisenda de Montcada, to King Jaume II of Aragon, who chose the town for the simple reason that royal weddings bestowed tax-free status on the town hosting it, and Vilabertran was small enough for this not to be a loss in income for the royal coffers. Crowned by a magnificent Lombard belfry, where three tiers of double arched windows on all four sides rise above the town, the church's heart is the tranquil twelfth-century cloister. Inside, an ornate fourteenth-century gold and silver cross rises almost two metres above the nave.

Vilabertran's prestigious Schubertiada festival (☎ 972 508 787; €15–21) features a series of concerts devoted to Schubert held in late August and early September.

For a bite to eat, aim for *L'Hostalet d'en Lons*, c/Concha 6 (closed Mon), a deceptively large **restaurant** inside an old house that serves very good Catalan fare.

Peralada

Some 5km northeast of Vilabertran, the road passes an intact Roman bridge before coming to the fortified medieval town of **PERALADA**, centred around an arcaded main square. Prime attraction is the splendid, moated Renaissance **Castell de Peralada**, which now houses vineyards and Catalonia's most stylish casino. The castle **museum** (July–Sept daily 10am–8pm; Oct–June Tues–Sun 10am–6.30pm; €4.50) holds a fine collection of glass and ceramics and a magnificent library containing 80,000 volumes, including 1000 versions of *Don Quixote* in dozens of languages; the ticket includes entry to the adjacent fourteenth-century **Convent de Sant Domènec** with its beautiful Romanesque cloister. You can buy wines produced by the castle, including good cavas, at the **Museu de Caves de l'Empordà**, in town at c/Dr Clos 4 (same hours).

There's a five-star **hotel**, *Golf Peralada* (℡972 538 287, ℻972 538 236, ⓦwww.golfperalada.com; 8x), alongside the golf course (see p.50), while **turisme rural** options include a two-bedroomed house at *La Costa*, c/Costa del Rector 6 (℡972 538 293; ❸), and rooms in the neighbouring hamlet of Vilanova de la Muga at *Mas Fresí*, L'Estanyol (℡972 502 003, ⓦwww.agroturisme.org/fresi; ❷).

A superb **meal** in the banquet hall of the *Casino Castell de Peralada*, c/St Joan (daily 9pm–12.30am; ℡972 538 125) will set you back around €54, while *Mas Molí* (closed Mon), in a restored farmhouse on the road to Vilabertran, charges similar prices for equally good Catalan cuisine. *Cal Sagristà*, c/Rodona 2 (closed Mon), offers much less expensive local home cooking.

Every July and August, the grounds of Peralada's casino and convent host a prestigious music festival (℡972 538 292, ⓦwww.festivalperalada.com; €3.60–€90).

AROUND FIGUERES

The Alt Empordà – north

The **northern** part of the **Alt Empordà** region is much more rugged than its neighbour to the south, a landscape where the wild grey of the Pyrenees meets the clear turquoise of the Mediterranean. Enjoying comparatively low-key tourism, catering mainly for Catalans, the region is still characterized by small-scale development and untouched inland villages. Boat and beach enthusiasts will find plenty of choice in the perfect waters of the dozens of generally uncrowded coves in the area, while walkers will relish days in the mountains and exploring the shoreline.

Map 3 at the back of the book covers
the whole Alt Empordà region.

Top draw is the arty, bohemian town of **Cadaqués**, made famous by having been Salvador Dalí's home for almost fifty years and still a magnet for artists and lotus-eaters. Separated from Cadaqués by the desolately beautiful **Cap de Creus** headland, the genteel, whitewashed town of

THE CAMÍ DE RONDA

Almost all of this stretch of coast can be walked. The Camí de Ronda (see p.49) leads from Portlligat (p.314) along the shore to Cap de Creus (p.319), from where the gruelling GR11 cuts across country to reach the shoreline again at Port de la Selva (p.320). North of here, the Camí de Ronda, with some sections following the road, is intact as far as Colera (p.335), where the GR92 takes over to scale the mountains to Portbou (p.339).

Port de la Selva sits quiet in a three-quarter-moon bay, while its inland parent of **Selva de Mar** remains unruffled by tourists. High on a mountain overlooking both is the **Monèstir de Sant Pere de Rodes**. At a crossroads between the coast and the **Serra de l'Albera** mountain range, the lively seaside town of **Llançà** is a curious split between its busy fishing port and sheltered inland settlement. The complexion changes with the tiny village of **Colera**, which has been all but missed out by tourism, and the old trading town and railway terminus of **Portbou**, on the French border.

Cadaqués and around

Often referred to as an island on the coast, the beautiful fishing village of **CADAQUÉS** has been protected from mass tourism by the tortuous route in through the mountains. Successive town councils have steadfastly resisted attempts to improve the access and there is still only one road in and out today.

Cadaqués was discovered by the likes of Picasso and Marc Chagall in the early 1900s, but its star quality was assured

CADAQUÉS AND AROUND

Roses ▲

Portlligat ▲

CADAQUÉS

DE ROSES

Es Arenella ▲

1 2 & A ◄

SOLITARI

SANTA BÀRBARA

DE LA PRUNA

DES COLOMER

NOU

DESTRO

EN SELVEN

TRILLA

SANT VICENÇ

DE L'HORTA VELLA

Bus
Station

Museu de
Cadaqués

SANT VICENÇ

DE LA FONT VELLA

CARITAT SERINYANA

CARITAT SERINYANA

LUÍS LLASSÓN

TERESA
MIRAMONT

SA RIERASA

DELS
AMETLLERS

DELS
LLEVANTOL

DELS
LLEVANTOL

C

D

Església de
Santa María

E

F

G

H 4

B

N

J

i

ST. ISIDRE

STA. MARGARIDA

BELLAIRE

STA. MARGARIDA

UNIÓ

SANT VICENÇ

SANT VICENÇ

EN GUILLEM DE BRUGUERA

PORTAL D'AMUNT

STA.
MARIA

DEL DR. CALLÍS

DEL DR. CALLÍS

DES VIGILANTS

Eduard
Marquina

RIBA NEMESI LLORENS

SILVI RAHOLA

RIBA NEMESI LLORENS

Port d'Alguer

Badia de Cadaqués

Es Baluard

Es Portal

Portixó

Salvador Dalí
Statue

Portixó

L

M

N

K

5

J

I

MIQUEL ROSSET

PALAU

PALAU

CARITAT SERINYANA

Es Poal

Es Pianc

PIANC

PIANC

PIANC

S. PERE

DE SA TORTORA

DE SA TORTORA

HORT D'EN SANÉS

DE LA MARGARIDA

CARRERÓ PUIG

PUIG

DEL DUC

OLIVERES

OLIGUERA

PUIG

CARBONERÓ PUIG

ANGELS PLANELLS

CARLES RIBA

CABRES

DEL DUC

DE PABLO RUIS PICASSO

DE LES CREUS

DE SANT ANTONI

SES FLORS

DEL FORN

PUIG VIDAL

PLAÇA
TORRE
LES CREUS

JOSEP PLA

PINTOR JOAN PONÇ

3

ACCOMMODATION

Hostal Cristina	5
Llané Petit	1
Playa Sol	2
Rocamar	2
Hostal Vehi	4

CAFÉS, BARS & RESTAURANTS

El Barroco	D	L'Hostal	K
Café de la Habana	A	La Sirena	G
Can Tito	L	Pizzeria Cesar	F
Casa Anita	I	Rincón de Marta	E
Casino	C	Si Té 7	B
Celeste	G	Tropical	N
La Frontera	J	Vehi	H

N

0   100 m

when **Salvador Dalí** settled at the neighbouring Portlligat cove in 1930; his home has now been turned into a fascinating **museum**. The focus of the town is the small hill dominated by its **church** overlooking the string of pretty pebble **coves** lining the enclosed bay. To the north, a minor road heads out to the wild **Cap de Creus** headland.

ARRIVAL AND INFORMATION

Cadaqués is reached along mountain **roads** from Roses to the south and Port de la Selva to the north, which meet 5km west of the town for the winding descent. Regular daily **buses** from Barcelona and Figueres, as well as two each from Girona, Roses and Port de la Selva, pull in at the bus stop near the large paying **car park** at the entrance to town. The nearest train stations are in Llançà and Figueres.

The small **tourist office**, c/Cotxe 2 (Mon–Sat 10am–1pm & 4–8pm; Easter–Oct also Sun 10am–1pm; ⊤972 258 315), is in an office behind the seafront Casino building.

ACCOMMODATION

Cadaqués has few **hotels**, so you should always reserve well in advance. AIC, Passeig 6 (⊤972 258 266, ⓕ972 258 145, ⓦwww.inmobiliariacadaques.com), has a fairly wide choice of **apartments**, most of which are the preserve of second-homers. **Campers** must rely on *Camping Cadaqués*, Ctra Portlligat 17 (⊤972 258 126, ⓕ972 159 383; April–Sept), an average-shaded site with good-sized plots near the Dalí house.

Hostal Cristina
c/Riera 5 ⊤ 972 258 138.
Closed Oct–Dec.

This cheerful *hostal* occupies an old veranda-fronted building a short distance from the main beach. The rooms are small but well furnished and have en-suite bathrooms. ❸

Llané Petit

c/Dr Bartomeus 37 ⓣ 972 258 050, ⓕ 972 258 778, ⓔ llanepetit@ctv.es.
Smart, friendly hotel that makes for a relaxing option overlooking a less crowded beach at the south end of town. Half of the rooms have splendid sea views, and all have air conditioning and spacious terraces. ❻

Misty

Ctra Portlligat ⓣ 972 258 962, ⓕ 972 159 090.
Closed Jan & Feb.
The low buildings of this hacienda-style hotel, in a residential area between Cadaqués and Portlligat, are grouped around a small swimming pool and well-tended gardens. Most bedrooms give onto the garden. ❹

Playa Sol

Pianc 3 ⓣ 972 258 100, ⓕ 972 258 054, ⓦ www.playasol.com.

Closed Oct–Dec.
Tasteful place with a large pool, located on a curve in the seafront north of the centre. Rooms with a sea view give the best panorama in town, although the alternative, looking over tranquil gardens behind, is almost as appetizing. ❼

Port-Lligat

Portlligat ⓣ 972 258 162, ⓕ 972 258 643.
Closed Nov–Dec.
At the top of a flight of steps overlooking the Casa-Museu Dalí, this tranquil hotel with pool is ideal for roaming Cadaqués or the Cap de Creus. ❺

Rocamar

c/Verge del Carme s/n ⓣ 972 258 150, ⓕ 972 258 650, ⓦ www.rocamar.com.
Tucked away in a cove south of town, this pleasant hotel with tennis courts, a large pool and diving school is full of oak-beamed charm, its pleasant, airy rooms giving onto either the sea or the gardens. ❼

Hostal Vehí
c/ Església 6 ☎ 972 258 470.
Closed Nov–Feb.
Friendly, excellent-value
hostal in a lovely central
location near the church.
Most of the rooms have great
views, but all share
bathrooms. **❶**

THE TOWN AND AROUND

The focal point of the town is a bronze waterfront **statue** of an aloof Salvador Dalí, standing with his back to the sea, staring haughtily down on all the artists, shoppers and street musicians. The **Casa-Museu Dalí**, once his home, lies in Portlligat, 1km northeast.

From the Dalí statue, Cadaqués' shoreline stretches right and left past the jumble of old houses and tiny tracts of pebble **beach** to larger, quieter **coves** lining the bay. Set back from the seafront, the old town rises through narrow, cobbled streets to the **Església de Santa Maria**, surrounded by galleries and artists' studios.

CADAQUÉS ACTIVITIES

The best of the English-speaking diving schools are Scuba World, c/Font Vella 5 (☎ 629 491 380, 🖷 972 259 163, 🌐 www.cdgir.com/scubaworld), and Diving Center Cadaqués, at *Hotel Rocamar* (☎ 972 258 989). Kayaking is organized by Ones, Es Portal (☎ 937 532 512, 🌐 www.onesinter.net), and Kayaking Costa Brava at Portlligat (☎ 972 773 806, 🌐 www.kayakingcb.com), which offers full-moon and sunrise trips along the coves. Kayaks and boats can also be rented at Animal Area, Es Poal (☎ 972 258 027) and Nàutica Viñas, Ctra Roses (☎ 972 258 069), while boat trips to Cap de Creus run from Portitxó, organized by Creuers Cadaqués, Ctra Portlligat 28 (☎ 972 159 462).

The old town

The most impressive way to enter Cadaqués is to climb up to the **old town** from the car park at the entrance to town – come here on a Monday and you'll pass through the **market** held on Riera Sant Vicens. Chaotic layers of whitewashed buildings scaled by rich pink and purple bougainvillea line the low hill, which is crowned by the church. Near the bottom is the **Museu de Cadaqués**, c/Narcís Monturiol 15 (opening hours and prices vary), a gallery staging very good exhibitions of local art or displays relating to unusual aspects of Dalí's work.

The short path to the top of the old town leads to the sixteenth-century **Església de Santa Maria**, whose simple exterior features a tall, uncluttered belfry. A wrought-iron door bearing symbols of the town and the sea opens to the ornate eighteenth-century altarpiece; among the gilded carvings are Atlas supporting the world, St Rita, patron saint of the impossible, and St Barbara, protector from storms and shipwrecks. The most interesting side chapel is the third on the left, which was painted by Dalí.

The Església de Santa Maria hosts classical music concerts every summer; for information and tickets (€15–30), contact the tourist office.

Below the church, the pretty streets around Dr Callis and des Call gradually become busier with smart clothes shops, restaurants and artists' studios and galleries before emerging into the tiny **Plaça Dr Trèmols**, where a narrow archway leads down to the seafront.

The seafront and beaches

Turning left at the archway from the old town leads directly to **Portitxó**, alongside **Es Portal**, which together comprise the main pebble beach, flanking the Dalí statue. Of the two very popular cafés (both daily 9am–2am) either side of the statue, *Boia*, to the south, is the friendlier and serves good breakfasts, while *Marítim* is trendier and better suited to a late–night tipple.

Facing the Dalí statue is the small but busy **Passeig**, lined with bars and restaurants, including the celebrated *L'Hostal* (see p.318), where – it is said – Dalí once spent a legendary night drinking with Gabriel García Márquez and Mick Jagger.

To Platja Sa Conca and beyond

South from the Dalí statue, the road winds past the small **Es Baluard** point, a popular after-dark hangout for local hippies. At a bend in the road, the small pebble beach at **Port d'Alguer** attracts a stylish crowd while, beyond it, the **Llaner Gros** beach caters more for families. Further on, Punta des Bau des Sortell is too litter-strewn for swimming; you'd do better to press on 300m along the road to the right of *Hotel Llané Petit* to the sheltered **Platja Sa Conca**. About 100m south along the shore, a footpath to the right leads through a slate and cactus gully to the ruined **Capella de Pius V**, built to commemorate the 1571 Battle of Lepanto. The tranquil little chapel has an intact domed roof and a bas-relief of Pope Pius V discernible on the back wall.

A signposted Camí de Ronda climbs steeply from Sa Conca for a thirty-minute trek and scramble to some good swimming at the medium-shelving beach of **Cala Nans**, nearly always virtually empty. Five minutes south of here, a **lighthouse** marks the boundary of the Badia de Cadaqués and gives wonderful open views.

Casa-Museu Dalí

Portlligat. Mid-June to mid-Sept daily 10.30am–9pm; rest of year
Tues–Sun 10.30am–6pm; closed Jan & Feb; last entry 50min before
closing. ☎ 972 251 015, ⓦ www.dali-estate.org. €8.

At **PORTLLIGAT**, 1km northeast of Cadaqués along a
well-signposted road starting opposite the car park, the simple beauty of the tiny cove is rendered even more enticing
by the presence of the superb **Casa-Museu Dalí**, the artist's
main residence for some fifty years. Dalí and his Russian
wife, Gala, set up home in 1930 in an old fisherman's hut;
over the next forty years, they bought up all the huts around
to create a labyrinthine house, now converted into by far the
most enthralling of the three Dalí museums in the region;
the others are in Figueres (see p.297) and Púbol (see p.238).

Visitor numbers are strictly limited: you should always
book in advance by phone. Small groups get ten minutes
with a guide in each of four areas, which is ample. Note
that although all the furniture in the house belonged to
Dalí and Gala, all the paintings are copies of the originals in
the Teatre-Museu Dalí in Figueres.

The experience starts outside the museum – which
stands on a small **beach** littered with fishing boats – where
a tree grows through an old boat; a brightly coloured door
opposite is where Dalí would ask the fishermen to brush
their paintbrushes dry after painting their boats, to create
spontaneous art.

Access is through the **Hall of the Bear**, the first hut the
artist bought, where a stuffed bear greets visitors. Pictures
of people with moustaches are dotted throughout the
house, reflecting one of Dalí's obsessions, while yellow St
John's Wort is also in abundance, a touch of Gala's; both can
be seen in the adjacent **Dining Room** and **Library**. The
latter gives onto a patio, marking the start of the Via Làctea
("Milky Way"), a private cliff-top path.

The second area, on the first floor past a reproduction of *Atomic Leda*, is where Dalí worked, housing the **Models' Room** and his **Studio**. Here and in subsequent rooms there are large picture windows admitting a tremendous amount of light, framing – in contrast with the surreal art – the natural beauty of the surroundings.

A yellow boat moored near the house – which once belonged to Dalí and Gala – can be rented for their favourite sea jaunt as far as Cap de Creus (daily 10am–7pm, on the hour; €6).

In the third area, the **Yellow Room** is remarkable for the view, but also for a giant snail clock and the mirror to the left of the window, angled so that the couple could watch the sun rise without getting out of bed. Above this room are the **Bird Room** and the **Bedroom**. The tiny cages in the former were for cicadas from Olot, as Dalí felt they sang the most sweetly. In the bedroom, the bed on the right was Dalí's, while the tiny chairs were his wife's taste as they were reminiscent of Russian dolls. The **Photo Room** holds images of celebrities visiting Dalí, such as Harpo Marx, Laurence Olivier and Gregory Peck. The last indoor room, the domed **Oval Room**, was Gala's retreat and has remarkable acoustics.

The final area, the **Summer Dining Room** and **Patio**, was where the couple would entertain. The shaded **garden** topped by eggs (to symbolize life) gives on to the phallic-shaped **swimming pool**, resembling the fountains in Granada's Alhambra, surrounded by some splendid examples of surreal art using everyday objects.

EATING

The seafront between Portitxó and Es Baluard boasts a string of moderately priced seafood **restaurants**, any of which is worth trying, while dotted about the old town and along c/Miquel Rosset are places to suit a wide range of tastes and budgets.

El Barroco

c/Nou s/n.

Nov–March closed Sun–Tues.

With a logo designed by Dalí, who used to dine here in the summer, this extravagantly decorated restaurant centres around a jasmine and geranium garden. Specialities include a tasty tenderloin in raspberry sauce and vegetarian lasagne, all to the accompaniment of live classical piano. Moderate.

Can Tito

c/Vigilant s/n.

Nov–March closed Mon–Thurs.

In what appears to be a small warehouse hollowed out of a building, this superb establishment specializes in progressive Catalan cuisine, with especially good grilled fish, *favetes a la menta* (broad beans in mint) and *escalivada* pie. Expensive.

Casa Anita

c/Miquel Rosset 16 ☎ 972 258 471.

Another of Dalí's favourite haunts, this rustic-chic restaurant is in the heart of Cadaqués' night quarter and is always heaving. Huge portions of traditional and filling Catalan food are accompanied by slabs of *pà amb tomàquet*. Moderate.

Celeste

c/Nou 1.

Nov–March closed Wed.

A cheap and cheerful old town bar–restaurant, decorated with wicker furniture and abstract paintings and specializing in four types of pasta in eleven types of sauce. They also serve great cocktails. Budget.

Pizzeria Cesar

c/Curós 11.

Daily 8pm–midnight;
Nov–March closed Sun–Tues.

Below the church, this labyrinthine restaurant is in a former cottage, with a whitewashed stone interior. Serving a wide selection of delicious pizzas and imaginative salads – notably chicory and walnut – it's justly popular. Inexpensive.

Rincón de Marta
c/Curós 10.
Daily 8pm–midnight;
Nov–March closed Mon.

Bright and popular restaurant a short walk below the church specializing in new takes on pasta, salads, meat and fish dishes, especially the macaroni *à la vodka* and spaghetti in cream and courgette sauce. Inexpensive.

La Sirena
c/Es Call s/n.
Closed Feb & Nov.

Owned by a perfectionist Croatian chef, this superb restaurant, in a tiny street, serves some of the best fish dishes in town. Especially good is the *suquet*, while the desserts, such as the lemon and vodka ice cream, are fabulous. Inexpensive.

Vehí
c/ Església 6.
Closed Nov–Feb.

Near the church, this lovely restaurant has views of the town and bay, and serves traditional local cuisine, where the tuna mousse in a red pepper sauce is top choice. There's also a range of *menús del dia* from €9 to €11.30. Expensive.

DRINKING AND NIGHTLIFE

Nightlife in Cadaqués is a pleasurable blend of laid-back supping on the seashore and stylish hobnobbing in the streets of the old town and, especially, the night quarter of c/Miguel Rosset.

Café de la Habana
Porta d'en Pampà.

Rustic Cuban furnishings and eclectic paintings help create the atmosphere in this cool café serving an amazing selection of cocktails. Live music by a singer-songwriter every night at 11pm adds to the mellow tone.

CADAQUÉS AND AROUND ●

Casino

Riba Nemesi Llorens s/n.
This old-fashioned social centre of the town features high ceilings and subtle lighting. The conservatory-style front room is great for morning breakfast or evening cocktails, while modernity is encroaching with an internet room off the bar.

La Frontera

c/ Miquel Rosset 20. Closed Nov–Easter.
One of the trendiest places in town, this lively, friendly bar serves top cocktails. The noisy interior contrasts nicely with a pleasant garden bursting with flowers.

L'Hostal

Pg del Mar 8.
Nov–March closed Mon.
The first bar of its kind in Catalonia when it opened in 1901, which subsequently became Dalí's favourite haunt. A vaguely surreal feel lingers, with bizarre artworks jostling for wall space with photos of the rich and famous who have passed through its doors. Live jazz and rock plays every night in the summer, while the outdoor terrace is the coolest place on the block.

Si Té 7

Riba d'en Pitxot.
Nov–March closed Mon & Tues.
In a great location overlooking the beach at Port d'Alguer, this tiny bar – with an amiable Catalan owner – is perfect for late-night mellowing to jazz, blues and reggae.

Tropical

c/Miquel Rosset 19.
A lush, candlelit garden leads into a cavernous interior where fish painted on driftboard line the natural rock painted to resemble the sea bed. In all, a fun place to sip a cocktail and listen to Spanish Caribbean tunes.

LISTINGS

Bike and scooter rental
Rent@bit, Avgda Caritat
Serinyana 7 ⓣ 972 251 023;
Animal Area, Platja Es Poal
ⓣ 972 258 027.
Health centre c/Nou ⓣ 972
258 807.
Internet Casino, Riba Nemesi
Llorens (daily 9pm–1am);
Estocafix, c/Miquel Rosset
(daily 11.30am–1.30pm &
5–9pm); on@, c/Miguel Rosset
3 (daily 10am–9pm); Rent@bit,
Avgda Caritat Serinyana 7 (daily
10am–1pm & 5–9pm).
Pharmacies Colomer, Ctra
Port-Lligat; Moradell, Pl
Frederic Rahola.
Police c/Vigilant 2 ⓣ 972 159
343.
Post office c/Rierassa (Mon–Fri
9am–2pm, Sat 9.30am–1pm).
Taxi Stand on corner of Passeig
and Avgda Caritat Serinyana
ⓣ 972 258 268.

CAP DE CREUS

From Portlligat, a spectacular road climbs 6km through a
lunar landscape to the wild **Cap de Creus** headland. Along
the way, the route passes secluded coves and a sand-
coloured rock formation after about 4km known as **El
Camell**, in the shape of a haughty, seated camel. Walkers
can take the spectacular if demanding **Camí de Ronda**
footpath, which follows the rocky shoreline from Portlligat
and offers lots of opportunities along the way to take a dip.

Alternative ways of getting to Cap de Creus from Cadaqués
include minibus (contact Passarella, Avgda Caritat Serinyana
23 ⓣ 972 258 771; €12), and the mini-train from Portitxó
beach (daily 10am–6pm, hourly; 2hr round trip; €9.80).

Best of the beaches en route are **Platja de Sant Lluís**,
reached by a twenty-minute signposted footpath through
olive terraces, where both nude and clothed bathers enjoy

CADAQUÉS AND AROUND

319

an uncrowded pebble beach. Almost at the headland, a yellow rambler sign by a crash barrier signals a parking place for the climb down to a pair of wild coves – **L'Infern** ("Hell") and the prettier **Cala Jugadora**, great for swimming.

The Cap de Creus **headland** itself (where you'll find plenty of parking) is the most easterly point in the Iberian peninsula, a fact celebrated by dawn revels every New Year's Day. A **lighthouse** dating from 1853 stands in juxtaposition with the false lighthouse built nearer the edge of the cliff for the 1971 film, *The Light at the End of the World* (see p.357). Crowning the clifftop, the *Cap de Creus* bar and **restaurant** (Mon–Thurs noon–8pm, Fri–Sun 11am–midnight) serves food, from Catalan to Indian, and has a great terrace.

Port de la Selva and around

Exuding a peeling-paint charm, the whitewashed town of **PORT DE LA SELVA**, tucked away in a small near-circular bay 13km northwest of Cadaqués, doesn't possess a single high-rise block. The town centres around the fishing and pleasure **ports** and an uncluttered **promenade**, while either side are a string of lovely **coves**, rugged to the north, gentler to the west. The inland parent town of **Selva de Mar** is quieter still and makes for a pleasant afternoon's visit, while the imposing **Monèstir de Sant Pere de Rodes** and even more atmospheric **Castell Sant Salvador** tower over the area from atop the craggy Serra de Rodes.

ARRIVAL AND INFORMATION

Port de la Selva is reached by a signposted turning off the winding **road** heading inland from Cadaqués, which joins the coast-hugging GI612 route heading southeast from Llançà 500m south of the town itself. There's **parking** to the right of the road and by the beach.

Six **buses** a day make the trip from Figueres and Llançà (the latter has the nearest train station), while a further two buses arrive from Cadaqués on their way to Barcelona. All buses stop on the seafront near the entrance to the town, a short distance past the car park.

There's a small **tourist office**, c/Mar 1 (June–Sept daily 8am–10pm; Oct–May Mon–Fri 8am–3pm, Sat 9am–1pm; ☎972 387 025, ⓦ www.ddgi.es/porselva), in the seafront town hall, past the fishing port.

ACCOMMODATION

The few **hotels** and **hostals** are of a high standard. *Porto Cristo*, c/Major 59 (☎972 387 062, ⑤972 387 529, ⓔ portocristo@retemail.es; ❼; closed Jan & Feb), is a sumptuous converted merchant's mansion on a quiet backstreet. Each room is unique, characterized by king-size beds, marble floors and circular baths. On a tiny street near the port is the smart *Pensió Sol y Sombra*, c/Nou 8–10 (☎972 387 060, ⑤972 387 527, ⓔ solisombra@oem.es; ❸), offering generous-sized rooms with air conditioning. Cheerful *Hostal La Tina*, c/Sant Baldiri 15 (☎972 387 149, ⑤972 126 013, ⓦ www.gna.es/hostallatina; ❷), one street back from the beach, has a broad choice of spacious rooms, all with a copious buffet breakfast thrown in; the owners also have apartments and a house for rent.

Finques Morell, c/Illa 2 (☎972 126 396, ⑤972 387 088, ⓔ agmorell@teleline.es), has the best range of **villas** and

apartments in the area. Top-choice **campsite** is shaded *Port de la Vall*, Ctra Llançà–Port de la Selva km6 (ⓣ & ⓟ972 387 186, ⓦwww.campingportdellavall.com; closed Oct–Easter), running down to the beach at the northern entrance to town.

THE TOWN AND AROUND

The town hugs a strip of the southern and eastern shores of its bay, but extends inland for barely more than two streets all the way along: walking distances are long, and yet the main attraction is in wandering among the town's simple whitewashed buildings.

From the car park and bus stop near the entrance to town, the road runs northeast alongside the blue-flag **Platja Gran**, a popular beach despite its steep shelving and occasional jellyfish warnings. From here, you'll stumble almost immediately onto the café-lined **Plaça Dr Oriol** and the short **promenade**, truncated by the bustling **fishing port**, which juts out squarely into the bay. Past here, the narrow road wends its way towards the end of the harbour.

North of the centre

The seaside road north passes the leisure marina before coming to a string of small beaches. The first, **Platja d'en Pas**, a steeply shelving pebble beach, boasts some of the cleanest water in the Mediterranean, but it does get busy. Some 200m north from here, the road ends and a footpath takes over to **Cala Tamariua**, a sheltered pebble cove favoured by clothed and nude bathers. The path picks up again the far side of the beach, hugging the shoreline for 700m to the tiny **Cala Cativa** inlet, where a fishermen's refuge stands on the water's edge. A quarter-hour of scrambling along the less stable path from here culminates in the delightful pebble beach of **Cala Fornells**, where an ancient lime kiln made of stones still stands.

The best way to see the isolated coves further east towards Cap de Creus is to take a cruise from Llançà (see p.331).

West around the bay

The **beaches** to the west of town – far less rugged than the coves to the north – can be reached along the Camí de Ronda. Some 2km from the town, a signposted turning to the right leads to a haphazard parking area on the **Punta de S'Arenella**, a scrubby headland surmounted by a solitary lighthouse, where the quiet little coves are good for snorkelling. The Cau del Llop beach in Llançà (see p.334) is 3km further north.

EATING

Choice of **restaurants** is limited. Both the *Pensió Sol y Sombra* and *Hostal La Tina* (see p.321) serve tasty staple food at reasonable prices, while terraces along the seafront either side of the fishing port serve a wide selection of snacks.

Ca l'Herminda
c/Illa 7.
Sept–June closed Mon & Tues.
In the cellars of an old fisherman's house near the fishing port, this bustling restaurant specializes in seafood and fresh fish, serving very good *suquet* and *sarsuela*. Expensive.

Club Nàutic
c/Moll Gros 1.
Daily noon–11pm; Sept–June closed Mon–Thurs.
With a large terrace, the marina restaurant serves a wide choice of food and has a reasonable *menú del dia* as well as set menus for two. For a cheaper option, try the tapas

and chunky sandwiches, available throughout the day. Expensive.

Llevantina
c/Illa s/n.
Daily 10am–11pm; Sept–June closed Mon.

With a terrace on the water's edge between the fishing port and the marina, this relaxing bar has tranquil views and serves great tapas. Budget.

Monterrey
c/Platja 5.
Daily noon–11.30pm; Sept–June closed Mon.

Opposite the beach, this terrace restaurant serves a wide range of tasty food, from seafood to pizzas, and lovely homemade desserts. It's also a bar (open until 3am), and makes great cocktails for an unhurried night-time drink. Inexpensive.

Porto Cristo
c/Major 59.
Closed Jan & Feb.

This cavernous restaurant in a nineteenth-century town mansion is hugely atmospheric. Specializing in Catalan cuisine, it is rightly famous for the chef's superb daily specialities and the delicious homemade desserts. Moderate.

DRINKING AND NIGHTLIFE

Port de la Selva's **nightlife**, while sedate, is still enticing and varied. There are several terrace bars strung along the seafront, including a couple of summer *xiringuitos* in the port.

Cal Sereno
c/Cantó dels Pescadors 4.
Sept–June closed Wed.

In a narrow street between the fishing and leisure ports, this semi-surreal bar gets joyously packed in the early hours. Set in the cellar of a 250-year-old fisherman's cottage, it's named after the former owner, who would serenade his wife on returning from sea so that she would let him in.

Café Espanya
c/Illa 1.

Daily 10am–3am; Sept–June closed Mon–Thurs.

This old-fashioned seafront café appeals to all sorts, from domino-playing elderly men to stylish youngsters. In the summer, it has a great terrace on the water's edge and serves anything from tapas to a late-night drink.

Gus
c/Lloia 1.

Daily noon–3am; Sept–June closed Tues.

Overlooking the pleasure marina, this cheerful bar has a great terrace and serves tapas and sandwiches along with cocktails. In the evening, the quiet veranda contrasts with the lively interior, where a younger crowd gathers around the pool table.

Mackintosh
Ctra Cadaqués.

Sept–June closed Mon–Thurs.

This unpretentious disco has all the spontaneous fun of a Catalan small-town nightspot, where a catholic selection of locals, with one or two tourists thrown in, strut their stuff to an eclectic musical choice.

SELVA DE MAR

The foothill setting of **SELVA DE MAR**, 2km inland from Port de la Selva, has contributed to preserving the unhurried peace of this medieval village, centred around the shaded terrace cafés of the **Plaça Camp de l'Obra**.

Turning right into the street at the top of the steps on Plaça Camp de l'Obra leads you past a fortified house and through a narrow alley to the start of a **walk**, indicated by a rambler signpost, which gives a complete tour of the outskirts. Follow the signs along a track leading upwards past vineyards until you come to an ancient **stone bench** decorated with lions. The trail leads down from here to the remains of a small **water mill** and the steep waterfall that

SELVA DE MAR

fed it – a lovely spot. Across a bridge by a small square with a fountain, the path climbs again through evergreen oaks to the twelfth-century fortified **Església de Sant Sebastià**, directly aligned with the church in Port de la Selva. The track back to the centre skirts the church to the right, descending past cultivated terraces to the edge of the village, where three tiny and ancient **stone bridges** span the rocky riverbed running through Selva de Mar.

From the Església de Sant Sebastià, a waymarked hike (4hr) leads to the monastery at Sant Pere de Rodes (see opposite).

Practicalities

Non-residents aren't permitted to take cars into Selva de Mar, but there's plenty of **parking** space in a field on the edge of the village. A small summer **tourist office** operates from the town hall, c/Camp de l'Obra (July & Aug Mon 9.30am–1pm & 4–8pm, Wed 4–8pm, Tues, Thurs & Fri 9.30am–1pm; ⊤972 387 228).

For **accommodation**, the atmospheric *Fonda Felip*, Plaça Camp de l'Obra 15 (⊤972 387 271; ❷; closed Oct–Easter), has pleasant double rooms, en suite and not. Its **restaurant** is good, as is that of the rustic *Ca L'Elvira*, c/Baix 1 (closed Oct–Easter), which serves excellent Catalan food and an inexpensive *menú del dia*. For a **snack** or **drink**, try the superb *El Celler de la Selva* (daily noon–3am) in a five-century-old tied house on Plaça Camp de l'Obra, which stages live music in the summer amid surreal art and luscious cocktails. This was a favourite haunt of Dalí's and the setting for one of his preferred pastimes of autographing women's bottoms.

SANT PERE DE RODES AND AROUND

Monastery open Tues–Sun: June–Sept 10am–8pm; Oct–May
10am–2pm & 3–5.30pm. €3.60, free on Tues.

Some 6km inland from Port de la Selva, off the road to
Selva de Mar, tortuous hairpin bends climb 675m to a trin-
ity of ancient buildings, dominated by the rambling
Benedictine **Monèstir de Sant Pere de Rodes**. There's
space for parking (€1.20) about 500m before you reach the
monastery, from where you'll have to proceed on foot.

Legend has it that, in the seventh century, in the face of
barbarian threats on Rome, **Pope Boniface IV** ordered a
safe haven to be found for countless holy relics. They were
hidden in this region by a trio of hapless **monks**, who then
forgot where, and so built a monastery rather than return to
face the pope's wrath. Historians, though, claim that this
was the site of an ancient **temple of Venus**. By the tenth
century the monastery had become wealthy: four centuries
of splendour ended in 1789 with the site's abandonment.

Sant Pere de Rodes used to be one of the most romantic
ruins in Catalonia but over-zealous restoration is robbing it
of a great deal of its charm. No original columns or capitals
remain in the **cloister** and the new pantiled roofs are just
too tidy. The redeeming feature, apart from the superb
views, is the **church**, which retains tenth- to fourteenth-
century stonework in its three naves, including delicate
carvings of animals on the capitals. Below the church are
atmospheric **lower cloisters**; excavations have turned up
traces of pre-Romanesque **murals**.

In July (Sun 8pm), there are classical piano recitals in
the Monèstir de Sant Pere de Rodes; get information and
tickets from the Port de la Selva tourist office.

Castell Sant Salvador

Far more spectacular than Sant Pere de Rodes is the smouldering silhouette of the ruined **Castell Sant Salvador**, perched on the summit of the mountain and reached by a steeply climbing footpath from outside the monastery. You'll need to be reasonably agile to make the thirty-minute ascent, especially the last few metres and the hop up into the castle walls; once at the top, you should take extreme care as there are no barriers between parts of the ruins and a sheer drop. What remains today dates from the tenth and eleventh centuries, primarily the perimeter walls and alternate semicircular and square towers. The **views** are breathtaking.

Llançà and around

About 7km northwest of Port de la Selva – and 14km south of the French border – the quiet town of **LLANÇÀ** is divided between the original tenth-century settlement, the **Vila**, built inland to escape the attentions of marauding pirates, and the **Port**. Southeast of the town, a string of busy coves stretches to Port de la Selva, while, to the north, initially crowded beaches lead to the desolate **Cap Ras** headland, indented with tranquil pockets of rock and sand, with less picturesque **Colera** a little north.

ARRIVAL AND INFORMATION

Llançà sits at the point where the N260 coastal **road** from Portbou cuts inland to Figueres; six **buses** a day from Figueres and two from Portbou stop in the Port and the

Vila. A local road snakes along the shore from Port de la Selva, and there's paid **parking** in the Port and Vila. The **train station**, 1km northeast of the town, has regular services from Portbou, Figueres and Girona.

A helpful **tourist office** lies halfway along the road connecting the Vila with the Port, at Avgda Europa 37 (July & Aug Mon–Sat 9.30am–9pm; rest of year Mon–Fri 9.30am–2pm & 4.30–8pm, Sat 10am–1pm & 5–7pm; ⊕972 380 855, ⊛www.llanca.net). There's a summer **office** in the Torre de la Plaça in the Vila (June–Sept Mon–Fri 5.30–9pm, Sat 6.30–9pm).

The **police** station is on c/Colomer in the Vila (⊕972 381 313). There's a **taxi** stand on c/Castellar near the Passeig Marítim at the Port (⊕689 393 939).

ACCOMMODATION

The beach **hotels** and **pensions** are good value. Numerous **apartments** are available in the Port or on the hillsides either side; the agency with the widest choice is Finques Palandriu, Avgda Pau Casals 25–27 (⊕972 120 568, ⊕972 120 074, ⊛www.palandriu.com).

Berna
Pg Marítim 13, Port ⊕972 380 150, ⊕972 121 509.
Closed Oct–April.
Great location on the beach opposite the port adds to the attraction of this pleasant hotel. All the rooms are spacious and most have large balconies giving onto the sea. ❹

La Goleta
c/Pintor Torroella 12, Port ⊕972 380 125, ⊕972 120 686, ⊕goleta@xecweb.com.
Fifty metres from the port, this charming hotel exudes a sense of tradition. The spacious antique-furnished rooms feature air conditioning and modern bathrooms. ❹

LLANÇÀ AND AROUND

329

Grimar

Ctra Portbou ⓣ 972 380 167,
ⓕ 972 381 200,
ⓔ grimar@speedcom.es.
Closed Oct–Easter.

This plush hotel outside town – with no public transport access – is set in its own extensive lawns, with tennis courts and a large pool. The rooms are simple but airy, boasting ceiling fans and wicker decor. ❺

Maria Teresa

c/Cabrafiga s/n, Vila ⓣ 972 380 004, ⓕ 972 380 276,
ⓦ www.hmteresa.com.
Closed Nov–April.

Between the town and the beach, this hotel is run on ecological principles, offering vegetarian and conventional cuisine and yoga and tai-chi classes. The rooms are rustic but comfortable and most give onto a pine wood. ❷

Miramar

Pg Marítim 7, Port ⓣ 972 380 132.
Closed Sept–Feb.

One of the earliest hotels in Llançà, in a perfect setting on the seafront – a family establishment which has been extensively renovated, with the added benefit of a very good restaurant. ❹

THE TOWN

A sharp turn-off from the Port de la Selva road heads southeast to Llançà's **Port**, site of the Wednesday **market**, leading past the shops and restaurants of **Carrer Castellar**. East of this, the modern **Passeig Marítim** follows the curve of the sandy **beach**; at the south end is the fishing port – much older and livelier than the rest of the quiet seafront. Crowning the port, the craggy **Es Castellar** point is a favourite place for an evening stroll; below it, the quiet **Platja de la Gola**, a medium-shelving beach, is good for swimming, but its waters get very choppy when the wind is up.

As well as diving courses, Centre d'Immersió Cap de Creus (☎ 972 120 000, ⓦ www.cicapcreus.com) runs spectacular cruises among the hard-to-reach coves around Llançà and Port de la Selva, as far east as Cap de Creus. SK Kayak (☎ 627 433 332, ⓦ www.skkayak.com) runs good kayak excursions from the port.

The small **Vila** revolves around the lively **Plaça Major**, where pavement cafés sit in the shade of the Arbre de la Llibertat, a huge plane tree planted in 1870 to commemorate freedom from France, and where locals flock for *sardanes* and live music through the summer. Adjacent to the square is the imposing fourteenth-century **Torre de la Plaça** (Mon–Fri 5.30–9pm, Sat 6.30–9pm), crowned by battlements and a pyramid-shaped roof; the remnants of a roof halfway up show that it was once part of a larger construction. During recent restoration work, medieval stocks were unearthed and are now on display on the ground floor; the top floor offers views over the port and the Serra de l'Albera mountains.

To the right of the tower, the **Museu de l'Aquarel.la Martínez Lozano** (June–Sept Mon–Sat 7–9pm, Sun 11am–1pm & 7–9pm; rest of year Sat & Sun 11am–1pm & 6–8pm; €1.80), the first museum in Spain devoted purely to watercolours, is a small-scale gem. A surprising variety of twentieth-century works jostles for attention, collected by local painter Martínez Lozano, whose own bustling streetscenes contrast with the measured realism and bold abstracts of the more modern painters and the earlier, traditional pieces.

EATING

Most good **restaurants** are in the Port rather than the Vila. Llançà has an abundance of good fresh fish and seafood eateries – in general, the busiest are the best – although you'll also find a variety of other cuisines.

La Brasa

Pl Catalunya 6, Port.

Oct–May closed Mon.

Behind c/Castellar away from the seafront, this family fish restaurant stands out for its lovely garden, excellent *fideuà*, a tasty couscous special every Thursday, and a reasonable range of *menús del dia*. Moderate.

Can Narra

c/Castellar 37, Port.

Sept–June closed Sun eve & Mon; also closed Oct.

The best of the traditional fish restaurants, overlooking the beach and serving top *suquet* and a huge *graellada de peix* (fish platter). Also a very reasonable *menú del dia* at €11.25. Moderate.

Celler de Llançà

c/Lepanto 5, Port.

Sept–June closed Mon.

This small tavern, serves outstanding Catalan food, including a wide variety of salads and platters of very tasty cheese, pâté and *embotit*,

just made for sharing. Vegetarians will find a good choice: plump for spinach cannelloni. Budget.

Els Pescadors

c/Castellar 41, Port.

Sept–June closed Sun eve & Mon; also closed Oct.

This popular terrace restaurant offers imaginative variations on standard fishy fare. Best of all are the light foie gras terrine in orange and vanilla sauce and the prawn carpaccio with truffle vinaigrette. Expensive.

Le Provençal

Pg Marítim 1, Port.

Sept–June closed Mon.

Pizzeria between c/Castellar and the beach serving inventive, succulent Italian food with a Provençal twist, including a very good octopus and seafood pizza and lovely baked camembert in redcurrant sauce. Inexpensive.

La Vela

Avgda Pau Casals 23, Port.

Sept–June closed Mon; also closed mid-Oct to mid-Nov. Plush restaurant, decorated in crisp white throughout, serving superb fish, especially the *graellada de peix*, and seafood, plus a range of innovative local meat dishes – duck with glazed figs, for instance. Moderate.

DRINKING AND NIGHTLIFE

Llançà's nightlife scene is easy-going, with a few trendy **bars** mingled with seafront terraces. Locals and Catalan holidaymakers favour having a meal and an early drink in the Port, before moving on to the Vila.

One out-of-town nightspot worth a visit is **Rachdingue** (Easter–Oct daily 11.30pm–5am; €8.50), which occupies a surreally decorated old house 9km southwest of Llançà between Vilajuïga and Pau. Once a favourite of Salvador Dalí, who designed the logo, it boasts a pool and two dance areas, playing techno, house, jungle and trip-hop; the mixture of Dalí and music gives it a broad appeal.

Café de l'Havana
c/Castellar 40, Port.
Daily 10am–3am.
The walls of this small, laid-back bar are covered in photos of old Llançà, old Havana and Che Guevara. A small pavement terrace copes with the overflowing clientele of all ages savouring *mojitos*.

Carajillo
c/Gardissó 17, Vila.
Daily 9am–3am.
This big, hip bar is adorned with Hopper prints and cool, young Spanish art and attracts an eclectic crowd. The lively interior, with pool table and a scattering of tables and chairs, contrasts with the mellow tranquillity of the garden.

Planetarium
Avgda Mestral 19, Port.
Sept–June closed Sun–Thurs.
Half a dozen shiny planets dangling from the ceiling mark the theme of this trendy bar, popular with a younger

LLANÇÀ AND AROUND

crowd. Its small dance floor hosts mainly house and garage.

summer terrace attracts a wider crowd.

Port de Nit
Avgda Pau Casals 25, Port. Sept–June closed Sun–Thurs. Abstract art in this designer bar reflects the trendy image of the twenty- and thirty-something clientele on the techno dance floor, while the

La Taverna del Pirata
c/Rafael Estela 19, Vila. An extravagant bar off Plaça Major decorated with a surreal-inspired hotchpotch of anything that came to hand. A favourite late-night haunt, especially for the live rock and reggae at weekends.

SOUTH TO CAU DEL LLOP

Beaches **south of Llançà** can be reached from steps climbing up to the headland from Platja de la Gola (see p.330), which lead past windblasted honeycomb rocks to the unpaved Camí de Ronda. Past a high unfenced cliff, the path drops down to small pebble beaches, which rarely get crowded and which offer great snorkelling amid the rocky inlets. The last of Llançà's beaches, gently shelving **Cau del Llop**, is the busiest of all owing to its good parking and proximity to apartments; the coarse grey sand boasts a bar and showers. Beyond it, the Camí de Ronda continues for 3km to the Punta de S'Arenella headland (see p.323), north of Port de la Selva.

CAP RAS AND BEYOND

The beaches **north of Llançà** on the 7km route to Colera can be reached by the Camí de Ronda, which hugs the water's edge, or by the main N260 road, which swoops in and out of the shoreline.

Some 3km from town, past the uninspiring Platja Grifeu, a signposted turn-off on the brow of a hill leads to the cluster of coves on the **Cap Ras** headland. Don't be put off by the number of cars, as the warren of little beaches can soak up a lot of bodies. Tracks crisscross the headland amid low pines, bamboo and scrub, dipping down to the sea. The **pebble beaches** on the south side get slightly busier but the shallow shelving is great for splashing about in. The tip of Cap Ras – almost always deserted – is thoroughly wild, with trees bent horizontal by past *tramuntanes* and rock pools and craggy inlets. Around the point, the trails clamber sharply down to sheltered **sandy beaches** on the north side, which are more steeply shelving and are very much the domain of nude bathers.

Past Cap Ras, the road picks up the shoreline again before descending to **Platja Garbet**, a pebble beach that gets extremely crowded – largely because of a superb (and expensive) seafood **restaurant** on the water's edge, the *Garbet* (Easter–Oct daily 11am–11pm; rest of year closed Mon–Thurs). Should you not fancy a full-on fish supper, though, you can fill up on tapas here.

COLERA

The sleepy town of **COLERA**, 7km north of Llançà, runs along a riverbed to the sea. It's an unprepossessing town dominated by the huge iron railway bridge passing high overhead, but is rendered inviting by its rugged beaches. The core of the town, **Plaça Pi i Margall**, is 200m back from the beach; here you'll find a pair of pavement cafés around the base of the sheltering Arbre de la Llibertat. Walking north along the sheltered pebble beach brings you to **Platja d'en Goixa**. Steep steps from here climb up to a small road, which leads about 650m north to wild, windblown **Punta de l'Escala**, reached by a public footpath

LLANÇÀ AND AROUND

leading precariously down beneath a house to the rocks below. The solitude is rewarding, but you need to be a confident swimmer to cope with the underwater currents.

Colera's **train station**, with only irregular services between Portbou and Llançà, is a five-minute walk northwest of the beach. At the top of a flight of steps off Plaça Pi i Margall, the **tourist office**, c/Labrun 34 (Easter–Sept Mon–Fri 10am–2pm & 4–8pm; ☏972 389 050), is on the first floor of the tiny town hall. The best **place to stay** is the modern *La Gambina*, Pg Marítim 5 (☏972 389 172; ⑤), on the beach, which doubles up as the top **restaurant**, serving excellent fish. Friendly *Hostal Mont Mercé*, c/Mar 107 (☏972 389 126; ③), has comfortable rooms, some with a sea view.

Parc Natural de l'Albera

With the lowest passes anywhere in the Pyrenees, the **Serra de l'Albera** mountains – occupying the hinterland between Figueres and the French border – have always been a thoroughfare. The **PARC NATURAL DE L'ALBERA** was granted protected status in 1986, creating safe havens for indigenous flora and fauna and helping to preserve an unspoilt environment of sheer escarpments and hidden villages. Perfect **walking** country, or for roaming by car, the region is home to secluded monastic ruins, Neolithic dolmens and a stunning variety of **wildlife**, including tortoises, a protected species of Albera cow, golden eagles and wild boar.

GARRIGUELLA

About 9km west of Llançà on the GI603 lies the thriving, thousand-year-old village of **GARRIGUELLA**, remarkable for its dissonantly large **Església de Santa Eulàlia de Noves**. First recorded in the tenth century, the present church was built in 1722 of unworked stone, belying its ornate interior. Based on the original Romanesque building, the large central nave is crowned by a pronounced vault supported on three arches.

Centre de Reproducció de Tortugues de l'Albera

Santuari del Camp. July–Sept daily 9am–1pm & 4–7pm; closed Nov–March; April–June hours vary. ℗ 972 552 245. €3.

A narrow, signposted road from Garriguella leads 500m to the fascinating **Centre de Reproducció de Tortugues de l'Albera** (Mediterranean Tortoise Reproduction Centre), which sets out to protect the creatures in their last remaining natural habitat in the Iberian peninsula. Over two hundred tortoises a year born in the centre are released with transmitters, in order to monitor them in an environment devastated each summer by forest fire, the main factor endangering their existence. The centre is laid out to recreate the different ecosystems in which the tortoises thrive. The circular path (about 90min) begins with the appealingly tiny newborns and moves through dryland and wetland habitats, taking in other endangered breeds of such as shy pond turtles and massive African spurred tortoises.

The tiny Santuari de Santa Maria del Camp, outside the tortoise centre, marks a legend that Charlemagne built a church here in the eighth century. The present chapel is sixteenth century but holds an intricate mural relating the story.

GARRIGUELLA

Practicalities

For **accommodation**, there are several good *turisme rural* houses in Garriguella, particularly the stone *Can Garriga*, c/Figueres 3 (⊗972 530 184; ❹), with airy bedrooms, and *Mas Hortus*, c/Despoblat 1 (⊗972 530 261, ⓔdecibelio36 @hotmail.com; ❻), which has two well-equipped apartments for rent. At the entrance to the village is the excellent *Vell Empordà* **campsite**, Ctra La Jonquera (⊗972 530 200, ⓕ972 552 343, ⓦwww.vellemporda.com). For a **meal**, *Can Battle*, Plaça de Baix (Oct–May closed Sun–Thurs), is famous for its fish and traditional cuisine.

ESPOLLA

ESPOLLA, a crisp mountain village 9km northwest of Garriguella in the centre of the park, is set around the leaning belfry of its eighteenth-century Església de Sant Jaume. Housed in the old presbytery is the excellent **Centre d'Informació del Parc de l'Albera**, c/Mossén Amadeu Sudrià (May–Oct Mon–Fri 8am–3pm, Sat 9am–2pm & 4–6pm, Sun 10am–2pm; Nov–April Sat 9am–2pm & 3–5pm, Sun 9am–2pm; ⊗972 545 039), where the fascinating display panels of flora, fauna and human history are complemented by a range of detailed maps and itineraries for any number of walks in the area, including the route from nearby Rabós d'Empordà to Sant Quirze de Colera (see box). The **restaurant** *Ca La Maria*, 3km south in Mollet de Peralada, c/Unió 5 (Oct–April closed Tues), is famous for its chunky, moderately priced Catalan fare.

Cabana Arqueta is a highly atmospheric dolmen dating from 2500 BC, standing alone in the shade of tall oaks 1km southwest of Espolla, 10min along a footpath to the right of the GI602 road towards Sant Climent Sescebes.

A SHORT WALK IN THE SERRA DE L'ALBERA

RABÓS D'EMPORDÀ village, 4km southeast of Espolla, provides the starting-point for one of the most rewarding walks in the park, taking in the breathtaking setting of the ruined monastery of Sant Quirze de Colera, well signposted 5km northeast. The route follows a tortuous, dusty track, passable on foot or by car, which winds through pine-carpeted valleys amid the stunning natural arena of the foothills; your only companions are likely to be cicadas. Rabós has a great place to stay, the comfortable self-catering *Cal Pastor* house, c/Pont 3 (☎ 972 563 247, ⓦ www.cal-pastor.com; ❷), and a fine, inexpensive Catalan restaurant, *Can Tomas*, Pl Pou Nou (closed Wed).

Founded more than a thousand years ago, the Benedictine monastery of Sant Quirze de Colera is currently being renovated. The solitary ruins nestle in the basin of a lush valley, dwarfed by the sheer height of the escarpment framing them. The building isn't open to the public at present, but you can still view the facade, including perfectly preserved arch windows bordering the cloisters; the four blocks rising up above are thought to have been part of the tenth-century church. An enterprising soul has located a restaurant (Easter–Sept daily 1–5pm) in the nearby stables, which serves good Catalan cooking in a perfect setting.

Portbou

The fortunes of **PORTBOU**, 7km north of Colera, are irrevocably linked to its location on the border between Spain and France. Once a semi-deserted haven, where fishermen would pull their catch ashore safe from storms,

Portbou was transformed by the construction of a huge railway station in 1872. For more than a century, the town made its living from border traffic and old money is still evident in the grand, if faded, Modernist buildings. The eighty-odd customs agencies disappeared almost overnight in 1995 following the elimination of border controls, and Portbou is trying to redefine itself as a holiday town.

THE TOWN

The protected bay, a natural amphitheatre of granite and water, shelters an uncrowded pebbly **beach**. From the north side of the beach, a footpath hugs the rocky shoreline to the adjacent **Tres Platgetes** and from there to **Platja del Pi**, a narrow inlet popular with nude bathers and the last easily accessible beach before France.

For details of kayaking among the bay's tiny inlets, contact the tourist office. The Centre d'Immersió Portbou, c/Mar 20 (Ⓦ www.chez.com/giry) offers diving excursions.

Framing the deep horseshoe of the bay, the small, café-lined **promenade** provides a picturesque backdrop for the *sardanes* and *havaneres* held here throughout the summer.

An easy five-minute climb from the beach to the **south cliff** overlooking the bay takes you to Israeli sculptor Dani Karavan's abstract *Passagen*, or **Walter Benjamin Memorial**, a bleak testimony to the plight of refugees that's named after a German Jewish philosopher who committed suicide in a hotel in Portbou in 1940 rather than be handed over to the Gestapo. A stark brown metal tunnel leads claustrophobically down steps towards the sea, open to the sky only for the last few metres, before coming to a glass barrier etched with an inscription by Benjamin in five languages: "It is more arduous to honour the memory of the nameless than that of the renowned. Historical construction is devoted to the memory of the nameless." Through the glass, all you can see is the sea crashing on the rocks below, while the only way out is back up through the stifling tunnel. The philosopher's grave lies alone in the town cemetery, a few metres away, on the second terrace on the right.

PRACTICALITIES

Portbou's vast **train station** (☎972 390 099), with trains from all over Spain and Europe, is 500m northwest of the beach through a pedestrian underpass. The winding N260 comes straight into town, and there are signs to the huge **car park** under the railway bridge. The small but helpful **tourist office** (May–Sept daily 9am–8pm; ☎972 390 284) is centrally located in a cabin on the seafront, Pg Sardana.

There's a good range of **hotels**. On the promenade itself, most of the cheerful rooms of the lovely *La Masia*, Pg Sardana 1 (☎972 390 372; ④), have large balconies giving onto the beach. On a quiet street back from the beach is the old charm of the *Comodoro*, c/Méndez Nuñéz 1 (☎972 390 187; ④; closed Oct–May). There's also the good-value *Hostal Juventus*, Avgda Barcelona 3 (☎972 390 241; ②), which has airy rooms and modern shared bathrooms, and the simple *Hostal Costa Blava*, c/Cervera 20–25 (☎972 390 003, ✉joangub@eresmas.net; ③).

The **restaurants** on Pg Sardana are overpriced and under-quality; best bet here is *L'Ancora*. Otherwise, *Hostal Juventus* serves appetizing, inexpensive snacks and pizzas, and *Art in Café*, c/Mercat 11 (daily 8am–1am), makes tasty crêpes, salads and juices while you surf the **internet**. You'll find pavement **bars** on Plaça Major, while the only late-night joint is the lively *El Recó*, c/Font del Moro 12 (daily 10pm–3am), done up with a Chaplin theme.

PORTBOU

CONTEXTS

CONTEXTS

A brief history

T he **history** of Catalonia, more than of many other regions in Europe, is one of swings in fortune. Standing at the threshold through which armies and ideas entered the Iberian peninsula, the **Costa Brava**, in the north of Catalonia, has both suffered and benefited from being batted back and forth between the civilizations that have laid claim to it – and from the centuries of border haggling between France and Spain.

From prehistory to the Romans

A 100,000-year-old **pre-Neanderthal** jawbone found in the Coves de Serinyà caves outside Banyoles provides the earliest sign of humans in the region. Dozens of dolmens and menhirs in the Serra de l'Albera mountains from between 3500 BC and 1800 BC comprise Catalonia's largest concentration of **Neolithic** monuments.

By the seventh century BC, the Indiketa tribe of **Iberian** settlers established the first town along modern lines in Ullastret. In 550 BC, the **Greeks** landed at Roses, founding settlements there and at Empúries, from where they established trading connections with the Indiketas and the rest of the peninsula. Three centuries later, with the Greek colonies still thriving, the region had become an important part of the **Carthaginian Empire**; Barcelona was founded in around 230 BC by Hamil Barca.

The **Romans** first landed at Empúries in 218 BC under Scipio, and subjugation of the peninsula began in earnest in 195 BC, although it was only after two centuries of fighting that the Iberian tribes capitulated. The Romans introduced olives and vines to the Costa Brava, along with many other new ideas, such as the notion of a main square – originally a forum, later a Plaça Major – at the heart of a town. Catalonia's great *masies*, rambling, fortified farmhouses, are the direct descendant of Roman villas.

By the fifth century AD, Rome's collapse had opened the door for the **Visigoths** from Gaul, who briefly established their capital in Barcelona in 531.

The making of Catalonia

The **Moors** – Muslim North Africans – invaded Spain in 711 and reached Catalonia six years later. Their rule there lasted less than a century, not long enough for their influence to be felt strongly. Far more important was the **Jewish** influence: by the thirteenth century, Girona had become one of Europe's leading centres of Jewish learning.

Catalonia was among the first regions taken back from the Moors. **Charlemagne** captured Girona in 785, and his son, Louis, took Barcelona in 801. This turned Catalonia into a buffer zone, known as the **Spanish Marches**, made up of small territories each ruled by a count and owing allegiance to the Frankish Empire. Also at this time, spoken Latin had taken on geographical pecularities and the Romance languages, including **Catalan**, began to develop: a document from 839 is regarded as the first Catalan text.

In 878, **Guifré el Pelós** (Wilfred the Hairy) took advantage of greater independence to establish a dynasty which was to rule for over five centuries. He made important territorial

gains in his lifetime, including Girona and Besalú. Then, in
1137, **Ramon Berenguer IV** married Petronella, the two-
year-old daughter of King Ramiro II of Aragon, thus uniting
the dynasties of Catalonia and Aragon and providing the
platform for rapid expansion over the next three centuries.

The golden age

Ramon Berenguer IV's son, **Alfons I**, inherited the title of
King of Aragon and added Roussillon and much of southern France to his empire, although the death of his son,
Pere el Católic – which left the country ruled by the five-
year-old **Jaume I** – left the door open for rivals to end
Catalonia's aspirations north of the Pyrenees. Despite these
setbacks, the 63-year rule of the remarkable Jaume I,
known as El Conquistador ("the Conqueror"), was marked
by expansion into the Balearics and Valencia, and the creation, with the **Corts Catalanes**, of one of Europe's first
parliamentary governments; a network of consulates in foreign ports protected Catalonia's interests.

Jaume's son, **Pere II**, gained Sicily, Malta, Corsica,
Sardinia and Naples with the help of his admirals Roger de
Flor and Roger de Llúria, the latter winning a famous vic-
tory against the French fleet near the Formigues islands off
Calella de Palafrugell in 1285. Catalan became a trading
language used throughout the Mediterranean.

In 1289, **Pere IV** created the Generalitat, a committee
within the Corts that is now the Catalan government,
which became responsible for administering public order
and which maintained a fleet for the defence of the king-
dom. This was an era of new building, particularly of great
cathedrals, as architecture progressed from Romanesque to
Gothic styles. In literature, Mallorcan missionary Ramon
Llull's *Llibre de Contemplació* (Book of Contemplation)
appeared a century before Chaucer's *Canterbury Tales*.

Dissent and decline

Catalonia's fortunes declined as Spain's rose. In 1479, Ferdinand of Aragon married Isabella of Castille; together they were known as **Els Reis Católics** ("The Catholic Monarchs"), uniting the two great Spanish houses. They took Granada from the Moors in 1492 and initiated a wave of Christian fervour, which brought with it the **Inquisition**, established in Catalonia in 1487, and the **expulsion of the Jews** in 1492. After Columbus's landfall in the New World, also in 1492, trade routes shifted and the Mediterranean ceded its position as a profitable market. Catalonia lost out to Seville and Cadiz, which were awarded the rights to the lucrative new trade, and it steadily became poorer throughout the sixteenth century.

The first open confrontation with the rest of Spain came in 1640 with the **Guerra dels Segadors** ("The War of the Harvesters"), when Catalonia placed itself under the protection of the French king. Barcelona eventually surrendered to the Spanish army in 1652, and the subsequent Treaty of the Pyrenees in 1659 sliced up the historical lands of Catalonia and created the border between Spain and France as it stands today. The revolt is remembered in the *Els Segadors* marching song, now Catalonia's national anthem.

Catalonia backed the wrong horse again in the **Spanish War of Succession**, won in 1714 by the Bourbon king Felipe V. As a reprisal, Felipe imposed a series of repressive measures, removing Catalonia's political and judicial systems, banning its language and suppressing its universities. Further hardship came in 1808, when Napoleon invaded Spain, heralding the **Peninsular War**. Girona held out in a heroic eight-month siege but it wasn't until 1814 that the French were finally driven out with the aid of the British.

Revival and Renaixença

Despite political emasculation, Catalonia in the nineteenth century enjoyed an **economic revival**, spearheading Spain's industrial revolution. On the coast, cork production became a boom industry and helped finance Spain's first railway. Language and literature flourished in the first stirrings of the Catalan **Renaixença**, or Renaissance; books in Catalan began to reappear after the prohibition of the language eased, and spoken Catalan became favoured once more by the urban bourgeoisie. Increasing wealth in the cities went hand in hand with movements in art and architecture, culminating in the influential **Modernist** school.

War and repression

Catalan cultural life in the early **twentieth century** was linked to the aspiration for long-lost independence: in 1931, Francesc Macià, leader of the Republican Left party, declared Catalonia an independent republic. Madrid naturally refused to accept the declaration. When the **Spanish Civil War** broke out in 1936, Catalonia was firmly Republican and became the last stronghold taken by the Fascists in 1939. Girona fell on February 5 and the Castell de Sant Ferran in Figueres was the last home of the Spanish Republic before its leaders fled into exile.

With defeat came **reprisals**. Once again, the language was outlawed, investment per capita was lower than elsewhere in Spain and **Franco** encouraged immigration from other regions in an attempt to dilute nationalist sentiments. To offset economic disaster, Franco and his new Ministry of Tourism initiated in the 1960s the **tourist boom**, based on a false pan-Spanish image of flamenco and bullfighting, to further erode regional differences.

Modern Catalonia

Catalan culture survived nonetheless, and when Franco died in 1975, **democracy** slowly returned. The **Generalitat** was re-established in 1978 and the **statute of autonomy** was signed in 1979, granting Catalonia the basis of some self-determination; the first regional elections took place the following year. The Catalan language returned quickly as road signs were rewritten, books and newspapers published and TV and radio stations set up. The region's clout is such that **Jordi Pujol**, Catalonia's president, has been able to negotiate dispensations well beyond the statute of autonomy, such as tax-raising powers and a regional police force.

Democracy and **devolution** have brought a huge upturn in economic fortunes, making Catalonia the most prosperous region in Spain, enjoying an enormous boost in fortune and image. A turning point came with the 1992 Barcelona Olympics and the subsequent projection of the city's image, which continues to have a positive effect on the whole of the region. No longer tainted with an image of tawdry commercialism, the Costa Brava is enjoying a revival that is staying faithful to the culture and qualities of the region.

Wildlife and the environment

D espite the popular image of package holidays and high-rise hotels, the Costa Brava and its hinterland are home to a wide variety of **wildlife**, influenced by the region's tremendous range of **habitats** and micro-climates. Growing environmental awareness has galvanized local people into demanding the preservation of natural areas and an end to rampant property development, while environmental groups and official bodies have contributed to creating a string of nature reserves and protected lands. Since 1998, a growing number of coastal towns have signed the **Carta de Tossa** (Tossa Charter), undertaking to match tourism with environmental protection.

The Catalan government **website** ⓦwww.gencat.es /mediamb gives the broad picture, while the Associació de Naturalistes de Girona at ⓦwww.grn.es/ang has the local lowdown.

Habitats

Spain's first maritime nature reserve was created in 1985

around the **Illes Medes**, off the coast at L'Estartit, providing a home to numerous fish and aquatic flora as well as a nesting ground for sea birds. An even greater ecological triumph was the wildfowl reserve at **Aigüamolls de l'Empordà**, extensive marshlands on the sweep of the Golf de Roses, which was saved by the locals from development.

To the north, the **Cap de Creus** headland is a haven for marine life and sea birds, while the **Serra de l'Albera** mountains are home to rare birds, mammals and reptiles; its park authority is very active in preserving endangered species. The volcanic **La Garrotxa** region inland is outstanding for its range of flora and animal life.

Mammals

Wild boar are present in the mountains in large numbers, while the large expanses of woodland provide shelter for a number of predators, including **beech martens** and **wildcats** in La Garrotxa and **badgers** and **stone martens** in the Serra de l'Albera. The rare and very shy **genet**, a nocturnal ring-tailed animal, lives in both parks, and the Serra de l'Albera is home to the endearing **Albera cow**, little over a metre tall, which roams free.

Birds

The Costa Brava has a wide range of resident and migratory birds. Everywhere you'll find the striking **hoopoe**, a brown and white bird with a fan-like crown, while dozens of **white egrets** strut around long tracts of the coastal strip.

On the coast, some 93 species, including the rare **Kentish plover**, **kingfisher** and **stone curlew**, favour the Aigüamolls de l'Empordà for nesting. The same park attracts over three hundred species of temporary visitor, such as **flamingoes**, **cranes** and **ibises**. The Illes Medes are home to **cormorants**, **grey herons** and the **shag**, while it's also possible to spot **kestrels** and **peregrine falcons**.

The mountain regions shelter numerous birds of prey. Foremost among these are the **golden eagle**, which inhabit the highlands of the Serra de l'Albera, where you might also spy **sparrowhawks**, **eagle owls** and the tiny **lesser kestrel**. Of the nearly 150 species in La Garrotxa, the **goshawk** stands out. Other woodland birds are the **great spotted woodpecker** and the **nuthatch**, while the highest reaches are inhabited by the very rare **wallcreepers**, which live on sheer cliff faces.

Reptiles

The best place for reptiles is the Serra de l'Albera, home to **green lizards** and several varieties of **snake**, while the streams and rivers are inhabited by **turtles** and **striped-necked terrapins**. The **Mediterranean tortoise** is an endangered species found only in this part of the Iberian peninsula, bred at Garriguella for release into the wild. La Garrotxa, meanwhile, is home to three types of **vipers**, which inhabit cavities in the volcanic rocks.

Marine flora and fauna

Roughly three-quarters of the three-thousand-plus Mediterranean species of marine flora and fauna can be found in the waters of the Costa Brava. Star of the show is the rare **sea horse**, often spotted at Cap de Creus. As the sea deepens, so different marine species occupy the different levels. Nearer the surface, predators such as **bream** hunt for **Chinese limpets** and **runner crabs** among **sea lettuce** and **anemones**. Transparent **gobies** are food for larger fish, mainly **bass**, **amberjacks** and **barracudas**. Around 15m down, brightly coloured **sponges** cling to the rocks which provide shelter for **lobsters** and **scorpion fish** and large predators such as **conger eels** and the huge **groupers**. The **coral beds** begin at around 20m, creating a micro-environment and home to some six hundred animal species, including, **great hermit crabs**, **dogfish** and the **marbled electric ray**.

Books and films

Very few **books** have been written in English about the Costa Brava. Books on specialist subjects are invariably in Spanish or Catalan, while the dozens of books and essays by the pre-eminent twentieth-century Catalan writer Josep Pla have not been translated. Following is a personal selection, with the publisher given in brackets. A British company, Books on Spain (PO Box 207, Twickenham TW2 5BQ ☎020/8898 7789, ⓦwww .books-on-spain.com), has an extensive selection, including many on Catalonia.

Since the 1950s, Hollywood **film**-makers have been coming to the Costa Brava, whether for its setting of Riviera-style beachlife or for the stunning natural beauty. Over the years, the coast has starred in what has become an unconscious chronicle of the changing pace of tourist development.

Books

Salvador Dalí *The Secret Life of Salvador Dalí* (Dover). Straight from the horse's mouth, this unputdownable book, written in 1942 and often reissued, is a fast and furious autobiography of Dalí's early life. Beautifully illustrated throughout, it reveals beguiling glimpses of the outrageous

BOOKS

snobbishness and self-adoration of an artist aware of his genius.

Ian Gibson *The Shameful Life of Salvador Dalí* (Faber). A revealing contrast to the artist's self-perception. Underlying Dalí's exhibitionism was an intense feeling of sexual shame, illustrated by the recurring theme in his paintings of the individual hanging his head.

John Hargreaves *Freedom for Catalonia* (Cambridge UP). A serious work on the nationalism of stateless countries in general and of Catalonia in particular, centring around how the 1992 Olympics raised existing tensions with Spain.

John Hooper *The New Spaniards: a Portrait of the New Spain* (Penguin). The best general introduction to post-Franco Spain, this highly readable book has captured the feel of the huge changes in society and the regions.

Norman Lewis *Voices from the Old Sea* (Faber). A highly personal and romanticized view of the changing complexion of the Costa Brava as tourism slowly began taking a hold, chronicling the summers of 1949, 1950 and 1951 which the author spent in the region.

George Orwell *Homage to Catalonia* (Penguin/Harcourt Brace). Absorbing account of Orwell's participation in left-wing revolution in Barcelona and his later disillusionment with Republican in-fighting during the Spanish Civil War.

Caroline Roe *The Isaac of Girona Chronicles* (Berkley). A collection of uneven but entertaining crime thrillers taking the supposedly real character of Isaac, a blind Jewish physician in fourteenth-century Girona, as its central protagonist.

Hugh Thomas *The Spanish Civil War* (Penguin/Touchstone). Written in 1961, this blow-by-blow chronological account of the Civil War is still the best, and includes large sections on the whys and wherefores of the conflict in Catalonia.

Films

Pandora and the Flying Dutchman (1951). A sensation-seeking American star, played by **Ava Gardner**, romances her way around Spain, in a movie credited with having put Tossa de Mar, and with it the Costa Brava, on the tourist map. In much-publicized events at the time, **Frank Sinatra** followed Gardner to the Costa Brava to court her; tales of her supposed flings still abound in towns from Tossa to Palamós.

The Spanish Gardener (1956). **Dirk Bogarde** stars as the eponymous worker, who becomes the role model for the young son of a widowed and increasingly jealous British diplomat (**Michael Hordern**). Filmed in Mas Juny, the home of Catalan artist Josep Maria Sert overlooking Platja Castell, the film shows how little has changed in an area protected from the developers.

Chase a Crooked Shadow (1957). The plot – an heiress (**Anne Baxter**) is duped into believing an impostor (**Richard Todd**) is her long-lost brother –
is less engaging than the wealth of mid-Fifties Costa Brava scenery. The corniche road between Tossa de Mar and Sant Feliu de Guíxols remains largely unchanged, but now-wealthy Tamariu back then was a row of huts on the beach, and Palamós makes an appearance without the bars and restaurants of today.

Light at the Edge of the World (1971). **Kirk Douglas** and **Yul Brynner** star in this adaptation of Jules Verne's novel about an evil-doer who builds a false lighthouse to lure ships to their doom. The star is the spectacular Cap de Creus headland, whose haunting, lunar landscape is perfect for the bleakness of the story.

Costa Brava (1995). Award-winning Catalan romantic comedy, filmed in English, telling the story of two women, a Catalan tour guide and an Israeli engineer who fall in love. The film is set against a backdrop of Barcelona and the more unspoilt beaches around Palamós and Begur.

FILMS

Language

Catalan – one of the four official languages in Spain – is spoken by some six million people in Catalonia, with variations spoken by a further three million in the Balearics, Valencia and French Catalonia, more than many better-recognized tongues such as Danish or Norwegian.

The vast majority of people on the Costa Brava speak Catalan as their first language: Girona, even more than Barcelona, is the heartland of Catalan culture and almost all schooling is now in Catalan, although, thanks to Franco – who outlawed the language and prohibited its teaching in schools and use in the media – many over-35s have difficulty in writing.

Many people working in the tourist industry speak English and most young people learn English at school, so all along the coast you'll be able to get by with little difficulty; inland, though, it's rarer to find English-speakers.

Catalan: a few rules

Catalan is pronounced quite differently from Castilian (Spanish), with much more neutral sounds, similar to those found in English – meaning that it's easier for native

English-speakers to master. In Catalan, *c* and *z* aren't lisped as they are in Spanish.

Rules of stress are convoluted but, as a rule of thumb, emphasis lies on the last syllable unless the word ends in a vowel or an "s", or if there's an accent (which marks the stress). Plurals of masculine nouns simply add "s", while feminine nouns ending in "a" drop it and add "es", so *cervesa* ("sairvaisa") becomes *cerveses*. Adjectives add a final "a" in the feminine.

Vowels

a as in m**a**t when stressed, as in **a**lone when unstressed.

e as in g**e**t when stressed, as in fath**e**r when unstressed.

i is long, as in ´pol**i**ce.

o varies, but usually as in d**o**g when stressed and t**oo** when unstressed.

u somewhere between sch**oo**l and r**u**le.

Consonants

c followed by *e* or *i* is soft as in fa**c**ile; otherwise hard as in ba**c**on.

ç is always soft, as in fa**ç**ade.

g followed by *e* or *i* is like the "s" in plea**s**ure; otherwise hard as in wa**g**on.

h is always silent.

ig as in do**dge**.

ix as in ba**sh**.

j is like the "s" in plea**s**ure.

l.l occurs in the middle of words, as in "aquare**l.l**a", and doubles the ordinary *l* sound.

ll is like the sound in the middle of co**ll**iery.

nt has a silent *t*: the word *cent* is pronounced "sen".

ny as in o**ni**on.

qu before *e* or *i* sounds like *k*; before *a* or *o* as in **qu**it.

r is rolled at the start or in the middle of a word; at the end, it's silent.

rr is doubly rolled.

s at the start or in the middle of a word as in **s**ee; at the end, as in **z**oo.

tx as in ba**tch**.

tz as in ba**ts**.

v is very soft, as if you're trying to say *b* without closing your lips.

w is similar to *v*.

x is halfway between *s* and x.

z as in **z**oo.

CATALAN: A FEW RULES

WORDS AND PHRASES

Basics

yes	*si*	good	*bó*
no	*no*	bad	*dolent*
OK	*val*	here	*aquí*
please	*sisplau*	there	*allí*
thank you	*gràcies*	open	*obert*
hello	*hola*	closed	*tancat*
goodbye	*adéu*	yesterday	*ahir*
good morning	*bon dia*	today	*avui*
good afternoon	*bona tarda*	tomorrow	*demà*
good evening	*bona nit*	Monday	*dilluns*
good night	*adéu bona nit*	Tuesday	*dimarts*
		Wednesday	*dimecres*
sorry	*ho sento*	Thursday	*dijous*
excuse me	*perdoni*	Friday	*divendres*
I (don't) understand	*(no) entenc*	Saturday	*dissabte*
		Sunday	*diumenge*
Do you speak English?	*Parla anglès?*		

Numbers

1	*u, un*	13	*tretze*
2	*dos, dues*	14	*catorze*
3	*tres*	15	*quinze*
4	*quatre*	16	*setze*
5	*cinc*	17	*disset*
6	*sis*	18	*divuit*
7	*set*	19	*dinou*
8	*vuit*	20	*vint*
9	*nou*	21	*vint-i-un*
10	*deu*	30	*trenta*
11	*onze*	40	*quaranta*
12	*dotze*	50	*cinquanta*

60	*seixanta*	100	*cent*
70	*setanta*	200	*doscents*
80	*vuitanta*	1000	*mil*
90	*noranta*		

Hotels, shops and directions

I'd like...	*Voldria...*
Do you have...?	*Teniu...?*
a (double) room	*una habitació (doble)*
with shower	*amb dutxa*
for one/two people	*per a una persona/dues persones*
for one/two nights	*per a una nit/dues nits*
for one week	*per a una setmana*
How much is it?	*Quant val?*
Where is ...?	*On és...?*
the bus station	*l'estació d'autobussos*
the train station	*l'estació de trens*
the nearest bank	*el banc més a prop*
the post office	*el correu*
the toilet	*el lavabo*
left	*a l'esquerra*
right	*a la dreta*
straight on	*tot recte*
How do I get to Púbol?	*Per on es va a Púbol?*
Where does the bus to Olot leave from?	*D'on surt l'autobus a Olot?*
Does this train go to Girona?	*Aquest tren va a Girona?*
What time does it leave/arrive?	*A quina hora surt/arriba?*
A (return) ticket to Portbou	*Un bitllet (d'anar i tornar) a Portbou*
A table for two	*Una taula per a dos*
menu	*carta*
The bill, please	*La compte, sisplau*
How much is it? (in a bar)	*Em cobra, sisplau?*

MENU READER

Basics

a l'ast	spit-roasted
a la brasa	chargrilled
a la planxa	grilled
a la romana	deep-fried in batter
al forn	oven-baked
all	garlic
allioli	garlic and olive oil mayonnaise
bikini	toasted cheese and ham sandwich
formatge	cheese
mantega	butter
oli	oil
ous	eggs
pà	bread
pà amb tomàquet	thick country bread, often toasted, smeared with fresh tomato and daubed with olive oil and salt
pebre	pepper
romesco	almond, tomato and garlic sauce
sal	salt
sofregit	basic tomato, olive oil and onion sauce
sucre	sugar
torrades	toasted country bread, often served as *pà amb tomàquet*

Soup (*sopa*) and salad (*amanida*)

amanida verda	green salad
amanida catalana	salad with cold cuts and cheeses
escalivada	roasted aubergine, red pepper and onion salad, drizzled in olive oil
escudella	broth with rice or pasta
esqueixada	salad of dried cod, red pepper, tomato, onion and olive

gazpacho	cold soup of tomatoes, green peppers, cucumber and onion

Starters (*entrants*)

canalons	cannelloni
entremesos	hors d'oeuvres of mixed meat and cheeses
espinacs a la catalana	spinach sautéed in olive oil with raisins and pine nuts
faves a la catalana	broad beans sautéed in olive oil and garlic with mushrooms and ham
pica-pica	a selection of different dishes for sharing, often seafood
salpicó de mariscos	cold shellfish salad with onions and peppers
truita (espanyola/ francesa)	omelette (potato/plain)
xamfaina	onion, tomato, pepper and aubergine stew

Rice dishes

arròs a banda	rice cooked in fish broth
arròs a la cubana	boiled rice with tomato sauce, egg and banana
arròs a la marinera	seafood paella
arròs negre	rice cooked in squid ink

Meat (*carn*)

bistec de vedella	veal steak
botifarra	Catalan sausage
cargols	snails, often served in a spicy sauce
conill	rabbit
embotits	cold cuts and cured sausages
fricandó	veal and wild mushroom fricassee
llom	loin of pork
mandonguilles	meatballs
niu	chunky stew of swordfish, cod tripe and wild fowl

pernil dolç	cooked ham
pernil Serrat	cured ham
pinxo	marinated pork kebab
pollastre	chicken
salxitxó	salami-type sausage
xai	lamb
xoriç	spicy sausage

Fish (*peix*) and seafood (*marisc*)

anxoves	anchovies
bacallà	cod
berberetxos	cockles
calamars	squid
cloïsses	clams
escamarlans	king prawns
fritada de peix	various fried fish
gambes	prawns
graellada de peix	various grilled fish
llagosta	lobster
llenguado	sole
lluç	hake
musclos	mussels
navalles	razor clams
peix espada	swordfish
pop	octopus
rap	monkfish
roger	red mullet
sard	sea bream
sarsuela	fish and shellfish stew
seitons	fresh anchovies
sípia	cuttlefish
suquet	fish casserole
tonyina	tuna
truita	trout

MENU READER

Desserts (*postre*)

crema catalana	egg custard with a caramelized topping
flam	crème caramel
gelat	ice cream
macedònia	fresh fruit salad
mel i mató	curd cheese and honey
tarta	cake

Vegetables (*verdures*)

albergínies	aubergine
ametlles	almonds
cebes	onions
cogombre	cucumber
espàrrecs	asparagus
mongetes	beans
pastanagues	carrots
pebres	peppers
pèsols	peas
rovellons	wild mushrooms
tomàquets	tomatoes
xampinyons	mushrooms

Fruit (fruita)

maduixes	strawberries
melò	melon
pera	pear
pinya	pineapple
plàtan	banana
poma	apple
préssec	peach
raïm	grape
síndria	watermelon
taronja	orange

Drinks (begudes)

aigua (mineral)	(mineral) water
amb/sense gas	sparkling/still
café	coffee
cava	champagne
cervesa	beer
chupito	tot of liqueur
llet	milk
suc	juice
te	tea
vi negre/blanc/rosat	red/white/rosé wine

Glossary

ajuntament town hall

aparcament parking

badia bay

Barroc Baroque – eighteenth-century style of architecture and design characterized by extravagant forms and dense, elaborate facades.

cala cove

Camí de Ronda coastal footpath

Ca'n "the house of", similar to the French *chez*

claustre cloister

correu post office

cova cave

entrada entrance, admission ticket

ermita hermitage or chapel

església church

estanc tobacconist that sells stamps

far lighthouse

festa festival

Gòtic Gothic – style of architecture of the thirteenth to sixteenth centuries, characterized by pointed arches, rib vaulting and octagonal towers

havaneres sea shanties brought back from Cuba in the nineteenth century

Indianos Catalans who made their fortune in the Americas in the nineteenth and twentieth centuries before returning home, also known as Americanos (see p.122).

jardí garden

mercat market

mirador belvedere

Modernisme Modernism – a purely Catalan art and architecture movement of the late nineteenth and early twentieth centuries, embracing painters, sculptors, furniture makers and, most famously, architects, who used tiles, wrought iron, brick and glass to re-create classical and vegetal forms characterized by fluidity and imaginative juxtapositions of materials and symbols.

monéstir monastery

museu museum

parròquia parish church

passeig boulevard, or an evening stroll

platja beach

pont bridge

pou well

puig hill

riu river

Romànic Romanesque – an early medieval architecture distinguished by rounded arches, multiple apses and tall, slender belfries.

sender footpath

serra mountain range

sortida exit

xiringuito beach bar

Index

H

I

internet

K

L

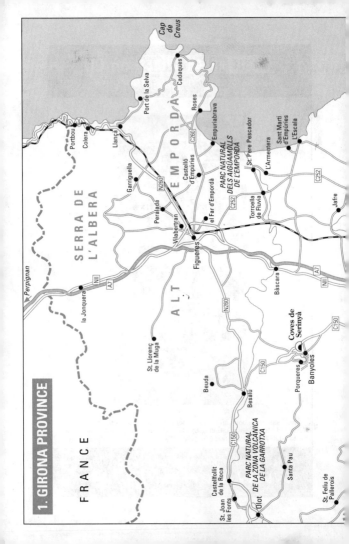

1. GIRONA PROVINCE

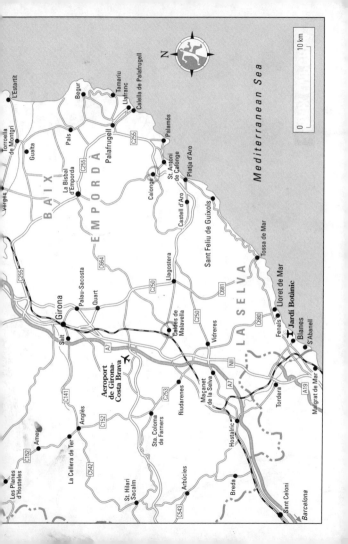

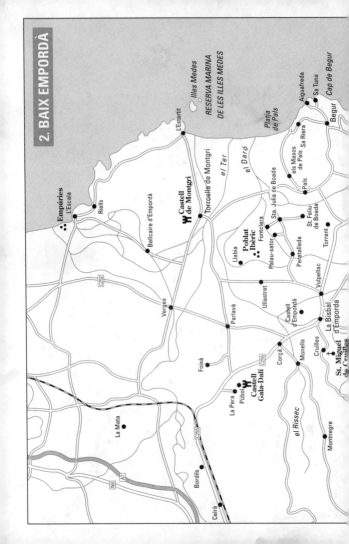

2. BAIX EMPORDÀ